CAMBRIDGE GREEK TESTAMENT FOR
SCHOOLS AND COLLEGES

THE EPISTLE OF PAUL THE APOSTLE

TO THE

PHILIPPIANS

CAMBRIDGE UNIVERSITY PRESS WAREHOUSE,

C. F. CLAY, Manager.

London: FETTER LANE, E.C.
Glasgow: 50, WELLINGTON STREET.

Leipzig: F. A. BROCKHAUS.
New York: THE MACMILLAN COMPANY.
Bombay and Calcutta: MACMILLAN AND CO., Ltd.

THE EPISTLE OF PAUL THE APOSTLE

TO THE

PHILIPPIANS

Edited by

H. C. G. MOULE, D.D.

Lord Bishop of Durham

WITH INTRODUCTION AND NOTES

CAMBRIDGE:
at the University Press
1906

First Edition 1897.   *Reprinted* 1906

PREFACE

BY THE GENERAL EDITOR.

THE Greek Text upon which the Commentaries in this Series are based has been formed on the following principles: Wherever the texts of Tischendorf and Tregelles agree, their readings are followed: wherever they differ from each other, but neither of them agrees with the Received Text as printed by Scrivener, the consensus of Lachmann with either is taken in preference to the Received Text: in all other cases the Received Text as printed by Scrivener is followed. It must be added, however, that in the Gospels those alternative readings of Tregelles, which subsequently proved to have the support of the Sinaitic Codex, have been considered as of the same authority as readings which Tregelles has adopted in his text.

In the Commentaries an endeavour has been made to explain the uses of words and the methods of construction, as well as to give substantial aid to the student in the interpretation and illustration of the text.

The General Editor does not hold himself responsible except in the most general sense for the statements made and the interpretations offered by the various contributors to this Series. He has not felt that it would be right for him to place any check upon the expression of individual opinion, unless at any point matter were introduced which seemed to be out of harmony with the character and scope of the Series.

J. ARMITAGE ROBINSON.

CHRIST'S COLLEGE,
February, 1893.

CONTENTS.

In thy Orcharde (the wals, buttes and trees, if they could speak, would beare me witnesse) I learned without booke almost all Paules Epistles, yea and I weene all the Canonicall Epistles, saue only the Apocalipse. Of which study, although in time a great part did depart from me, yet the sweete smell thereof I truste I shall cary with me into heauen: for the profite thereof I thinke I haue felte in all my lyfe tyme euer after.

BISHOP RIDLEY, to Pembroke Hall (Pembroke College), Cambridge.

From *A letter which he wrote as his last farewel to al his true and faythefull frendes in God*, October, 1555, a few days before he suffered. Transcribed from Coverdale's *Letters of Martyrs*, ed. 1564.

INTRODUCTION.

CHAPTER I.

PHILIPPI : ST PAUL'S CONNEXION WITH IT.

THE site of Philippi is near the head of the Archipelago (*Mare Ægœum*), eight miles north-westward of the port of Kavala, or Kavalla, probably the ancient Neapolis. Just south of it runs the 41st parallel of north latitude; a little to the west, the 24th parallel of east (Greenwich) longitude. The place is at present a scene of ruins. A village hard by, also in ruins, still bears the name of *Philibedjik*[1]. In the first century the town occupied the southern end of a hill above a fertile plain, and extended down into the plain, so as to comprise a higher and a lower city. These were divided by the great Egnatian road, which crossed Roman Macedonia from sea to sea. The higher town contained, among other buildings, the citadel, and a temple, built by the Roman colonists, to the Latin god Silvanus. The lower town contained the market-place, and the forum, a smaller square on which opened the courts of justice. Four massive columns are still standing at the foot of the hill, probably marking the four corners of the forum. A little more than a mile to the west of the town the small river Bounarbachi, anciently Gangas, Gangîtes, or Angîtes, and still called, at least at one part of its course, Angista, flows southward into a fen which borders the plain of the city, and to the south of which

[1] Lewin, *Life and Epistles of St Paul*, Vol. i. p. 208.

again rise the heights of Mount Pangæus, now Pirnári, rich of
old in veins of gold and silver, and covered in summer with
wild roses. The whole region is one of singular beauty and
fertility.

The geographical position of Philippi was remarkable. It lay
on a great thoroughfare from west to east, just where the
mountain barrier of the Balkans sinks into a pass, inviting the
road-builders of Greek, Macedonian, and Roman times. It was
this which led Philip of Macedon (B.C. 359—336) to fortify the
old Thracian town of Daton[1], or Crenîdes (*Fountains*). To the
place thus strengthened he gave his name, and, by pushing his
border eastward into Thrace, converted it from a Thracian into
a Macedonian town[2].

This position of Philippi accounts for the one great event
in its secular history, the double battle in which (B.C. 42) some
ninety-five years before St Paul first saw Philippi, the combined armies of Brutus and Cassius were defeated by Octavius
(afterwards Augustus) and Marcus Antonius. Cassius en-
camped on Pangæus, south of the town, plain, and fen, Brutus
on the slopes to the north, near the town ; thus guarding from
both sides the pass of the Egnatian road. First Cassius was
routed, and two days later Brutus. Each in succession was
slain, at his own command, by the hand of a comrade, and
with them died the cause of the great republican oligarchy of
Rome.

Augustus erected Philippi into a colony (*colonia*, κολωνία,
Acts xvi. 12), with the full title *Colonia Augusta Julia Victrix
Philipporum*, or *Philippensis*[3]. A colony, in the Roman sense,
was a miniature Rome, a reproduction and outpost of the
City. The colonists were sent out by authority, they marched
in military order to their new home, their names were still

[1] Lewin, I. 207.

[2] To Philip it was important not only for military strength but as
a place of mines. He is said to have worked the old and almost
abandoned mines so vigorously as to have drawn from them 10,000
talents yearly. Long before the Christian era, apparently, the supply
of precious ore was finally exhausted.

[3] On this form see note on Phil. iv. 15.

enrolled among the Roman tribes, they used the Latin language and Latin coinage, their chief magistrates were appointed from Rome, and were independent of the provincial governors[1]. These magistrates were two in each colony, *Duumviri*, and combined civil and military authority in their persons. At Philippi we find them assuming the grandiose title of commandants, prætors, στρατηγοί (Acts xvi. 20), and giving their constables the title of lictors, ῥαβδοῦχοι (ver. 35). They posed, in effect, as the more than consuls of their petty Rome. Much of the narrative of Acts xvii. comes out with double vividness when the *colonial* character of Philippi is remembered.

In Acts xvi. 12 we find Philippi called, in the Authorized Version, "the chief city of that part of Macedonia." The better rendering of the best-attested reading is, however, "a city of Macedonia, first of the district." This may mean, grammatically, either that Philippi first met the traveller as he entered the region of Macedonia where it lay, or that it was the political capital of that region. Mr Lewin (i. 202, 206) advocates the latter view, and holds that Philippi succeeded Amphipolis as the capital of the "first," or easternmost, of the four Roman "Macedonias." Bp Lightfoot (*Philippians*, p. 50) prefers decidedly the former view, maintaining that the fourfold Roman division was, by St Paul's time, long disused. We incline, however, to an explanation nearer to Mr Lewin's view; that Philippi is marked by St Luke as first, in the sense of most important, of its district; not officially perhaps, but by prestige.

We may remark in passing that the geographical position of Philippi is incidentally illustrated by the presence there of Lydia, the purple-merchant from Asiatic Thyatira, come to this important place of thoroughfare between her continent and Roman Europe. And the colonial, military, character of Philippi explains in a measure the comparative feebleness of its Jewish element, with their humble *proseucha*, or prayer-house (Acts xvi. 13), outside the walls.

On the story of St Paul's work at Philippi there is little need

---

[1] Britain, like other frontier provinces, had its *coloniæ;* e.g. *Lindum Colonia*, *Lin-coln*.

to dwell in detail, so full and vivid is the narrative of Acts xvi., from the unobtrusive opening of the mission (A.D. 52) by the Apostle, with his coadjutors Silas, Timothy, and probably Luke[1], to the moment when Paul and Silas quit the house of Lydia, and, probably leaving Luke behind them, set out westward along the Egnatian road for Amphipolis. It is enough to say here that the whole circumstances there depicted harmonize perfectly with the contents and tone of our Epistle ; with its peculiar affectionateness, as written to witnesses and partners of tribulation, with its entreaties to the disciples to hold together in the midst of singularly alien surroundings, and, we may add, with its allusions to the "citizen-life" of the saints whose central civic home is (not Rome but) heaven.

Twice after A.D. 52, within the period covered by the Acts, we find St Paul at Philippi. Late in the year 57 he left Ephesus for Macedonia (Acts xx. 1 ; cp. 2 Cor. ii. 12, 13, vii. 5, 6), and undoubtedly gave to Philippi some of his "much exhortation." In the spring of 58, on his return eastward from Corinth by Macedonia, he spent Passover at Philippi (Acts xx. 6), lingering there, apparently, in the rear of the main company of his fellow-travellers, "that he might keep the paschal feast with his beloved converts[2]."

Intercourse with Philippi was evidently maintained actively during his absences. Our Epistle (iv. 16) mentions two messages from the converts to St Paul just after his first visit, and the frequent allusions to Macedonia[3] in the Corinthian Epistles indicate that during the time spent at Ephesus (say 55—57) Philippi, with the other "churches of Macedonia," must have been continually in his heart and thoughts, and kept in contact with him by messengers.

---

[1] The narrative (Acts xvi. 1—17) is in the first person. On the "*we* sections" of the Acts see Salmon, *Introduction to the N.T.*, pp. 371 &c. We may assume Timothy's presence from Acts xvi. 1 &c. and xvii. 14, 15.

[2] Lightfoot, p. 60.

[3] The word "Macedonia" in the Roman period embraced Macedonia Proper, Epirus, and Thessaly. "Achaia" (as a province) denoted the rest of Greece Proper, north and south of the Gulf of Corinth.

Before leaving the topic of St Paul's intercourse with Philippi, we may notice two points in which distinctively *Macedonian* traits appear in the Christian life of the mission Church. The first is *the position and influence of women.* We have women prominent in the narrative of Acts xvi., and in Phil. iv. 2 we find two women who were evidently important and influential persons in the Church. And similar indications appear at Thessalonica (Acts xvii. 4) and Beroea (*ib.* 12). Bp Lightfoot has collected some interesting evidence to shew that Macedonian women generally held an exceptionally honoured and influential position. Thus it is common, in Macedonian inscriptions, to find the mother's name recorded instead of the father's; and Macedonian husbands, in epitaphs upon their wives, use terms markedly reverent as well as affectionate. The Gospel doctrine of woman's dignity would find good soil in Macedonia. The other point is the *pecuniary liberality* of the Philippians, which comes out so conspicuously in ch. iv. This was a characteristic of the Macedonian missions, as 2 Cor. viii., ix., amply and beautifully prove. It is remarkable that the Macedonian converts were, as a class, very poor (2 Cor. viii. 1); and the parallel facts, their poverty and their open-handed support of the great missionary and his work, are deeply harmonious. At the present day the missionary liberality of poor Christians is, in proportion, vastly greater than that of the rich.

The post-apostolic history of Philippi is very meagre. We know scarcely anything of it with the one exception that St Ignatius passed it, on his way from Asia to his martyrdom at Rome, about the year 110. He was reverently welcomed by the Philippians, and his pathetic visit occasioned communications between them and Ignatius' friend Polycarp, bishop of Smyrna, who then wrote to the Philippian Christians his one extant Epistle (see below, ch. v.). "Though the see is said to exist even to the present day," writes Bp Lightfoot (*Philippians*, p. 65), "the city itself has long been a wilderness….Of the church which stood foremost among all the apostolic communities in faith and love, it may literally be said that not one stone stands upon another. Its whole career is a signal monument of the inscrutable counsels of God. Born into the world with the brightest promise, the Church of Philippi has lived without a history and perished without a memorial." (See further, Appendix O.)

As we leave the ruins of Philippi, it is interesting to observe that among them have been found, by a French archæological mission (1864), inscriptions giving the names of the promoters of the building of the temple of Silvanus, and of the members of its "sacred college." Among them occur several names familiar to us in the Acts and Epistles ; Crescens, Secundus, Trophimus, Urbanus, Aristobulus, Pudens, and Clemens— this last a name found in our Epistle.

CHAPTER II.

DATE AND OCCASION OF THE EPISTLE.

IT may be taken as certain that the Epistle was written from Rome during the two years' imprisonment recorded by St Luke (Acts xxviii. 30); that is to say, within the years 61—63. It is true that some scholars, notably Meyer[1], have made Cæsarea Stratonis (Acts xxiv. 23—27) the place of writing of the *Philippians*, *Ephesians*, and *Colossians;* and some who hesitate to assign the two latter epistles to the Cæsarean captivity assign the *Philippians* to it (see Lightfoot, p. 30, note). But the reasons on the other side seem to us abundantly decisive. Bp Lightfoot gives them somewhat as follows (pp. 30, 31, note). (1) The notice of "Cæsar's household" (iv. 22) cannot naturally apply to Cæsarea. (2) The notice (i. 12 &c.) of the progress of the Gospel loses point if the place of writing is not a place of great importance and a comparatively new field for the Gospel. (3) St Paul looks forward, in this Epistle, to an approaching release, and to a visit to Macedonia. This does not agree with his indicated hopes and plans at Cæsarea, where certainly

---

[1] His reasons are fully stated, and answered, in Alford's Prolegomena to the *Ephesians*.

his expectation (Acts xxiii. 11) was to visit Rome, under whatever circumstances, most probably as a prisoner on appeal.
The chief plea, in the *Philippians*, for Cæsarea is that
the word πραιτώριον (i. 13) corresponds to the *prætorium*, or
residency, of Herod at Cæsarea (Acts xxiii. 35). But here
again we may remark that the allusion in the Epistle indicates
an area of influence remarkable and extensive, conditions
scarcely fulfilled at Cæsarea. And Rome affords an obvious
and adequate solution of the problem, as we shall see at the
proper place in the text.

The subordinate question arises, When within the two years of
the Roman captivity was our Epistle written? Was it early or
late, before or after the *Ephesians* and the *Colossians?* which
are plainly to be grouped together, along with the private letter
to the Colossian Philemon.

A widely prevalent view is that the *Philippians* was written
late, not long before St Paul's release on the final hearing of his
appeal. The main reasons for this view are

(1) the indications in the Epistle that the Gospel had made
great progress at Rome ;

(2) the absence in the Epistle of the names Luke and
Aristarchus, who both sailed from Syria with St Paul (Acts
xxvii. 2) and who both appear in the *Colossians* and *Philemon;*

(3) the lapse of time after St Paul's arrival at Rome demanded by the details of Epaphroditus' case (Phil. ii. iv.),
which seem to indicate that the Philippians had heard of St
Paul's arrival ; had then despatched their collection (perhaps
not without delay, iv. 10) to Rome by Epaphroditus ; had then
heard, from Rome, that Epaphroditus had been ill there (ii. 26),
and had then somehow let it be known at Rome (*ibid.*) that the
news had reached them ;

(4) the tone of the Epistle, in its allusions to St Paul's strict
imprisonment and to his entire uncertainty, humanly speaking,
about the issue of his appeal ; allusions said to be inconsistent
with the comparative freedom indicated by the Acts, but consistent with a change for the worse in the counsels of Nero,

such a change as would have occurred when (A.D. 62) the wicked Tigellinus succeeded the upright Burrus in command of the Guard.

Bp Lightfoot on the other hand takes the view that the *Philippians* was the earliest of the Epistles of the Captivity. And he meets the above arguments somewhat as follows.

(1) There is good evidence, both in the Acts and the Epistle, and above all in the *Romans*, for the belief that "a flourishing though unorganized Church" existed at Rome before St Paul's arrival. Already, three years earlier, he had addressed his greatest Epistle "to all that were in Rome, beloved of God, called saints"; and there is strong reason to think that many of the Christians greeted in that Epistle (ch. xvi.) were identical with "the saints of the Household" of our Epistle (see on Phil. iv. 22), and so that those "saints" were pre-Pauline converts, at least in many instances. And when he lands at Puteoli, in 61, he finds there too Christians ready to greet him. And on the other hand the allusions in our Epistle to the progress of the work at Rome must not be pressed too far, as if the whole population of the City was being stirred. What is meant is that a distinct and vigorous "new departure" was being made by the Roman Christians, as willing evangelists, and that the warders of the Apostle were carrying out the strange and inter-esting news of his doctrine and character among their fellow Prætorians and "people in general" (οἱ λοιποὶ πάντες). But all these notes excellently suit a time not long after the Apostle's arrival, when the stimulus of his presence among the Christians would be powerful in its novelty, and when of course already the "soldiers that kept him" would be among his hearers, and not seldom, by the grace of God, his converts. Even the allu-sion (i. 15) to internal opposition suits such a time better than a later, "when...antagonism...and...devotion...had settled down into a routine" (Lightfoot, p. 34).

(2) As regards the absence from the *Philippians* of the names Luke and Aristarchus, this is in the first place an argu-ment from silence only, which cannot be conclusive. The two disciples may be included under the "brethren" and

"saints" of iv. 21, 22. But further, it is at least doubtful whether Aristarchus, though he sailed from Syria with St Paul, landed in Italy with him. He was a Thessalonian, and the vessel in which St Paul sailed was an Adramyttian, from the Ægæan, in which Aristarchus may have been on his way not to Rome but to Thessalonica[1]. From Macedonia he may easily have joined St Paul in Italy later, associating himself so closely there with the imprisoned Apostle as to earn the title of his "fellow-prisoner of war" (Col. iv. 10). As for Luke, it is obvious that at any time he might have left Rome on a temporary errand, to Puteoli perhaps, or some other outlying mission. And of course the same remark may be made of Aristarchus, supposing him to have been after all in Italy.

(3) The argument from the case of Epaphroditus is not strong. It is not necessary to suppose that a special message went from Rome to Philippi to announce St Paul's arrival. Very possibly through Aristarchus (see just above), if not by some other means, the Philippians may have heard that he was far on his way, and may have acted on probabilities. Epaphroditus may even have left Philippi, with the collection, before St Paul reached Italy. And a month, under favourable circumstances, would suffice for a journey from Philippi to Rome, by Brundisium (Brindisi), Dyrrachium (the Illyrian port), and the Egnatian road across Macedonia[2]. Thus if the *Philippians* was written only four months after St Paul's arrival the time would amply include all we need infer under this head.

(4) The tone of the Epistle, with its suspense, its allusions to rigour of confinement, and on the other hand its expectations of release, is not conclusive for a late date. The imprisonment as depicted in it is, after all, no less and no more severe than Acts xxviii. 16 implies. And the references to the trial and its uncertain issue would probably be at least as appropriate in the

---

[1] Indeed, the first intention of the centurion Julius may have been that his prisoners should be conveyed to Rome by way of the Ægæan, Macedonia, and the Adriatic (Lightfoot, p. 35, note).

[2] See Lightfoot's interesting proofs, p. 38, note.

early stages of its progress, or under early experiences of its delays, as later. Doubtless the Epistle depicts trials and sorrows where the Acts speaks only of opportunity and success; but Bp Lightfoot well remarks that this is perfectly truth-like. The *historian* reviews the sum total of a very fruitful period of influence; the *letter-writer* speaks under the immediate pressure of the day's, or the week's, chequered circumstances. St Paul's expectation of release is discussed in the notes (ii. 24); it certainly affords no decisive note of time. As for the pro-motion of Tigellinus, Lightfoot justly says that such changes in the Imperial court would make little difference, for better or worse, in the case of an obscure provincial prisoner, the mis-sionary of a *cultus* which had not yet come to be thought politically dangerous.

If these arguments for a late date for the Epistle may be fairly answered thus, we have meanwhile positive evidence for an earlier date in the doctrinal affinities of the *Philippians*. These point towards the great central group of Pauline Epistles (*Romans, Corinthians, Galatians*), and especially towards the *Romans*, the latest written of that group. In Phil. iii. we have in prominence the doctrine of Justification, in the precise form of the doctrine of Imputed Righteousness, the believer's refuge and peace in view of the absoluteness of the Divine Law. Now this is the characteristic topic of the Roman and Galatian Epistles, and in a minor degree of the Corinthian (1 Cor. i. 30, iv. 4, vi. 11; 2 Cor. iii. 9, v. 19—21). But it is absent, as regards just *this form* of presentation, from the Ephesian and Colossian Epistles, in which St Paul was led by the Holy Spirit to deal more expressly with the closely related, but dif-ferent sides of truth conveyed in such words as Union, Life, Indwelling, Universal Church. This is strong evidence for an approximation of the *Philippians* to the *Romans*, &c., in point of time, as near as other considerations allow. Certainly it makes it likely that the *Ephesians* and its group were not interposed between the *Romans* and the *Philippians*.

And on closer examination we find many links of thought and expression between the *Romans* and the *Philippians*,

besides this main link. Bp Lightfoot (pp. 43, 44) collects the
following parallelisms of this sort :

Compare PHIL. i. 3—8   with ROM. i. 8—11 :

—	— i. 10	—	— ii. 18 :
—	— ii. 2—4	—	— xii. 10, 16—19 :
—	— ii. 8—11	—	— xiv. 9—11 :
—	— iii. 3	—	— ii. 28, i. 9, v. 11 :
—	— iii. 4, 5	—	— xi. 1 :
—	— iii. 10, 11, 21	—	— vi. 5 :
—	— iii. 19	—	— vi. 21, xvi. 18 :
—	— iv. 18	—	— xii. 1.

And he notes the following words and phrases as occurring
in the two Epistles, and not elsewhere : ἀποκαραδοκία, σύμμορφος,
ἐξ ἐριθείας, ἄχρι τοῦ νῦν, προσδέχεσθαι ἐν Κυρίῳ.

On the whole, we may date the Epistle, with great pro-
bability, late in the year 61 or early in 62. See further *The
Epistle to the Ephesians*, in this *The Camb. Bible for Schools*, &c.,
Introduction, pp. 19—22.

Of the occasion of writing, little needs to be said ; the
Epistle itself speaks clearly on the subject. The arrival of
Epaphroditus bringing the Philippian gift, his illness at Rome,
and his anxiety to return to Philippi, appear to have given the
immediate suggestion and made the opportunity. We gather that
besides this Epaphroditus had reported, as the one serious defect
of Christian life at Philippi, a tendency to party-spirit, or at least
to personal antagonisms and differences, especially in the case
of two well-known female converts. See i. 2, 27, ii, 2, 3, 14, 26,
iv. 2, and notes. And meanwhile St Paul takes the occasion
to warn his beloved Philippians against errors of doctrine and
practice which, if not already rife at Philippi, were sure to find
their way there ; the errors both of the Pharisaic legalist
(iii. 2—11), and of the antinomian would-be Paulinist (iii.
13—19).

So, occasioned on the one hand by present circumstances,
and on the other guided by the secret working of the Holy
Spirit to form a sure oracle of God for the Church for ever,
the Letter was dictated, and the greetings of the Writer's

visitors were added, and the manuscript was given over to
Epaphroditus, to be conveyed across Italy, the Adriatic, and
Macedonia, to the plain and hill of Philippi[1].

CHAPTER III.

AUTHENTICITY OF THE EPISTLE.

No trace of doubt on this subject appears in early Christian
literature. Amongst direct testimonies, and taking the later
first, we may cite *Tertullian* (cent. 2—3). He (*de Resurrectione
Carnis*, c. xxiii.) quotes Phil. iii. 11—13[2], as "written by Paul
to the Philippians." He mentions (*de Præscriptione*, c. xxxvi.)
Philippi among the Churches which possessed "authentic
apostolic epistles," that is, apparently, letters received at first
hand from Apostles. In his *Reply to Marcion*, bk. v., taking
up the Pauline Epistles one by one for evidence against the
Gnostic theory of Christianity taught by Marcion, he comes
(c. xx.) to "the Epistle to the Philippians," and quotes, or refers
to, i. 14—18, ii. 6—8, iii. 5—9, 20, 21. It will be observed that
this latter evidence is doubly valuable, as it assumes his op-
ponent's agreement with him about the authenticity.

Irenæus (late cent. 2) quotes (*de Hæresibus*, iv., c. xviii. 4)
Phil. iv. 18 as the words of "Paul to the Philippians."

Clement of Alexandria (late cent. 2) repeatedly quotes the
Epistle. He brings (*Pædagogus*, i., c. vi., ed. Migne) Phil.
iii. 12—14 to refute those who "call themselves 'perfect' and
'gnostic'." In the *Stromata*, iv., c. iii., he refers to Phil. iii.
20, in the words "having obtained citizenship in heaven"; c. v.,
he quotes i. 13, 14 as the "words of the Apostle"; c. xiii. he
quotes i. 7, 29, 30, ii. 1, 2, 17, 20, 21, and refers to the Philippians
as addressed by "the Apostle" in these passages.

---

[1] For further particulars of St Paul's life and work at Rome see
Appendix A.

[2] With one curious variation of reading: *persequor ad palmam
incriminationis*; as if reading τὸ βραβεῖον τῆς ἀνεγκλήσεως.

In the contemporary *Letter of the Churches of Lyons and Vienne*, describing the martyrdoms of A.D. 177[1], the sufferers are said to have striven to "imitate Christ, who being in the form of God, thought it not robbery to be equal with God." The Greek is verbatim as Phil. ii. 6.

Polycarp, in his Epistle to the Philippians (very early cent. 2), both refers (c. iii.) to the Epistle which St Paul had addressed to them, and manifestly echoes its phraseology. He speaks indeed of "Epistles." But the plural is often used for the singular of this word; see Lightfoot in his Edition of Polycarp (*Apostolic Fathers*, Pt. II.; Vol. ii., sect. ii., p. 911). Polycarp's Epistle is given below, nearly in full; Introduction, ch. v.

Ignatius, on his way to martyrdom (about A.D. 110), wrote a series of Epistles. In that to the Romans, c. ii., he speaks of his desire to be "poured out as a libation (σπονδισθῆναι) to God"; to the Philadelphians he writes (c. viii.), "do nothing in a spirit of faction," κατ᾽ ἐριθείαν, Phil. ii. 3); to the Smyrnæans (c. iv.), "I endure all things, for He, the perfect Man, strengtheneth me"; and (c. xi.), "being perfect, be ye also perfectly minded." These passages, taken together, are good evidence for Ignatius' knowledge of the Epistle.

All the ancient Versions (see below, p. xxx) contain the Epistle.

Such evidence, combined on the one hand with the total absence of ancient negative testimony, and on the other with the perfect naturalness, and intense and tender individuality, of the Epistle itself, is abundantly enough to satisfy all but the ultra-scepticism which, however ingenious, really originates in *à priori* views. Such surely is the account to be given of the theory of F. C. Baur (1796—1860)—that the Epistle is a fabrication of the second century, betraying a development of doctrine[2] and life later than the age of St Paul, and aiming at a reconciliation between divergent Church parties (see on iv. 2 below). His objections to the Epistle have, however,

[1] Preserved by Eusebius, *Hist. Eccl.*, v. cc. i.—iv. The quotation is from c. ii.

[2] See further, Appendix F.

been discarded as futile even by rationalizing critics, such as Hilgenfeld, Pfleiderer, and Renan[1]. Alford (*Greek Test.*, iii. p. 27) says, "To those who would see an instance of the very insanity of hypercriticism I would recommend the study of these pages of Baur [*Paulus, der Apostel Jesu Christi*, pp. 458—475]. They are almost as good, by way of burlesque, as the 'Historic Doubts respecting Napoleon Buonaparte' of Abp Whately. According to [Baur] all *usual* expressions prove its spuriousness, as being taken from other Epistles ; all *unusual* expressions prove the same, as being from another than St Paul, &c." Lightfoot says (*Phil.*, p. 74), "I cannot think that the mere fact of their having been brought forward by men of ability and learning is sufficient to entitle objections of this stamp to a serious refutation." Salmon says (*Introd. to N. T.*, pp. 465, 6), "Baur has pronounced this Epistle dull, uninteresting, monotonous, characterized by poverty of thought, and want of originality. But one only loses respect for the taste and skill of the critic who can pass such a sentence on one of the most touching and interesting of Paul's letters. So far is it from shewing signs of having been manufactured by imitation of the other Epistles that it reveals aspects of Paul's character which the other letters had not presented...Elsewhere we are told how the Apostle laboured with his own hands for his support, and declared that he would rather die than let the disinterestedness of his preaching be suspected ; here we find (iv. 10—19) that there was no false pride in his independence, and that when there was no likelihood of misrepresentation, he could gracefully accept the ungrudged gifts of affectionate converts. Elsewhere we read only of his reprobation of Christian teachers who corrupted the simplicity of the Gospel ; here we are told (i. 18) of his satisfaction that, by the efforts even of those whose motives were not pure, the Gospel of Christ should be more widely published."

[1] Dr Harnack, in his *Chronology of Early Christian Literature*, 1897, pt. i. p. 239, makes no doubt about accepting the *Philippians* as genuine, and considers that it was written from Rome.

CHAPTER IV.

RELATION OF THE EPISTLE TO THE OTHER EPISTLES OF THE FIRST IMPRISONMENT.

WE have pointed out the strong doctrinal link of connexion between the Philippian Epistle and the *Romans* with its attendant Epistles. We find in the *Philippians* on the other hand indications of similar connexion with the *Ephesians* and the *Colossians*, and such indications as to harmonize with the theory advocated above (p. xvi) that these Epistles were dated some time later in St Paul's captivity.

In two directions chiefly these connexions appear; (*a*) in the view of the Church as a City or Commonwealth, and (*b*) in the view of Christ's personal Glory.

Under the first head, cp. Phil. iii. 20 with Eph. ii. 12, 19, remembering that nowhere in the Epistles written before the Roman imprisonment is this view of the Church distinctly presented.

Under the second head, cp. Phil. ii. 5—11 with Eph. i. 17—23, ii. 8, &c.; Col. i. 15—19, &c. And cp. Phil. ii. 10 with Eph. i. 20; Col. i. 20. In the earlier Epistles the Apostle was guided to the fullest statements of the salvation wrought out by Christ, especially in its judicial and propitiatory aspects. But this exposition of the grace and wonder of His personal majesty, personal self-abasement, and personal exaltation after it, is in a great measure a new development in the revelations given through St Paul.

Observe in connexion with this the insistence on the blessedness of "*knowing Him*" (iii. 10), compared with the glowing language of Eph. iii. 19 "to *know* the love of Christ, &c."). Most certainly the idea is present everywhere in the Epistles of St Paul; but it reaches its full prominence in this group of Epistles, as other sides of truth do in the *Romans* and the *Galatians*.

Among minor notes of kinship in these Epistles observe the view of faith as the "*gift of God*" (Phil. i. 29; Eph. ii. 8); the mention of the Divine "*good pleasure*," or gracious sovereign purpose (Phil. ii. 13; Eph. i. 4); the phrase "*preach Christ*" (Phil. i. 16, 18; Col. i. 28); the Apostle's "*joy*" in his trials (Phil. i. 18; Eph. iii. 13; Col. i. 24); the Divine "*inworking*" in the saints (Phil. ii. 13; Col. i. 29; cp. Eph. ii. 10); and the following words or phrases peculiar to these among the Pauline Epistles—ταπεινοφροσύνη (Phil. ii. 3; Eph. iv. 2; Col. iii. 12), σπλάγχνα οἰκτιρμῶν (or nearly so) (Phil. ii. 1; Col. iii. 12; cp. Philem. 7, 12, 20); ὀσμὴ εὐωδίας (Phil. iv. 18; Eph. v. 2); ἐπι-χορηγία (Phil. i. 19; Eph. iv. 16; cp. Col. ii. 19).

CHAPTER V.

The Epistle of Polycarp to the Philippians.

This Epistle, the only other extant letter addressed to the Church of Philippi, has been already mentioned (p. xxi). For the text, fully edited with notes, see Lightfoot's *Apostolic Fathers*, Part II. Vol. ii., sect. 2, pp. 898, &c. We give a translation of the Epistle slightly abridged. It is interesting to observe the wealth of N. T. quotations, and the frequent tacit allusions to the copies of St Paul's Epistle. All clear Scripture quotations are italicized, as well as phrases apparently suggested by Scripture.

———

Polycarp and his elders to the Church of God sojourning at Philippi; grace and peace be multiplied from God Almighty and Jesus Christ our Saviour.

i. *I rejoiced greatly with you in the Lord,* in your joy on welcoming those Copies[1] (μιμήματα) of the True Love, chained with those holy fetters which are the diadems of the elect; and that your long-renowned faith persists, and bears fruit to Christ,

———

[1] Ignatius and his companion Confessors.

who for our sins died and rose, *in whom, not having seen Him, you rejoice with joy unspeakable and full of glory,* a joy into which many long to enter, knowing that *by grace ye have been saved, not of works,* but by the will of God in Christ.

ii. So *gird up your loins,* forsake the prevalent specious errors, *believe on Him who raised our Lord from the dead and gave Him glory,* to *whom* (Christ) *all things in heaven and earth are subjected,* to whom every living thing (πνοή) does service, who comes *to judge the quick and dead,* whose blood God will require of the unbelieving. He who raised Him *will raise us also,* if we walk in His ways, abstaining from all injustice, avarice, and evil-speaking, *not rendering evil for evil or railing for railing;* remembering how the Lord said, *Judge not, that ye be not judged; blessed are the poor, and the persecuted for righteousness' sake, for theirs is the kingdom of God.*

iii. I write thus concerning righteousness, not of my own motion but because you have invited me. Neither I nor any like me can approach the wisdom of the blessed and glorious Paul, who when among you, face to face with the men of that day, taught accurately and with certainty the word concerning the truth, who also when absent wrote to you letters[1], which if you study diligently you shall be able to be built up into the faith given you ; which faith is *the mother of us all,* followed by hope, and by hope's forerunner, love to God, to Christ, and to our neighbour. For if any one is given to these, he hath fulfilled the precept of righteousness. He who hath love is far from all sin.

iv. *Now the beginning of all evils is the love of money. We brought nothing into the world, and can carry nothing out.* Let us *put on the armour of righteousness* and teach one another to walk in the precept. Teach your wives too to walk in the faith, love, and purity given them, faithful to their husbands in all truth, amiable to all around them in true modesty, training their children in the fear of God. Let your widows be sober in

---

[1] See p. xxi.

the faith, instant in intercession, holding aloof from evil-speaking, from avarice, and from all wrong. They are God's altar, and He inspects the victim to see if it has any blemish.

v. *God is not mocked;* let us *walk worthy* of His precept and glory. Let the deacons (διάκονοι, ministers) be blameless before Him, as ministers of God and Christ, avoiding likewise evil-speaking, and avarice, and unkindness, before Him who was *minister of all.* If we please Him in this world we shall receive the world to come ; if we *walk* (πολιτευσώμεθα) *worthy of Him, we shall reign with Him,* if we believe. Let the juniors too walk in holy strictness. Every *lust warreth against the spirit; fornicators* and such like *shall not inherit the kingdom.* So let them watch and abstain ; let them submit to the presbyters and deacons. And let the virgins walk in holiness.

vi. The presbyters should be compassionate, watchful over the erring, the weak, the widows, orphans, and poor, *providing always for that which is good before God and men,* renouncing wrath, partiality, avarice, and rash judgment. If we ask remission, we must remit. *We must all stand before the judgment seat of Christ, and give account each of himself.* Let us do Him bond-service, as He bade us, and His Apostles, and the Prophets who *shewed before of His coming.* Be zealous for good ; avoid offences, and false brethren, who deceive the careless.

vii. For *whosoever confesseth not that Jesus Christ is come in the flesh is antichrist.* Whosoever confesses not the mystery of the Cross is of the devil. Whosoever perverts the Lord's oracles to his lusts, and says that there is neither resurrection nor judgment, is Satan's firstborn. So let us forsake the current vain doctrines, and turn to the once-delivered Gospel, *watching unto prayer,* persevering in fastings, praying the all-seeing God *not to lead us into temptation;* as the Lord said, *The spirit is willing, but the flesh is weak.*

viii. Let us hold fast to our hope and to *the earnest* of our righteousness, which earnest is Christ Jesus, *who bore our sins in His own body to the tree; who did no sin, neither was guile*

found in His mouth; who bore all that we might live in Him.
Let us imitate His patience. If we suffer for Him, let us
glorify Him.—He left us this *example* (ὑπογραμμὸν ἔθηκεν).

ix. All of you obey the word of righteousness, and practise
true endurance, which you have seen exemplified before you
not only in blessed Ignatius, Zosimus, and Rufus, but in others
of your own body, and in Paul himself and the other Apostles.
You know that they all *did not run in vain.* They have gone,
in the path of faith and righteousness, to their promised
(ὀφειλόμενον) place, beside the Lord with whom they suffered.

x. Stand fast then, according to His example, *steadfast and
unmoveable in the faith, kindly affectioned one to another with
brotherly love;* sharing together in truth, in the Lord's gentleness[1] *preferring one another. When able to do good,* defer it
not, *for almsgiving rescueth from death* (Tobit iv. 11, xii. 9).
*All being subject to one another, have your conversation honest
among the Gentiles, that by your good works* you may obtain praise,
and the Lord be not blasphemed. Teach all men true sobriety.

xi. I am exceedingly grieved for Valens, once made an elder
among you, that he so ignores the position given him. Do you
avoid avarice; be pure, be true. He who cannot steer himself
aright in such duties, how can he preach them? If he avoids
not avarice he will be defiled by idolatry, and judged as one of
the Gentiles. *Know we not that the saints shall judge the world?*
as Paul teaches. I never heard of such sins in you, among
whom the blessed Paul toiled, who were his *"(living) epistles"*[2]
in the first (days of the Gospel). About you he *glories in the
churches* which knew the Lord before we knew Him. I am
deeply grieved for Valens, and for his wife; God grant them
repentance. *Count them not as enemies,* but restore them as
diseased and wandering members, that your whole body may be
in safety.

---

[1] *Mansuetudine,* perhaps representing ἐπιεικείᾳ, Phil. iv. 5. Ch. x—
xii., xiv., are preserved only in a Latin version.

[2] So Lightfoot explains the difficult sentence: *ego autem nihil tale
sensi in vobis, vel audivi, in quibus laboravit beatus Paulus; qui estis
in principio epistolæ ejus.*

xii. You know the holy Scriptures perfectly ; a knowledge not granted to me. Only, (I know that) it is there said, *Be angry and sin not; let not the sun go down upon your wrath.* Now the God and Father of our Lord, and He, the eternal High-Priest (*Pontifex*), (our) God[1], Jesus Christ, build you up in all holiness, and give you part and lot among His saints, and to us with you, and to all everywhere who shall believe on our Lord and God Jesus Christ, and on His *Father who raised Him from the dead. Pray for all the saints, and for kings and rulers, and for them that persecute you,* and for *the enemies of the Cross,* that your *fruit* may be *manifest in all things,* that ye may be perfect in Him.

xiii. Both you and Ignatius have asked me that, if a messenger is leaving us for Syria, he may carry your letter with ours. This I will do, in person or by delegate. The letter of Ignatius to us, and all others in our hands, we have sent you, as you desired, attached to this letter. They will greatly benefit you spiritually. Report to us anything you hear of Ignatius' companions.

xiv. My letter-bearer is Crescens, whom again I commend to you, as a blameless Christian. His sister too I commend to you, in prospect. Farewell in the Lord Jesus Christ, in grace, with all who are yours. Amen.

CHAPTER VI.

The Greek Text in this Edition.

No attempt whatever is made here to discuss general principles of textual criticism. All that is intended is to explain the terms and signs used in the critical notes, and to state the rule of construction of the text.

[1] So Lightfoot ; in preference to the reading *Dei Filius,* which he thinks to be later.

A.

The following are the Manuscripts, Versions, Fathers, and modern Editors, referred to in the Critical (and occasionally other) Notes, and the English Versions frequently quoted in the general Notes.

i. Uncial Manuscripts, i.e. copies written in Greek capital letters, a style much more used in the early Christian centuries than later.

ℵ. *Codex Sinaiticus.* Found by Tischendorf in the Convent of St Catharine, Mount Sinai; now at St Petersburg. Cent. 4. It was corrected cent. 6 and 7, and later.

A. *Codex Alexandrinus.* In the British Museum; given by Cyril Lucar, once Patriarch of Alexandria, to Charles I. Cent. 5.

B. *Codex Vaticanus.* In the Vatican Library. Of the same date as ℵ, and probably by one of the scribes of ℵ.

C. *Codex Ephraemi.* At Paris. Cent. 5, retouched cent. 6 and 9. It is fragmentary, and in Philippians gives only i. 22 to iii. 5 inclusive. Palimpsest, with works of St Ephraim in Greek as the upper writing.

D₂. *Codex Claromontanus.* Greek and Latin. Found by Theodore Beza (cent. 16) at Clermont; now at Paris. Cent. 6, probably. It contains the Pauline Epistles. (It must be carefully distinguished from the famous MS. of the Gospels and Acts, also found by Beza, now at Cambridge, and known as D, *Codex Bezæ.*)

G₂. *Codex Boernerianus.* At Dresden. Probably cent. 9: perhaps written by Irish scribes at St Gallen in Switzerland.

K₂. *Codex Mosquensis.* Probably cent. 9. (K denotes another MS., *Codex Cyprius,* of the Gospels.)

L. *Codex Angelicus.* At Rome. Not earlier than middle of cent. 9.

P. *Codex Porphyrianus.* At St Petersburg. Cent. 9.

ii. Cursive Manuscripts, i.e. copies written in "running" hand. Of the vast number of these extant, none probably is older than cent. 10 or at earliest 9. Their evidence is of a secondary but often high value.

They are denoted by numbers, and a separate numeration is given to those which contain St Paul's Epistles.

Of those cited, 17 (at Paris, bound up with the noteworthy Codex 33 of the Gospels) is of the tenth century. The remainder are of cent. 11, or later.

iii.   ANCIENT VERSIONS, from the Greek.

Vulgate. This word commonly denotes the Latin Version of the Bible produced by Jerome (331—420); completed 404. This version was in parts a new rendering from the Hebrew, in parts a revision of the Old Latin Version (cent. 2)[1]. This latter is the character of the Vulgate of the N.T.; in the Acts and Epistles the revision is less thorough than in the Gospels. Among important MSS. of the Vulgate we have referred to that of *Fulda*, in Prussia; written in Italy, cent. 6.

Gothic. A version from the Greek by Ulphilas (311—381)[2], for the Visigoths. It is fragmentary, and of Philippians gives only i. 14—ii. 8, ii. 22—iv. 17.

Syriac (a), Peshitto (i.e. "Simple"). Perhaps cent. 4.

Syriac (b), Harkleian. Cent. 7. A revision by Thomas of Harkel (Heraclea) of a version (the *Philoxenian*) made cent. 6 for Philoxenus of Hierapolis.

Egyptian or Coptic (a), the *Memphitic,* also called *Bohairic.* The version of the Bohaira, a district near Alexandria. Date uncertain, perhaps cent. 3 or 4.

Coptic (b), the *Thebaic,* or *Sahidic* (Phil. iii. 16). The version of Upper (i.e. Southern) Egypt. This is fragmentary. Date uncertain, perhaps cent. 3.

Armenian. Cent. 5.

Æthiopic, or *Old Abyssinian.* Still used in Abyssinian worship, though the language is no longer spoken. Some time cent. 4—6.

iv.   FATHERS: Writers in the early centuries of the Christian

---

[1] In some Apocryphal books the Old Latin appears unrevised.
[2] It is uncertain whether Ulphilas was the translator of the *Old* Testament.

Church, whose frequent quotations from Scripture give evidence
on readings. The date in each case is that of the death.

(a) *Writers in Greek.*

    Clement, of Rome, *cir.* 110.

    Clement, of Alexandria, *cir.* 210.

    Origen, of Alexandria, 253.

    Eusebius, of Cæsarea Stratonis, *cir.* 340.

    Athanasius, of Alexandria, 373.

    Basil, of Cæsarea, in Cappadocia, 379.

    Epiphanius, of Cyprus, 403.

    Chrysostom, of Antioch and Constantinople, 407

    Cyril, of Alexandria, 444.

    Theodoret, of Cyrus, in Syria, 457.

    Damascene (John of Damascus), *cir.* 780.

    Theophylact, of Greece and Bulgaria, *cir.* 1107.

(b) *Writers in Latin.*

    Irenæus, of Asia Minor and Gaul (placed here because his
        great extant work, *Against Heresies*, is preserved mainly
        in a Latin Version), *cir.* 200.

    Tertullian, of N. Africa, *cir.* 230.

    Cyprian, of N. Africa, 258.

    Hilary, of Gaul, 354.

    Victorinus, of N. Africa, *cir.* 382.

    Ambrose, of Milan, 397.

    Ambrosiaster or pseudo-Ambrose (Hilary the Deacon, of
        Rome), *cir.* 400.

    Jerome, of Dalmatia and Palestine, 420.

    Augustine, of N. Africa, 430.

v. MODERN EDITORS OF THE TEXT.

C. Lachmann, 1793—1851. The first critical editor to desert
the *Textus Receptus* as an authority in favour of ancient evidence only. For his text (1842—1850) he used only Uncials, the
Vulgate, certain other Latin Versions, and certain Fathers of
cents. 2, 3, 4.

C. Tischendorf, 1815—1874. His life was devoted to the
research and editing of MSS., in which he did a vast work. As

many as eight editions of his Greek Testament appeared ; the 8th has been used for the present work.

S. P. Tregelles, 1813—1875. He published in instalments a Greek Text founded on the oldest MSS., the Versions to cent. 7, and Fathers of cent. 1—4.

H. Alford, 1810—1871. He followed Tischendorf and Tregelles on the whole : but gave more weight to internal evidence.

Chr. Wordsworth, 1807—1885. *The Greek New Testament,* 1856—1860 ; ed. 2, 1872.

J. B. Lightfoot, 1828—1890. *The Epistle to the Philippians,* 1868 ; ed. 7, 1883.

C. J. Ellicott. *Philippians, Colossians, and Philemon,* 1857 ; ed. 2, 1861.

B. F. Westcott and F. J. A. Hort. *The New Testament in Greek,* 1881. In this recension the highest value is assigned to B.

vi. ENGLISH VERSIONS OF THE NEW TESTAMENT.

J. Wyclif, or Wiclif, 1314 ?—1384. The whole Bible, 1382.

W. Tindale (so he always spells his name), 1484 ?—1536. The New Testament, 1525, 1526.

"Cranmer's" Bible, 1539. So called because its second edition, 1540, had a preface by the Archbishop. It is otherwise known as the Great Bible. It was the first "authorized" English Version.

The Genevan Version. By English exiles at Geneva ; the New Testament, 1557. For more than half a century this was the *popular* English Bible.

The "Authorized" Version, 1611.

The Revised Version ; the New Testament, 1881.

B.

The Text in this Edition is based on the texts of Tischendorf (Leipzig, 1872) and Tregelles. Their agreement is treated as decisive. Where they differ, the agreement of either with Lachmann is treated as decisive. In other cases the decision is given by the agreement of either with the *Textus Receptus* as printed by Dr Scrivener (Cambridge, 1876). The Editor has been careful to point out where this general method produces results which, from other points of view, are in his opinion open to criticism.

The *Textus Receptus* is that produced by the great French printer and scholar, Robert Estienne (Stephanus, Stephens); Paris, 1546—1550. His work was largely based on the later editions (1527, 1535) of Erasmus' Greek Testament, editions in which Erasmus had modified his earlier work (first issued 1516) by the edition called the Complutensian, published (1521 or 1522) at Complutum, i.e. Alcalá, in Spain, under the patronage of Card. Ximenes, Abp of Toledo (1436—1517). The MSS. used by Ximenes, Erasmus, and Stephens were neither numerous nor of the highest authority; and they are not always followed in the *Textus Receptus*.

CHAPTER VII.

Argument of St Paul's Epistle to the Philippians.

Ch. I. 1—2. PAUL and Timotheus, servants of Jesus Christ, greet the Christians of Philippi and their Church-officers, invoking blessing on them from the Father and the Lord Jesus Christ.

3—11. Paul assures them that his whole thought of them is full of thanksgiving, his every prayer for them full of joy, in view of their warm, steadfast cooperation from the first in his evangelical labours. He is quite sure [on this bright evidence] that the work of grace in them will reach its consummation in glory. His affectionate regard for them is but just, so fully have they claimed his heart by their identification of themselves with him in the trials of captivity and the toils of Christian witnessing and teaching. God knows with what yearning tenderness, drawn from the heart of Christ, he misses them and longs for them. [And his affection expresses itself above all things in prayer], the prayer that their love [of which he for one has had such proofs] may increasingly be guided and fortified by a quick spiritual perception, sifting truth from error, holiness from sin, and forming a character which at the Great Day should prove pure in principle, and rich in the fruit [of the Spirit], fruit generated by communion with Christ, and bringing glory to God.

12—20. As regards his own present circumstances, he rejoices to inform them that they are conducing to the advance of the Gospel at Rome. [His imprisonment is in itself a mission]; its connexion [not with political or social offences but] with Christ is now well known throughout the Imperial Guard [which supplied his warders] and among the Romans in general. And the Roman Christians, for the most part, have felt a spiritual impetus [after a time of depression]. His captivity has nerved them to bear a bolder witness among their heathen neighbours. [True, there is a shadow across this light]; some thus proclaim Christ [with new energy] from motives of opposition to Paul, while others do so in loyal sincerity. On the one side is love, which sees in the imprisoned Apostle a centre of action, set there by Christ, for the propagation of the Gospel; on the other side is the spirit of the partizan and of self, defiling the motive of the work, actually wishing to make his imprisonment doubly trying [by intercepting enquirers and converts]. Does it matter to him? [No—and] yes. [No, so far as his peace in God is concerned], yes, [*happily* yes, so far as the spread of the primary Gospel truth is concerned]. For thus in every way Christ is being proclaimed. Here is cause of joy for Paul; and here *shall be* cause of joy [even in the eternal future]; for the situation shall only animate the Philippians to earnest prayer for him, and this shall bring him a new fulness of the Holy Spirit, and so shall promote his grace and glory. Yes, it shall forward the realization of his longing anticipation, that at this crisis, as at all others, Christ shall be glorified, whether through his body's living energies, or through his submission to his body's death.

21—26. For indeed life is for him identified with, summed up in, Christ; and death, [as the introduction to Christ's fuller presence] is gain [even over such a life]. If [it is his Lord's will that] he should live on, [the prolonged life] will mean only larger work with richer fruit. And indeed the case is one of blessed dilemma. Personal preference is for dying, dying into the presence of Christ; a far, far better state [than the best here]; while duty, manifested in the needs of his converts, is for living patiently on. And thus he feels sure that he will live on, for the spiritual benefit of his converts, and particularly in order that his restoration to them in bodily presence may give them fresh occasion for triumph in Christ.

27—30. Meanwhile, let them live a life of holy practical consistency. Above all, let him see, or let him hear, as the case may be, that they are standing firm, and standing *together*, cordially at one in Christian witness and work, and calm amidst opposing terrors. Such calmness [under such circumstances] will be an omen of their opponents' ruin and their own coming heaven. God has thus adjusted things, God who has granted them not only faith in Christ but also the privilege of suffering for Him; a conflict one with that which they had seen in Paul's case [at Philippi] and now hear of in his case [at Rome].

Ch. II. 1—4. [Yes, let them above all things *hold together*, watching against a tendency towards internal dissension; a tendency which he fears has shewn itself, however faintly, amongst them.] By the common blessings of believers, by the pity of their human hearts, he begs them to crown his joy in them with the joy of an assurance that they are living in holy harmony; shunning the spirit of self, taking each the lowest room, entering with unselfish love into each other's needs.

5—11. Let them remember, and reflect, the supreme Self-forget-fulness of their Saviour. He, [in His preexistent glory,] being and seeming God, [looked indeed on the things of others]. He dealt with His true and eternally right Equality with His Father [in nature and majesty] not as a thing held, like a prize of strength or guile, anxiously and for Himself, [but as a thing which admitted of an act of most gracious sacrifice for others' good]. In a marvellous "Exinanition" [He laid by the manifested glories of Deity], and willed to be, and to seem, [as Man], the Bondservant [of God], putting on the visible garb of embodied manhood, [while always also more than man]. Aye, and having thus presented himself to men as man, He bowed yet lower, [in His supreme outlook "upon the things of others,"] in His supreme obedience to His God; He extended that obedience to the length of dying, dying on a Cross, [that last degradation in the eyes of Gentile and Jew]. [So He "pleased not Himself," and now, what was the result?] The Father raised Him to the eternal throne [in His now double glory, God and Man], giving to Him [as the once-abased One] the rights of supreme Majesty, that all creation in all spheres should worship Him, and the Father through Him, all beings confessing that Jesus Christ is "I am," to the Father's glory.

12—18. [With such an Example in view] let the beloved Philippians, now as always obedient to Paul's appeals, so watch, so live, in tender, solemn earnestness (and more than ever now, in the absence of their Apostle) [whose presence might have *seemed* to excuse in them a lack of such care] as to realize and carry out the plan of their salvation. [And to promote at once their solemn care and their restful hope let them remember that] it is God who is personally effecting in them [in the regenerate life] both their holy desires and their just works, in order to accomplish His own blessed purposes. Let them renounce all mutual murmurings and dissensions; seeking to prove their spiritual sonship by a perfectly consistent walk, in the midst of a rebellious world, in whose darkness they are seen as spiritual stars; offering the news of Christ to their neighbours' notice. So Paul would rejoice at the Great Day, looking back on his course of toil, that he had not lived in vain. [Aye, and that he had not *died* in vain]; for what if he should after all shed his blood as a libation on the altar at which the Philippians offered themselves a living sacrifice? He would rejoice, and would congratulate his converts. Let them rejoice, and congratulate him.

19—30. [But to turn to another subject;] he hopes to send Timothy ere long, to report to him (it will be a cheering report) on their state. None of the Christians round him is so entirely in sympathy with him and with Philippi. Others of his friends might otherwise go, but alas their devotedness to the Lord's will proves too partial. As for Timothy, the Philippians know by old experience how he had done bondservice to the Lord, with Paul, [in their very midst,] in a perfectly filial spirit. Immediately on Paul's learning the issue of the trial, Timothy shall thus be sent. And he trusts ere long to follow personally to Philippi. Epaphroditus meanwhile, Paul's fellow-labourer, and the bearer of the Philippians' bounty to him, is to be spared and sent immediately, as a matter of duty. That duty is made plain by Epaphroditus' state of feeling—his yearning to revisit Philippi, his sore trouble at the thought of the grief which must have been caused at Philippi by news there of his serious illness. He has indeed been ill, almost fatally. But God has spared him the grief [of premature removal from his work, and of being the cause of mourning at Philippi], and has spared Paul too the grief of bereavement added to his other trials. So he has taken pains to send him [in charge of the present Epistle], to the joy of the Philippians and the alleviation of Paul's own sadness. Let them give their messenger a glad Christian welcome back again. Let them shew their esteem for him and such as him. For Christ's work's sake he has all but lost his life; he has run great hazards with it, in order to do for them, in their loving assistance to Paul, what in person they could not do.

Ch. III. 1—3. Now to draw to a close. Let them rejoice in the Lord [as their all in all, cherishing a joyful insight into His fulness as their Righteousness and Life]. In effect, he has been saying this all along. But to emphasize it again is welcome to him and wholesome for them. Let them beware of the Pharisee-Christian, [cruelly exclusive, while] really excluding himself from the true Israel; of the advocate of salvation by works, himself a bungling workman; of the assertors of a circumcision that is only now a physical maltreatment. We Christians are the true circumcised Israel, worshipping by the rites of the Spirit, making Christ Jesus our boast, renouncing all trust in self.

4—11. If indeed such self-trust ever has just grounds, *Paul* claims it. He can surpass the claims of any such theorists [on their own principles,] in point of sacrament, pedigree, education, school of ascetic piety, tremendous earnestness, punctilious observance. These things were once his hoarded gains; but he has now decisively judged them to be one great loss, in the light of that Christ [to whose glory they blinded him]. Yes, and he holds that judgment now, concerning not these things only, but all things whatever [that can obscure his view of] the surpassing bliss of knowing Him as Saviour and as Lord. For Him he has been deprived of his all, and treats it now as refuse, that he may [in exchange] gain CHRIST for his, and be found [by the Judge] in living union with Him, presenting to the Eternal Holiness not a satisfying claim of his own, based on fulfilment of the Law as covenant of life, but the satisfying claim, which consists of Christ for him, appropriated by humble trust; God's way of acceptance, thus made good for Paul. [And is this to terminate in itself, in acceptance of his guilty person, and no more? No;] its true, its necessary issue is that he gets to know his Redeemer spiritually [in His personal glory and beauty], and to experience the power of His resurrection [as conveying assurance of peace and hope of glory, and also in the inflow of His blessed Risen Life], and the joy of entrance, [in measure,] into His experience as the Sufferer, [bearing the cross daily after Him], growing thus into ever truer conformity to His willingness to die. And all this, with the longing to attain [in the path of holiness], at any cost [of self-surrender], to the resurrection of glory [in Him who died to rise again].

12—16. [Meantime—there is reason why he should say it—] he is not yet at the goal, not yet perfected. He is pressing on, aiming to grasp that crown which Christ who grasped him [in conversion] converted him that he might grasp. [Others may say of themselves and their perfection what they will]; *Paul* does not think of himself as having grasped that crown. His concentrated purpose is to renounce all complacency in attainment, and to seek for ever higher things, and to take for his aim nothing short of that eternal glory which is the Divine Arbiter's award at the close of that life of heavenly conversion which is ours in Christ. Are any of us *perfect* Christians, then? [Christians mature and ideal?] Let us shew it [among other things] by such humbling views [of our personal imperfection, and of the greatness of our goal]. Should their views in this matter still differ from his own, he leaves them with calmness to the sure processes of God's enlightening grace [in experience]. Only, up to present light and knowledge, let harmony of conviction, and so of behaviour and action, be cherished by Apostle and converts alike.

17—21. [Nay, let him solemnly appeal to them to] become imitators, one and all, of his principles and practice, and to take for their visible models those among them who manifestly lived those principles out. For there were many [so-called Christians abroad whose life was a terrible and ensnaring travesty of the Gospel of free grace, antinomian claimants of a position in Christ lifted above the holy moral law, men] of whom he often warned them at Philippi, and warns them now, even with tears [over their own ruin and over the deadly mischief they do]. These men are the real enemies of the Cross [which won our pardon, but only that we might be holy]. Their end [in such a path] is eternal perdition. Their God is [not He with whom they claim special intimacy but] their own sensual appetites. They boast [of their insight and experience], but their lofty claims are their deepest disgrace. Their interests and ideas, [pretending to soar above the skies], are really " of the earth, earthy." [Such teachings, and lives, are utterly alien to those of Paul and his true followers.] The seat and centre of *their* life is in heaven, whose citizens they are [free of its privileges, " obliged by its nobility"]. And from heaven they are looking, [in a life governed by that look,] for the Lord Jesus Christ, as Saviour [of body as well as of soul]. He shall transfigure the body which now abases and encumbers us into true and eternal likeness to the Body He now wears upon the throne. [Do they ask, how can this be?] It is a possibility measured by His ability to subdue to His will, and to His purposes, nothing less than all things.

Ch. IV. 1—7. [With such a present, and such a future], let the dear and sorely missed Philippians [cleanse themselves from all pollution, and to that end] let them keep close to Christ, or rather dwell in Christ. [Let them in particular renounce the spirit of self; and here] he entreats two Christian women, Euodia and Syntyche, to renounce their differences. And let his truehearted yoke-fellow [Epaphroditus?] help these two persons to a loving reconciliation, remembering how they toiled and strove for the cause of Christ, by Paul's side, [in the old days]; and let Clement, and Paul's other fellow-labourers, whose names the Lord has marked for heaven, do the like kind service [for Euodia and Syntyche]. Let all rejoice always in the Lord; yes, let them indeed *rejoice* in Him! Let all around them find them self-forgetful, void of self; the Lord's [remembered] presence is the way to this. Let them be anxious in no circumstance; everything must be taken at once to God in prayer, with thanksgiving. Then the peace of God, [the glad tranquillity caused by His presence and rule in the heart], shall encircle as with walls their inner world and its actings, as they dwell in Christ.

8—9. In conclusion, let their minds, [thus shielded, not lie idle, but] be occupied with all that is true, honourable, right, pure, amiable; with all that man truly calls virtue, all that has the praise of his conscience.

And once more, let them practise the principles they have learned of Paul, and seen exemplified in him. So the God of peace, [peace in the soul and in the community], shall be with them.

10—20. [He must not close without loving thanks for a gift of money, for himself and his work, received lately from them.] It has given him holy joy to find that their thought about him has burst into life and fruit again after an interval. Not that they had ever forgotten him; but for some time (he knows) no means of communication had been found. Not, again, that he has been feeling any painful deficiency; for himself, he has learned the lesson of independence of circumstances. He understands the art of meeting poverty and plenty [in equal peace]. He has been let into the secret how to live so. [And the secret is—Jesus Christ.] In living union with Him and His spiritual power, Paul can meet *every* incident of the will of God, [to bear it, or to do it]. Not that he does not warmly feel their loving participation [by this gift] in his trials. But [there was no need of this particular gift to assure him of their affection]; they will remember that when he first evangelized Macedonia, and was now leaving it, they were the only Church which aided him with money; more such gifts than one reached him even when he was no further off than Thessalonica. Do not let them think that he is hunting for their money [by such reminiscences]; no, [so far as he welcomes their money at all] it is because such gifts are deposits bearing rich interest of blessing for the givers. But he has indeed been supplied, and over-supplied, in this contribution now sent by Epaphroditus' hands; this sweet incense from the altar [of self-sacrificing love to Christ in His servant]. For himself, [he can send back no material present, but] his God shall supply their every need, out of the wealth of eternal love and power, lodged for the saints in Christ Jesus. To our God and Father be the glory for ever. Amen.

21—23. Let them greet individually from him every Christian of their number. The Christians associated with him greet them. So do all the Roman believers, especially those connected with the Imperial household.

May the grace of the Lord Jesus Christ be with their inmost being.

A SCHEME OF THE EPISTLES OF ST PAUL

(from Bishop Lightfoot's *Biblical Essays*, p. 224).

PERIOD	EPISTLES	DATES	CHARACTERISTICS
1. Second Missionary Journey	1 and 2 Thessalonians	A.D. 52, 53	Christ the Judge *or* The Tribunal
2. Third Missionary Journey	1 and 2 Corinthians Galatians Romans	57, 58	Christ the Redeemer *or* The Cross
3. First Roman Captivity	Philippians Ephesians Colossians Philemon	62, 63	Christ the Word *or* The Throne
4. After the Release, including the second Roman Captivity	1 Timothy Titus 2 Timothy	67, 68	Church Organization *or* The Congregation

Cynexωc akoyωn anaгinωckomenωn tωn enictoλωn toy makapioy Παyλoy .. χaipω thc caλnirroc anoλayωn thc πneymatikhc .. kai θepmainomai tωi noθωi thn emoi φiλhn eniriνωckωn φωnhn .. enteyθen ta myria eφyh kaka, ano thc tωn гpaφωn arnoiac· enteyθen h noλλh tωn aipecewn eβλacthce λymh, enteyθen oi hmeλhmenoi βioi, enteyθen oi akepδeic nonoi.

S. CHRYSOSTOMUS, *Proœm. in Ep. ad Romanos.*

ΠΡΟΣ ΦΙΛΙΠΠΗΣΙΟΥΣ

1 ¹Παῦλος καὶ Τιμόθεος δοῦλοι Χριστοῦ Ἰησοῦ πᾶσιν τοῖς ἁγίοις ἐν Χριστῷ Ἰησοῦ τοῖς οὖσιν ἐν Φιλίπποις, σὺν ἐπισκόποις καὶ διακόνοις· ²χάρις ὑμῖν καὶ εἰρήνη ἀπὸ θεοῦ πατρὸς ἡμῶν καὶ κυρίου Ἰησοῦ Χριστοῦ.

³Εὐχαριστῶ τῷ θεῷ μου ἐπὶ πάσῃ τῇ μνείᾳ ὑμῶν, ⁴πάντοτε ἐν πάσῃ δεήσει μου ὑπὲρ πάντων ὑμῶν μετὰ χαρᾶς τὴν δέησιν ποιούμενος ⁵ἐπὶ τῇ κοινωνίᾳ ὑμῶν εἰς τὸ εὐαγγέλιον ἀπὸ τῆς πρώτης ἡμέρας ἄχρι τοῦ νῦν, ⁶πεποιθὼς αὐτὸ τοῦτο, ὅτι ὁ ἐναρξάμενος ἐν ὑμῖν ἔργον ἀγαθὸν ἐπιτελέσει ἄχρις ἡμέρας Χριστοῦ Ἰησοῦ, ⁷καθώς ἐστιν δίκαιον ἐμοὶ τοῦτο φρονεῖν ὑπὲρ πάντων ὑμῶν, διὰ τὸ ἔχειν με ἐν τῇ καρδίᾳ ὑμᾶς, ἔν τε τοῖς δεσμοῖς μου καὶ ἐν τῇ ἀπολογίᾳ καὶ βεβαιώσει τοῦ εὐαγγελίου συγκοινωνούς μου τῆς χάριτος πάντας ὑμᾶς ὄντας. ⁸μάρτυς γάρ μου ὁ θεός, ὡς ἐπιποθῶ πάντας ὑμᾶς ἐν σπλάγχνοις Χριστοῦ Ἰησοῦ. ⁹καὶ τοῦτο προσεύχομαι, ἵνα ἡ ἀγάπη ὑμῶν ἔτι μᾶλλον καὶ μᾶλλον περισσεύῃ ἐν ἐπιγνώσει καὶ πάσῃ αἰσθήσει, ¹⁰εἰς τὸ δοκιμάζειν ὑμᾶς τὰ διαφέροντα, ἵνα ἦτε εἰλικρινεῖς καὶ ἀπρόσκοποι εἰς ἡμέραν Χριστοῦ, ¹¹πεπληρωμένοι καρπὸν δικαιοσύνης τὸν διὰ Ἰησοῦ Χριστοῦ, εἰς δόξαν καὶ ἔπαινον θεοῦ.

¹²Γινώσκειν δὲ ὑμᾶς βούλομαι, ἀδελφοί, ὅτι τὰ κατ᾽
ἐμὲ μᾶλλον εἰς προκοπὴν τοῦ εὐαγγελίου ἐλήλυθεν,
¹³ὥστε τοὺς δεσμούς μου φανεροὺς ἐν Χριστῷ γενέσθαι
ἐν ὅλῳ τῷ πραιτωρίῳ καὶ τοῖς λοιποῖς πᾶσιν, ¹⁴καὶ
τοὺς πλείονας τῶν ἀδελφῶν ἐν κυρίῳ πεποιθότας τοῖς
δεσμοῖς μου περισσοτέρως τολμᾶν ἀφόβως τὸν λόγον
τοῦ θεοῦ λαλεῖν. ¹⁵τινὲς μὲν καὶ διὰ φθόνον καὶ ἔριν,
τινὲς δὲ καὶ δι᾽ εὐδοκίαν τὸν Χριστὸν κηρύσσουσιν·
¹⁶οἱ μὲν ἐξ ἀγάπης, εἰδότες ὅτι εἰς ἀπολογίαν τοῦ εὐαγγελίου κεῖμαι, ¹⁷οἱ δὲ ἐξ ἐριθείας τὸν Χριστὸν καταγγέλλουσιν οὐχ ἁγνῶς, οἰόμενοι θλῖψιν ἐγείρειν τοῖς δεσμοῖς
μου. ¹⁸τί γάρ; πλὴν ὅτι παντὶ τρόπῳ, εἴτε προφάσει
εἴτε ἀληθείᾳ, Χριστὸς καταγγέλλεται, καὶ ἐν τούτῳ
χαίρω. ἀλλὰ καὶ χαρήσομαι· ¹⁹οἶδα γὰρ ὅτι τοῦτό μοι
ἀποβήσεται εἰς σωτηρίαν διὰ τῆς ὑμῶν δεήσεως καὶ
ἐπιχορηγίας τοῦ πνεύματος Ἰησοῦ Χριστοῦ, ²⁰κατὰ τὴν
ἀποκαραδοκίαν καὶ ἐλπίδα μου ὅτι ἐν οὐδενὶ αἰσχυνθήσομαι, ἀλλ᾽ ἐν πάσῃ παρρησίᾳ ὡς πάντοτε καὶ νῦν μεγαλυνθήσεται Χριστὸς ἐν τῷ σώματί μου, εἴτε διὰ ζωῆς εἴτε
διὰ θανάτου. ²¹Ἐμοὶ γὰρ τὸ ζῆν Χριστὸς καὶ τὸ ἀποθανεῖν κέρδος. ²²εἰ δὲ τὸ ζῆν ἐν σαρκί, τοῦτό μοι καρπὸς
ἔργου· καὶ τί αἱρήσομαι οὐ γνωρίζω· ²³συνέχομαι δὲ
ἐκ τῶν δύο, τὴν ἐπιθυμίαν ἔχων εἰς τὸ ἀναλῦσαι καὶ
σὺν Χριστῷ εἶναι· πολλῷ γὰρ μᾶλλον κρεῖσσον· ²⁴τὸ
δὲ ἐπιμένειν τῇ σαρκὶ ἀναγκαιότερον δι᾽ ὑμᾶς. ²⁵καὶ
τοῦτο πεποιθὼς οἶδα, ὅτι μενῶ καὶ παραμενῶ πᾶσιν ὑμῖν
εἰς τὴν ὑμῶν προκοπὴν καὶ χαρὰν τῆς πίστεως, ²⁶ἵνα
τὸ καύχημα ὑμῶν περισσεύῃ ἐν Χριστῷ Ἰησοῦ ἐν ἐμοὶ
διὰ τῆς ἐμῆς παρουσίας πάλιν πρὸς ὑμᾶς.

²⁷Μόνον ἀξίως τοῦ εὐαγγελίου τοῦ Χριστοῦ πολιτεύεσθε, ἵνα εἴτε ἐλθὼν καὶ ἰδὼν ὑμᾶς εἴτε ἀπὼν ἀκούω

τὰ περὶ ὑμῶν, ὅτι στήκετε ἐν ἑνὶ πνεύματι, μιᾷ ψυχῇ
συναθλοῦντες τῇ πίστει τοῦ εὐαγγελίου, ²⁸καὶ μὴ πτυρόμενοι ἐν μηδενὶ ὑπὸ τῶν ἀντικειμένων, ἥτις ἐστὶν
αὐτοῖς ἔνδειξις ἀπωλείας, ὑμῶν δὲ σωτηρίας, καὶ τοῦτο
ἀπὸ θεοῦ· ²⁹ὅτι ὑμῖν ἐχαρίσθη τὸ ὑπὲρ Χριστοῦ, οὐ
μόνον τὸ εἰς αὐτὸν πιστεύειν ἀλλὰ καὶ τὸ ὑπὲρ αὐτοῦ
πάσχειν, ³⁰τὸν αὐτὸν ἀγῶνα ἔχοντες οἷον εἴδετε ἐν ἐμοὶ
καὶ νῦν ἀκούετε ἐν ἐμοί.

2 ¹Εἴ τις οὖν παράκλησις ἐν Χριστῷ, εἴ τι παραμύθιον ἀγάπης, εἴ τις κοινωνία πνεύματος, εἴ τις σπλάγχνα
καὶ οἰκτιρμοί, ²πληρώσατέ μου τὴν χαράν, ἵνα τὸ αὐτὸ
φρονῆτε, τὴν αὐτὴν ἀγάπην ἔχοντες, σύμψυχοι, τὸ ἓν
φρονοῦντες, ³μηδὲν κατ' ἐριθείαν μηδὲ κατὰ κενοδοξίαν,
ἀλλὰ τῇ ταπεινοφροσύνῃ ἀλλήλους ἡγούμενοι ὑπερ-
έχοντας ἑαυτῶν, ⁴μὴ τὰ ἑαυτῶν ἕκαστοι σκοποῦντες,
ἀλλὰ καὶ τὰ ἑτέρων ἕκαστοι. ⁵τοῦτο φρονεῖτε ἐν ὑμῖν
ὃ καὶ ἐν Χριστῷ Ἰησοῦ, ⁶ὃς ἐν μορφῇ θεοῦ ὑπάρχων
οὐχ ἁρπαγμὸν ἡγήσατο τὸ εἶναι ἴσα θεῷ, ⁷ἀλλὰ ἑαυτὸν
ἐκένωσεν μορφὴν δούλου λαβών, ἐν ὁμοιώματι ἀνθρώπων
γενόμενος· καὶ σχήματι εὑρεθεὶς ὡς ἄνθρωπος ⁸ἐταπεί-
νωσεν ἑαυτὸν γενόμενος ὑπήκοος μέχρι θανάτου, θανάτου
δὲ σταυροῦ. ⁹διὸ καὶ ὁ θεὸς αὐτὸν ὑπερύψωσεν καὶ
ἐχαρίσατο αὐτῷ τὸ ὄνομα τὸ ὑπὲρ πᾶν ὄνομα, ¹⁰ἵνα
ἐν τῷ ὀνόματι Ἰησοῦ πᾶν γόνυ κάμψῃ ἐπουρανίων καὶ
ἐπιγείων καὶ καταχθονίων, ¹¹καὶ πᾶσα γλῶσσα ἐξομολογήσεται ὅτι κύριος Ἰησοῦς Χριστὸς εἰς δόξαν θεοῦ
πατρός.

¹²Ὥστε, ἀγαπητοί μου, καθὼς πάντοτε ὑπηκούσατε,
μὴ ὡς ἐν τῇ παρουσίᾳ μου μόνον ἀλλὰ νῦν πολλῷ
μᾶλλον ἐν τῇ ἀπουσίᾳ μου, μετὰ φόβου καὶ τρόμου τὴν
ἑαυτῶν σωτηρίαν κατεργάζεσθε· ¹³θεὸς γάρ ἐστιν ὁ

ἐνεργῶν ἐν ὑμῖν καὶ τὸ θέλειν καὶ τὸ ἐνεργεῖν ὑπὲρ τῆς εὐδοκίας. ¹⁴πάντα ποιεῖτε χωρὶς γογγυσμῶν καὶ δια- λογισμῶν, ¹⁵ἵνα γένησθε ἄμεμπτοι καὶ ἀκέραιοι, τέκνα θεοῦ ἄμωμα μέσον γενεᾶς σκολιᾶς καὶ διεστραμμένης, ἐν οἷς φαίνεσθε ὡς φωστῆρες ἐν κόσμῳ, ¹⁶λόγον ζωῆς ἐπέχοντες, εἰς καύχημα ἐμοὶ εἰς ἡμέραν Χριστοῦ, ὅτι οὐκ εἰς κενὸν ἔδραμον οὐδὲ εἰς κενὸν ἐκοπίασα. ¹⁷Ἀλλὰ εἰ καὶ σπένδομαι ἐπὶ τῇ θυσίᾳ καὶ λειτουργίᾳ τῆς πίστεως ὑμῶν, χαίρω καὶ συνχαίρω πᾶσιν ὑμῖν· ¹⁸τὸ δὲ αὐτὸ καὶ ὑμεῖς χαίρετε καὶ συνχαίρετέ μοι.

¹⁹Ἐλπίζω δὲ ἐν κυρίῳ Ἰησοῦ Τιμόθεον ταχέως πέμψαι ὑμῖν, ἵνα κἀγὼ εὐψυχῶ γνοὺς τὰ περὶ ὑμῶν. ²⁰οὐδένα γὰρ ἔχω ἰσόψυχον, ὅστις γνησίως τὰ περὶ ὑμῶν μεριμνήσει· ²¹οἱ πάντες γὰρ τὰ ἑαυτῶν ζητοῦσιν, οὐ τὰ Χριστοῦ Ἰησοῦ. ²²τὴν δὲ δοκιμὴν αὐτοῦ γινώσκετε, ὅτι ὡς πατρὶ τέκνον σὺν ἐμοὶ ἐδούλευσεν εἰς τὸ εὐαγ- γέλιον. ²³τοῦτον μὲν οὖν ἐλπίζω πέμψαι ὡς ἂν ἀφίδω τὰ περὶ ἐμὲ ἐξαυτῆς· ²⁴πέποιθα δὲ ἐν κυρίῳ ὅτι καὶ αὐτὸς ταχέως ἐλεύσομαι.

²⁵Ἀναγκαῖον δὲ ἡγησάμην Ἐπαφρόδιτον τὸν ἀδελ- φὸν καὶ συνεργὸν καὶ συνστρατιώτην μου, ὑμῶν δὲ ἀπόστολον καὶ λειτουργὸν τῆς χρείας μου, πέμψαι πρὸς ὑμᾶς, ²⁶ἐπειδὴ ἐπιποθῶν ἦν πάντας ὑμᾶς, καὶ ἀδημονῶν διότι ἠκούσατε ὅτι ἠσθένησεν. ²⁷καὶ γὰρ ἠσθένησεν παραπλήσιον θανάτῳ· ἀλλὰ ὁ θεὸς ἠλέησεν αὐτόν, οὐκ αὐτὸν δὲ μόνον ἀλλὰ καὶ ἐμέ, ἵνα μὴ λύπην ἐπὶ λύπην σχῶ. ²⁸σπουδαιοτέρως οὖν ἔπεμψα αὐτόν, ἵνα ἰδόντες αὐτὸν πάλιν χαρῆτε, κἀγὼ ἀλυπότερος ὦ. ²⁹προσδέχεσθε οὖν αὐτὸν ἐν κυρίῳ μετὰ πάσης χαρᾶς, καὶ τοὺς τοιού- τους ἐντίμους ἔχετε, ³⁰ὅτι διὰ τὸ ἔργον Χριστοῦ μέχρι θανάτου ἤγγισεν, παραβολευσάμενος τῇ ψυχῇ, ἵνα

ἀναπληρώσῃ τὸ ὑμῶν ὑστέρημα τῆς πρός με λειτουργίας.

3 ¹Τὸ λοιπόν, ἀδελφοί μου, χαίρετε ἐν κυρίῳ. τὰ
αὐτὰ γράφειν ὑμῖν ἐμοὶ μὲν οὐκ ὀκνηρόν, ὑμῖν δὲ
ἀσφαλές. ²Βλέπετε τοὺς κύνας, βλέπετε τοὺς κακοὺς
ἐργάτας, βλέπετε τὴν κατατομήν. ³ἡμεῖς γάρ ἐσμεν
ἡ περιτομή, οἱ πνεύματι θεοῦ λατρεύοντες καὶ καυχώμενοι ἐν Χριστῷ Ἰησοῦ καὶ οὐκ ἐν σαρκὶ πεποιθότες,
⁴καίπερ ἐγὼ ἔχων πεποίθησιν καὶ ἐν σαρκί. εἴ τις
δοκεῖ ἄλλος πεποιθέναι ἐν σαρκί, ἐγὼ μᾶλλον, ⁵περι-
τομῇ ὀκταήμερος, ἐκ γένους Ἰσραήλ, φυλῆς Βενιαμείν,
Ἑβραῖος ἐξ Ἑβραίων, κατὰ νόμον Φαρισαῖος, ⁶κατὰ
ζῆλος διώκων τὴν ἐκκλησίαν, κατὰ δικαιοσύνην τὴν ἐν
νόμῳ γενόμενος ἄμεμπτος. ⁷ἀλλὰ ἅτινα ἦν μοι κέρδη,
ταῦτα ἥγημαι διὰ τὸν Χριστὸν ζημίαν. ⁸ἀλλὰ μενοῦνγε
καὶ ἡγοῦμαι πάντα ζημίαν εἶναι διὰ τὸ ὑπερέχον τῆς
γνώσεως Χριστοῦ Ἰησοῦ τοῦ κυρίου μου, δι᾽ ὃν τὰ πάντα
ἐζημιώθην, καὶ ἡγοῦμαι σκύβαλα ἵνα Χριστὸν κερδήσω
⁹καὶ εὑρεθῶ ἐν αὐτῷ, μὴ ἔχων ἐμὴν δικαιοσύνην τὴν ἐκ
νόμου ἀλλὰ τὴν διὰ πίστεως Χριστοῦ, τὴν ἐκ θεοῦ
δικαιοσύνην ἐπὶ τῇ πίστει· ¹⁰τοῦ γνῶναι αὐτὸν καὶ τὴν
δύναμιν τῆς ἀναστάσεως αὐτοῦ καὶ κοινωνίαν παθημάτων αὐτοῦ, συμμορφιζόμενος τῷ θανάτῳ αὐτοῦ, ¹¹εἴπως
καταντήσω εἰς τὴν ἐξανάστασιν τὴν ἐκ νεκρῶν.

¹²Οὐχ ὅτι ἤδη ἔλαβον ἢ ἤδη τετελείωμαι, διώκω δὲ
εἰ καταλάβω, ἐφ᾽ ᾧ καὶ κατελήμφθην ὑπὸ Χριστοῦ
Ἰησοῦ. ¹³ἀδελφοί, ἐγὼ ἐμαυτὸν οὔπω λογίζομαι κατει-
ληφέναι· ¹⁴ἓν δέ, τὰ μὲν ὀπίσω ἐπιλανθανόμενος, τοῖς
δὲ ἔμπροσθεν ἐπεκτεινόμενος, κατὰ σκοπὸν διώκω εἰς
τὸ βραβεῖον τῆς ἄνω κλήσεως τοῦ θεοῦ ἐν Χριστῷ
Ἰησοῦ. ¹⁵ὅσοι οὖν τέλειοι τοῦτο φρονῶμεν· καὶ εἴ τι

ἑτέρως φρονεῖτε, καὶ τοῦτο ὁ θεὸς ὑμῖν ἀποκαλύψει· [16]πλὴν εἰς ὃ ἐφθάσαμεν, τῷ αὐτῷ στοιχεῖν.

[17]Συμμιμηταί μου γίνεσθε, ἀδελφοί, καὶ σκοπεῖτε τοὺς οὕτως περιπατοῦντας καθὼς ἔχετε τύπον ἡμᾶς. [18]πολλοὶ γὰρ περιπατοῦσιν οὓς πολλάκις ἔλεγον ὑμῖν, νῦν δὲ καὶ κλαίων λέγω, τοὺς ἐχθροὺς τοῦ σταυροῦ τοῦ Χριστοῦ· [19]ὧν τὸ τέλος ἀπώλεια, ὧν ὁ θεὸς ἡ κοιλία καὶ ἡ δόξα ἐν τῇ αἰσχύνῃ αὐτῶν, οἱ τὰ ἐπίγεια φρονοῦντες. [20]ἡμῶν γὰρ τὸ πολίτευμα ἐν οὐρανοῖς ὑπάρχει, ἐξ οὗ καὶ σωτῆρα ἀπεκδεχόμεθα κύριον Ἰησοῦν Χριστόν, [21]ὃς μετασχηματίσει τὸ σῶμα τῆς ταπεινώσεως ἡμῶν σύμμορφον τῷ σώματι τῆς δόξης αὐτοῦ, κατὰ τὴν ἐνέργειαν τοῦ δύνασθαι αὐτὸν καὶ ὑποτάξαι αὐτῷ τὰ πάντα.

4 [1]Ὥστε, ἀδελφοί μου ἀγαπητοὶ καὶ ἐπιπόθητοι, χαρὰ καὶ στέφανός μου, οὕτως στήκετε ἐν κυρίῳ, ἀγαπητοί.

[2]Εὐοδίαν παρακαλῶ καὶ Συντυχὴν παρακαλῶ τὸ αὐτὸ φρονεῖν ἐν κυρίῳ. [3]ναὶ ἐρωτῶ καὶ σέ, γνήσιε σύνζυγε, συνλαμβάνου αὐταῖς, αἵτινες ἐν τῷ εὐαγγελίῳ συνήθλησάν μοι μετὰ καὶ Κλήμεντος καὶ τῶν λοιπῶν συνεργῶν μου, ὧν τὰ ὀνόματα ἐν βίβλῳ ζωῆς.

[4]Χαίρετε ἐν κυρίῳ πάντοτε· πάλιν ἐρῶ, χαίρετε. [5]τὸ ἐπιεικὲς ὑμῶν γνωσθήτω πᾶσιν ἀνθρώποις· ὁ κύριος ἐγγύς. [6]μηδὲν μεριμνᾶτε, ἀλλ᾽ ἐν παντὶ τῇ προσευχῇ καὶ τῇ δεήσει μετὰ εὐχαριστίας τὰ αἰτήματα ὑμῶν γνωριζέσθω πρὸς τὸν θεόν. [7]καὶ ἡ εἰρήνη τοῦ θεοῦ ἡ ὑπερέχουσα πάντα νοῦν φρουρήσει τὰς καρδίας ὑμῶν καὶ τὰ νοήματα ὑμῶν ἐν Χριστῷ Ἰησοῦ.

[8]Τὸ λοιπόν, ἀδελφοί, ὅσα ἐστὶν ἀληθῆ, ὅσα σεμνά, ὅσα δίκαια, ὅσα ἁγνά, ὅσα προσφιλῆ, ὅσα εὔφημα, εἴ τις ἀρετὴ καὶ εἴ τις ἔπαινος, ταῦτα λογίζεσθε· [9]ἃ καὶ

ἐμάθετε καὶ παρελάβετε καὶ ἠκούσατε καὶ εἴδετε ἐν
ἐμοί, ταῦτα πράσσετε· καὶ ὁ θεὸς τῆς εἰρήνης ἔσται
μεθ᾽ ὑμῶν.

[10] Ἐχάρην δὲ ἐν κυρίῳ μεγάλως ὅτι ἤδη ποτὲ ἀνεθάλετε τὸ ὑπὲρ ἐμοῦ φρονεῖν· ἐφ᾽ ᾧ καὶ ἐφρονεῖτε,
ἠκαιρεῖσθε δέ. [11] οὐχ ὅτι καθ᾽ ὑστέρησιν λέγω· ἐγὼ
γὰρ ἔμαθον ἐν οἷς εἰμὶ αὐτάρκης εἶναι. [12] οἶδα καὶ
ταπεινοῦσθαι, οἶδα καὶ περισσεύειν· ἐν παντὶ καὶ ἐν
πᾶσιν μεμύημαι καὶ χορτάζεσθαι καὶ πεινᾶν, καὶ
περισσεύειν καὶ ὑστερεῖσθαι. [13] πάντα ἰσχύω ἐν τῷ
ἐνδυναμοῦντί με. [14] πλὴν καλῶς ἐποιήσατε συνκοινωνή-
σαντές μου τῇ θλίψει. [15] οἴδατε δὲ καὶ ὑμεῖς, Φιλιππήσιοι, ὅτι ἐν ἀρχῇ τοῦ εὐαγγελίου, ὅτε ἐξῆλθον ἀπὸ
Μακεδονίας, οὐδεμία μοι ἐκκλησία ἐκοινώνησεν εἰς
λόγον δόσεως καὶ λήμψεως εἰ μὴ ὑμεῖς μόνοι, [16] ὅτι καὶ
ἐν Θεσσαλονίκῃ καὶ ἅπαξ καὶ δὶς εἰς τὴν χρείαν μοι
ἐπέμψατε. [17] οὐχ ὅτι ἐπιζητῶ τὸ δόμα, ἀλλὰ ἐπιζητῶ
τὸν καρπὸν τὸν πλεονάζοντα εἰς λόγον ὑμῶν. [18] ἀπέχω
δὲ πάντα καὶ περισσεύω, πεπλήρωμαι, δεξάμενος παρὰ
Ἐπαφροδίτου τὰ παρ᾽ ὑμῶν, ὀσμὴν εὐωδίας, θυσίαν
δεκτὴν εὐάρεστον τῷ θεῷ. [19] ὁ δὲ θεός μου πληρώσει
πᾶσαν χρείαν ὑμῶν κατὰ τὸ πλοῦτος αὐτοῦ ἐν δόξῃ ἐν
Χριστῷ Ἰησοῦ. [20] τῷ δὲ θεῷ καὶ πατρὶ ἡμῶν ἡ δόξα εἰς
τοὺς αἰῶνας τῶν αἰώνων· ἀμήν.

[21] Ἀσπάσασθε πάντα ἅγιον ἐν Χριστῷ Ἰησοῦ. ἀσπάζονται ὑμᾶς οἱ σὺν ἐμοὶ ἀδελφοί. [22] ἀσπάζονται
ὑμᾶς πάντες οἱ ἅγιοι, μάλιστα δὲ οἱ ἐκ τῆς Καίσαρος
οἰκίας.

[23] Ἡ χάρις τοῦ κυρίου Ἰησοῦ Χριστοῦ μετὰ τοῦ
πνεύματος ὑμῶν.

NOTES.

CHAPTER I.

Title. Πρὸς Φιλιππησίους. So אABK₂ and many cursives. D₂G₂ read αρχεται προς Φιλιππησιους (D₂, -ησιους). L has του αγιου αποστολου Παυλου επιστολη προς Φιλιππησιους ; and several other forms of the title appear, all considerably later than that given in the text.

1. Χριστοῦ Ἰησοῦ. So אBD₂ 109 copt : Ἰησοῦ Χριστοῦ is the order of G₂ and the large majority of other copies vulg syr (pesh and harkl). St Paul's love of the order X. Ἰ. inclines us to it in this case, though the adverse documentary evidence is weighty. LTTr Ell Ltft WH Χριστοῦ Ἰησοῦ.

5. ἀπὸ τῆς πρώτης ἡμέρας. So אABP with some other (scanty) evidence. D₂G₂K₂L, and most cursives, with good patristic support, give ἀ. πρ. ἡμ. This is here *durior lectio*, and, possessing considerable documentary evidence, seems to us the better. Ell Ltft πρώτης, LTTr WH τῆς πρώτης.

7. συγκοινωνούς. Συνκοινωνούς is the spelling of אAB*D₂G₂. So σύνψυχοι (ii. 2) and other similar words. WH (*N. T. in Gr.* § 393—404) deal with the question of spelling in MSS. generally, and conclude that the spellings of the best MSS. are the most trustworthy within our reach ; more likely to be transmitted from the autographs than introduced at the date of transcription.

11. καρπὸν...τὸν. So אABD₂G₂K₂L, several cursives, vulg (fuld καρπῶν) and some Greek fathers. P, the great majority of cursives, some copies of vulg syr (pesh and harkl) copt, Chrys Theophylact read καρπῶν...τῶν. St Paul elsewhere tends to use the singular rather than the plural of καρπός, and this, with the documentary evidence, inclines the scale to καρπὸν here. LTTr Ell Ltft WH καρπὸν...τὸν.

14. λ. τοῦ θεοῦ. So אABD₂*P, several cursives, vulg goth syr (pesh and harkl) copt and some other versions, Chrys (in two places) and some other fathers. The large majority of cursives omit τοῦ θεοῦ.

16, 17. οἱ μὲν ἐξ ἀγάπης...οἱ δὲ ἐξ ἐριθείας. The documentary evidence is strong for this order of the clauses, reversing that of A.V. So

אABD*₃G₂P, the important cursives 17 37 73 80, and several others,
vulg goth copt syr (pesh) (omitting the words οἱ μὲν ἐξ ἀγάπης)
and some other versions, and quotations by Basil Tertull and
some other fathers. The other order is read (in certain recensions)
in D₂KL (with some difference in detail), the great majority of cursives,
and quotations by Chrys Theodoret Damasc. To the favourable
documentary evidence must be added that of the subsequent context;
ver. 18 follows much more naturally on the ver. 17 of this order than
on the ver. 17 of the other. So all recent Editors.

18. πλὴν ὅτι. So אAG₂P, 17 and several other cursives, sah
Athan Cyr Theophyl. πλὴν alone is given by D₂KL, the great
majority of cursives, syr (pesh and harkl) arm æth, Chrys Theodoret.
LTTr Ltft WH πλὴν ὅτι. Ell om. ὅτι.

23. συνέχομαι δὲ. Many cursives, syr (pesh) Theodoret and
Origen (translated), read συν. γὰρ. But the evidence for δὲ is decisive.
So all recent Editors.

πολλῷ γὰρ. So אᵃABC, the important cursives 17 67 and five
others, Clem Alex Or Ambrst Aug (who makes use of *enim* in
an argument, *de Doctr. Chr.* iii. 2). Γὰρ is omitted by א*D₂FGKLP,
the great majority of cursives, vulg syr (pesh and harkl) and
some other versions, Chrys Theodoret and some other fathers. LTTr
Ltft WH πολλῷ γὰρ. Ell πολλῷ. The evidence of copies and
versions on the whole is for the omission of γὰρ.

25. παραμενῶ. So אABCD*₃G₂, 17 67 80 and a few other
cursives, arm. Meanwhile συμπαραμενῶ is read by D₃ᶜKLP, the great
majority of cursives, Chrys (who dwells on the word: συμπαρα-
μενῶ· τοῦτ' ἐστίν, ὄψομαι ὑμᾶς), Theodoret and other Greek fathers.
Συμπαραμενῶ thus has considerable support, and is recommended
besides by its comparative unlikelihood. It is easier to suppose
the unusual double compound shortened to παραμενῶ than παραμενῶ
expanded without any obvious call from the context. All recent
Editors παραμενῶ.

28. ἐστὶν αὐτοῖς. So אABCD*₃G₂, the important cursives 17 178
and two others, vulg (some copies) goth arm. D₂ᶜP, 47 and some
other cursives, Chrys Theophyl, read ἐστὶν αὐτοῖς μὲν. KL, the
great majority of cursives, syr (harkl), Theodoret Damasc read
αὐτοῖς μέν ἐστιν. All recent Editors ἐστὶν αὐτοῖς.

ὑμῶν. So אABC²P, 17 and three other cursives, arm syr
(pesh), Chrys Aug. D₂ᶜKL, the great majority of cursives, vulg
copt goth æth, Theodoret Ambrst and other fathers, read ὑμῖν,
which is also attested indirectly by C*D*G₂, which read ἡμῖν.
All recent Editors ὑμῶν. Ltft says of ὑμῖν and αὐτοῖς μέν ἐστιν,
"These are obviously corrections for the sake of balancing the clauses
and bringing out the contrast." They are thus rejected on the
principle of preferring the *durior lectio*, which certainly ὑμῶν is.
Otherwise, both rejected readings have considerable support, ὑμῖν
especially.

Ch. I. 1—2. Greeting.

1. Παῦλος. The name first appears Acts xiii. 9. It was probably
from the first the alternative name (for use in intercourse with Gentiles)
of Saul; given him as bearing a sound resembling his Hebrew home-
name. It seems to have been a favourite name at Tarsus (Lewin, *Life
&c. of St Paul*, i. 6).

He adds no allusion to his apostleship here (nor in the Ep. to
Philemon). Affectionate and untroubled intimacy with his correspondents made it needless.

Τιμόθεος. Named 24 times in N.T. See esp. Acts xvi. 1; 1 Cor. iv.
17, xvi. 10, 11; 1 Tim. i. 2; 2 Tim. i. 4, 5; below, ii. 19—22. Timotheus' connexion with Philippi was close. See Acts xvi., xvii., where
it is implied that he was St Paul's habitual companion till (xvii. 14)
they parted for a time at Beroea. He must thus have been present
during the stormy days of the first visit to Philippi, though for unknown reasons he did not share the maltreatment of Paul and Silas.
Later, Acts xx., he accompanied St Paul from Macedonia to Asia
Minor, and Philippi (ver. 6) was visited then again.

His name is similarly linked with St Paul's in 2 Cor., Col., 1 Thess.,
2 Thess. Here, but not in those other places, the Apostle at once
goes on to speak in his own person alone to his correspondents.

δοῦλοι. "Bondmen, slaves." So St Paul designates himself (alone
or in company) Rom. i. 1; Gal. i. 10; Tit. i. 1. Such he was, not only
as Apostle, but as Christian; see e.g. Luke xvii. 7—10; Rom. vi. 19;
but he loves to emphasize the fact in connexion with his special mode
of service.—The bondservice of the heavenly Master is not forced
labour, against the will, but it *is* the labour of those who do not con-
tract, but belong. Meanwhile, *Illi servire est regnare*.

Χριστοῦ 'Ιησοῦ. The order X. 'I. (see critical note) is almost
peculiar to St Paul, and he uses it more often than the other order.
The slight emphasis thus given to Χριστός suggests a special reference
to the Lord in glory.

ἁγίοις. "Holy Ones," separated from sin to God. Ἅγιος appears to
be connected linguistically not with ἅγνυμι, as if it implied *a breach,
a severance*, but with ἅγος or ἄγος, *a matter of sacred awe*. The ἅγιος
should thus mean *the devotee* of his God. Usage affirms this, and
thus sanctions in effect the suggestion of *separation* given by the older
(ἅγνυμι) derivation.

The Apostle constantly denotes the Christian community and its
members by this term, as equally true of all converts. He takes
them on their profession; not to lower the true meaning of the word,
but using it on a well-understood hypothesis. The ἅγιος is not the
professed Christian merely, but the professed Christian assumed to
be what he professes to be. Otherwise he is not in deed but only in
designation "a saint," "faithful," &c.

ἐν Χριστῷ 'Ιησοῦ. United to Him, as the branch is "in" the tree.
The ἅγιοι are what they are as they are veritably in contact with the

Holy One, by covenant and in eternal life. Cp. 1 Ccr. vi. 17; 1 Job. v. 12.

ἐν Φιλίπποις. See Introduction, ch. i.

σὺν ἐπισκόποις καὶ διακόνοις. "With *the* bishops and deacons," though the article is absent. Context in a case like this sufficiently defines; the persons of the classes named are self-evidently those at Philippi. So we in English could say, "bishops, deacons, and all," as readily as "*the* bishops, &c."

For further remarks on the offices here mentioned, see Appendix C.

2. χάρις ὑμῖν κτλ. Χάρις is a near equivalent to the English "favour," with its alternative meanings of comeliness and goodwill, of pleasingness and pleasure. The latter is its far commoner direction in LXX. and N.T., the former in the Greek Apocrypha. Linguistically, the word seems to be connected first with the thought of *brightness*, then with that of *beauty*, and so passes into that of the *kindly pleasure* given by the sight of beauty. By usage in didactic passages in the N.T. it denotes specially the *unbought* favour of the Holy One towards the sinful and helpless, whether in pardon, in gift of Divine life, or in development of it. It is the antithesis to ἔργον and to the whole idea of merit and payment. Cp. esp. Rom. xi. 6. And *in itself*, as the act is never apart from the Agent, χάρις in our acceptance is *God for us*, in our new life and power it is *God in us*.

εἰρήνη. The word is probably cognate to εἴρω, to join. "Peace" is essentially a harmony, an adjustment. Here it denotes the enjoyment of harmony with God; His reconciled favour, resulting in the Christian's and the Church's inward rest and happiness.

θεοῦ. The Father; see the immediate context. Not that to St Paul the Father is more Divine than the Son, but that He is the FATHER, in whom Deity is as in the Fountain, while it is in the Son as in the Stream. Hence the frequent distinctive use of θεός where He is in view.—See Pearson, *Exposition of the Creed*, marginal p. 40.

κυρίου. Without the article, as frequently. Usage has given the word an adequate self-definition. Here the Lord Christ is equally with His Father the Giver of eternal blessing; a deep indication of the apostolic belief about Him.

3—11. THANKSGIVING AND PRAYER FOR THE PHILIPPIAN SAINTS.

3. Εὐχαριστῶ. So also in the opening of Rom., 1 Cor., Eph., Col., 1 Thess., Philem. His "thanksgivings" for the two Macedonian Churches, Philippi and Thessalonica, are peculiarly warm and full.

τῷ θεῷ μου. The phrase is almost peculiar in N. T. to St Paul. In O. T., cp. Psal. xxii. 1 (appropriated by the Crucified Lord), lxiii. 1, &c.—The phrase speaks a profound individual appropriation and realization.

ἐπὶ πάσῃ τῇ μνείᾳ ὑμῶν. "In (or more literally "on") all my re-membrance of you." The article may best be represented here by "my"; it was not possible to write both genitives, μου and ὑμῶν.— Cp. Rom. i. 9; Eph. i. 16; 1 Thess. i. 2; 2 Tim. i. 3; Philem. 4.

4. δεήσει. "Request, petition"; a narrower word than προσευχή, which may and often does denote *worship* at large.

μετὰ χαρᾶς. Emphatic words by position. They strike a note continually repeated in the Epistle.

τὴν δέησιν. "*The* request" just mentioned.

ποιούμενος. The middle suggests a personal fulness in the action. The request comes from the depth of the man and relates to a welfare dear to him as his own. Only it is impossible to explain this in English without a certain exaggeration of the delicate Greek.

On the other hand ποιεῖσθαι is often used with a substantive by way of periphrasis, to express what would be more simply stated by a verb. E.g. Luke xiii. 22, πορείαν ποιούμενος (cf. ix. 51, πορεύεσθαι). Instances of ποιεῖν thus used are very rare. Thus explained the phrase here nearly equals δεόμενος, though still, surely, adding a certain fulness.

5. ἐπὶ τῇ κοινωνίᾳ ὑμῶν. "Over (on account of) your fellowship," your making yourselves one with me, whether in deed or in spirit. See further just below, ver. 7 and notes. The immediate but by no means whole reference was no doubt to their generous gifts of money; cp. iv. 10—19.

εἰς τὸ εὐαγγέλιον. "For the Gospel"; i.e. for its furtherance. For the phrase cp. 2 Cor. ii. 12, and below, ii. 22. For εὐαγγέλιον denoting *practically* the work of evangelization cp. 2 Cor. viii. 18; Gal. ii. 7; below, ii. 22, iv. 3, 15; 1 Thess. iii. 2.

ἀπὸ τῆς πρώτης ἡμέρας. On the reading, see critical note. If ἀπὸ πρ. ἡμ. is read, cp. Acts x. 30, xx. 18, for such absence of the article; it is perhaps an unconscious *nuance* of idiom, refusing analysis. See Lightfoot however on this verse: "the article is frequently omitted, because the numeral is sufficiently definite in itself." With this assertion of the Philippians' original and steady sympathy cp. ch. iv. 15, 16.

6. πεποιθώς. "Feeling confident." The word sometimes denotes *reliance*, on sure grounds, expressed or not (so e.g. Matt. xxvii. 43; 2 Cor. i. 9; below, ii. 24, iii. 3, 4); sometimes a more arbitrary *assurance* (Rom. ii. 19); in every case, a feeling of personal certainty. This expression of "confidence" about their future is perhaps occasioned by the words just previous, about their preserving consistency "*until now.*"

αὐτὸ τοῦτο. A characteristic Pauline expression; the firm touch of an intent mind. See e.g. Rom. ix. 17, xiii. 6; 2 Cor. ii. 3, v. 5; Gal. ii. 10; Eph. vi. 18; Col. iv. 8. Elsewhere in N. T. it appears only in 2 Pet. i. 5, in a disputed reading.

ὁ ἐναρξάμενος. We may perhaps render, "He who did inaugurate." Ἐνάρχεσθαι in Greek of the golden age (e.g. Eurip., *I. A.* 435) habitually means the *solemn opening* of the sacrificial ritual, the taking the barley from the basket. And in the Apocrypha it seems to tend on occasion to a certain *solemnity*; e.g. Ecclus xxxviii. 16, τέκνον, ἐπὶ νεκρῷ...ὡς δεινὰ πάσχων ἔναρξαι θρῆνον. But there are cases enough to justify the simpler rendering "He who did begin," if it is otherwise preferred.—The aorist participle points of course to the biographical crisis of their evangelization and conversion, when the Giver of grace made His message effectual in them. Cp. Gal. iii. 3, ἐναρξάμενοι πνεύματι νῦν σαρκὶ ἐπιτελεῖσθε; There the crisis of conversion is viewed from the *convert's* side.

ἔργον ἀγαθὸν. We may perhaps render "*the* good work"; so plainly is "the work of works" in view, defined by its own greatness.

ἐπιτελέσει, "Will complete it." The verb, like ἐνάρχεσθαι, has occasionally a religious solemnity of meaning; e.g. Hdt. ii. 63, θυσίας ἐπιτελέουσι. But Biblical Greek usage hardly warrants our pressing such a meaning here. Cp. again Gal. iii. 3: "are ye now *being completed*, ἐπιτελεῖσθε, by the flesh?"—The thought here is that of Psal. cxxxviii. 8, where it appears as the individual believer's personal assurance. (Aquila and Symmachus there have ἐπιτελέσει.)

ἄχρις ἡμέρας Χ. Ἰ. I.e., the process issuing in "completion" will go on till then, and be then summed up. "The day" is the goal, because not till then will *the whole being* of the Christian, body (Rom. viii. 23) as well as spirit, be fully "redeemed" from the results of sin. The mention of "the day" is thus equally in point, whether or not the Lord should be coming soon. In either case it, and no previous date, is the point of "completion."—"The day" is mentioned below, i. 10, ii. 16, and altogether, in St Paul, about twenty times. The Lord uses the word of His own Return, Matt. vii. 22, and in some fourteen other places in the Gospels, including Joh. vi. 39, 40, 44, 55.

7. Ver. 6 is a parenthesis in the thought, suggested probably by the last words of ver. 5. We now take up the thread of vv. 4, 5; the thankful remembrance, the glad prayer, occasioned by their "fellowship in the Gospel." He now justifies the assertion in detail.

δίκαιον. Not "meet" only, but "right." He feels a delightful *duty*.

ἐμοὶ. The emphatic form; "for *me*," whatever is right for others.

φρονεῖν. Almost, "to feel" this gratitude and joy. Φρονεῖν, a favourite word with St Paul, nearly always denotes a mental state or habit, not explicit thinking. See e.g. Rom. viii. 5, 6, 7, 27; below, iii. 15, 19; Col. iii. 2. For another shade of meaning see below, iv. 10.

ὑπὲρ πάντων ὑμῶν. "On behalf of you all," R.V. Ὑπέρ c. gen. properly means "over," and so suggests, first and most surely, attention, concern, interest; as when a man is busy "over" his work. This of course lends itself, in fit contexts, to such special meanings as "on behalf of," or even "in the place of"; but these need a context to develope them. The context of *prayer* above (ver. 4) justifies R.V. here.

διὰ τὸ ἔχειν με ἐν τῇ καρδίᾳ ὑμᾶς. We might render, of course, "Because you have me, &c." But with that meaning he would probably write ἐν ταῖς καρδίαις: and the following context makes *his* affection *for them* the prominent thought.

ἔν τε τοῖς δεσμοῖς μου κτλ. His first allusion to imprisonment. We can connect these words, in grammar, with either the previous or following sentences. But a connexion with the following is, in reason, the much more probable. To St Paul, his δεσμά and his ἀπολογία were practically one experience; to the Philippians, they would seem two distinct calls for loving fellowship.

ἐν τῇ ἀπολογίᾳ καὶ βεβαιώσει. Two words linked by one definite article. They cover together his missionary work at Rome. His ἀπολογία (cp. Acts xxii. 1, xxv. 16; below, 16; and esp. 1 Pet. iii. 15) was the explanation and vindication of the Gospel to the unconvinced; his βεβαίωσις, the development of "the reason of the hope" in the minds of convinced disciples, and also perhaps the practical "planting" of the Church for orderly work and witness.

μου τῆς χάριτος. Comparing Rom. i. 5, Eph. iii. 2, 8, we see a reference here not to Divine grace in general (God in Christ, *for* and *in* the saints; see on ver. 2 above) so much as to the special gracious gift of apostleship. So were the Philippians bound to him, alike in Divine life and in human love, that in his apostolic sufferings and labours they were his fellows, identified with him in everything, and by love, prayer, and gifts, working as it were through him.

The words συγκοινωνούς μου...ὄντας, in apposition to the ὑμᾶς above, may be rendered as if almost *absolute;* "you all being copartners of my grace."

Observe in this whole context the iteration of πάντες ὑμεῖς. It has been suggested that he has in view the slight inner dissensions at Philippi, and thus delicately deprecates them. But the motive seems too artificial to be quite in place in this warm passage; the language is that of unreserved affection.

8. μάρτυς...ὁ θεός. Cp. Rom. i. 9; 1 Thess. ii. 5, 10; and see 2 Cor. i. 18; for similar solemn appeals, characteristic of an ardent heart, often tried by unkind suspicions.

ἐπιποθῶ. The word is not common in classical Greek, nor in Biblical Greek before the N.T., where it, with its cognates, is used 11 times by St Paul (Rom. i. 11, xv. 23; 2 Cor. v. 2, vii. 7, 11, ix. 14; Phil. ii. 26, iv. 1, and here; 1 Thess. iii. 6; 2 Tim. i. 4), once by St James (iv. 5), and once by St Peter (1. ii. 2). In all the Pauline places it indicates a *homesick* yearning; in 2 Cor. v. 2 the "home" is the heavenly rest. Here the verb breathes the deep family affection of the Gospel.

ἐν σπλάγχνοις X. Ἰ. In classical Greek the σπλάγχνα are commonly (not invariably: e.g. Æsch., *S. c. T.* 1022) the *viscera nobiliora,* including the heart. The LXX. in their (rare) use of the word do not so limit it; they render by it the Heb. *rach'mim,* the bowels, viewed as the seat of affection. But the question is one not of anatomy but of current reference, and our word "heart" is thus the best rendering.

"In the heart of Christ Jesus":—the phrase is deeply significant. The Christian's personality, never lost, is yet so united to his Lord (see 1 Cor. vi. 17) that the emotions of the regenerate member are as it were in continuity with those of the ever-blessed Head. There is more than sympathy; there is communication.

9. καὶ τοῦτο προσεύχομαι. He defines thus the "request" of ver. 4.

ἵνα κτλ. Here ἵνα c. conj. denotes rather *purport* than *purpose;* less the aim than the idea of his prayer. This usage, as distinct from the strictly *final* usage, belongs to the later classical and the Hellenistic Greek, and is very frequent in N.T. A kindred but not identical usage appears e.g. Joh. xvii. 3, where the Greek means, in effect, that "the life eternal is, in the true *import* of the words, to know &c."

ἡ ἀγάπη ὑμῶν. Of which St Paul has had such warm proofs.

περισσεύῃ. He loves the thought of spiritual growth and overflow; see e.g. below, ver. 26, iv. 12, 18; and, for a close parallel here, 1 Thess. iv. 1.

ἐν ἐπιγνώσει. So Rom. xv. 13, εἰς τὸ περισσεύειν ὑμᾶς ἐν τῇ ἐλπίδι. He prays that their love may be ever "richer in knowledge and perception" as its safety and aid. The use and construction here of περισσεύειν belongs to later classical and Hellenistic Greek.

ἐπιγνώσει. Ἐπίγνωσις is a word of later classical and Hellenistic Greek. (In LXX. and Apocrypha the noun does not occur, but the verb is frequent.) In N.T., (more than in other Biblical Greek), it tends by usage to denote *full* (or *true*) *knowledge, in spiritual things.* St Paul uses it 15 times, besides Heb. x. 26; St Peter 4 times.

πάσῃ αἰσθήσει. Πάσῃ, with reference to the manifold demands for its exercise. Αἴσθησις is used only here in N.T., and cognates to it only Luke ix. 45; Heb. v. 14. In LXX. it is frequent in Proverbs as a rendering for *da'ath*, "knowledge." The A.V. rendering, "judgment," (R.V., "discernment"), a word which we often use of the criticism of e.g. works of art, and of practical insight, is a fair equivalent to the Greek here.

10. εἰς τὸ δοκιμάζειν. "With a view to (to qualify you for) testing."

τὰ διαφέροντα. See Rom. ii. 18 for the same phrase.—Τὰ διαφέροντα may be either "the things which *excel,*" or "the things which *differ*" (as in margin R.V.). On the whole we prefer this latter, partly as agreeing better with the (scanty) use of the verb in older Biblical Greek and in most of the N.T. examples; and more, as more obviously agreeing with the just previous thought of a growth of "judgment." The Greek commentator Theophylact (cent. xi.) explains the words by τί δεῖ πρᾶξαι καὶ τί δεῖ μὴ πρᾶξαι.

ἵνα ἦτε. The "judgment" was always to issue in character and conduct.

εἰλικρινεῖς. "Pure, singlehearted." Three derivations of εἰλικρινής (occasional in Attic; in N.T. only here and 2 Pet. iii. 1) are suggested; (1) εἴλη, κρίνειν: a test by sunlight; (2) εἴλειν, κρίνειν: a test by rolling or racking; (3) εἴλη (ἴλη), κρίνειν: a separation, or assortment, as in ranks or troops, with the thought of the disentanglement, simplification, of motive and conduct. This latter is favoured by Lightfoot. The Latin rendering is sinceri ("unadulterated"); and it is worth while to notice that this has a possible linguistic connexion with "sin-gle."

ἀπρόσκοποι. The word may mean either (1) "feeling no stumbling-block" (προσκοπή, πρόσκομμα; Lat. offendiculum, whence our word "offence" in its antiquated meaning), or (2) "laying no stumbling-block" in the way of others. The word is not classical, and nowhere common. The only two other N.T. examples, Acts xxiv. 16; 1 Cor. x. 32 (both Pauline); are exactly divided as evidence for the meaning here; and thus we are left to the context. This on the whole decides for (1); the Apostle is mainly concerned with the inward life of the Philippians; he prays that they may be so "sincere" with God as never to "stumble over" a wrong motive.

εἰς ἡμέραν Χριστοῦ. "Unto the day"; against it, in view of it, as the crisis of absolute disclosure. So ii. 16, where see note. On the phrase ἡμέρα Χ. see above on ver. 6.

11. πεπληρωμένοι. The perfect participle seems to anticipate "the day." He sees the Philippians as they will be then, "having been filled," and therefore then full; trees whose every branch had put forth, in their earthly life, "the fruit" described Gal. v. 22, 23.—On the reading, see critical note.—The accusative is "of reference."—Here, as in Gal., l.c., the singular (καρπόν) is significant. The results of grace are manifold, yet as to their material they are one; and each is necessary to the fulness of the rest.

δικαιοσύνης. So Jas iii. 18. And in LXX. see Prov. xi. 30, xiii. 2; Amos vi. 12. The "fruit" is a result yielded by "righteousness." "Righteousness" is here probably the rightness of the regenerate will, regarded as in accord with Divine law. But there is a possible reference also, in a Pauline writing (see further on ch. iii. 9), to that aspect of the word so prominent in the Roman Epistle, satisfactoriness to the law in respect of the atoning Satisfaction of Christ; so that the "fruit" would be the outcome not only of a renewed will but of an accepted person.

διὰ Ἰησοῦ Χριστοῦ. Who is alike, by His merit, the procuring Cause of the new life, and so of its fruits, and, by His Life, the true Basis of it.

εἰς δόξαν κτλ. The true goal of the whole process of salvation. "To Him are all things; to Whom be glory for ever. Amen" (Rom. xi. 36).—On the use of θεός here, distinctively, as often, for the Eternal Father, see above on ver. 2.

12—20. St Paul's Present Circumstances and Inward Experience.

12. τὰ κατ' ἐμέ. "The things relating to me, my position, my affairs." For the phrase cp. Rom. i. 15; Eph. vi. 21; Col. iv. 7. It does not appear in LXX. or Apocrypha, and is not common in classical Greek. The special reference is to his imprisonment, as an unlooked for advantage for his missionary work.

μᾶλλον. "Rather" than otherwise, against à priori calculation.

προκοπὴν τοῦ εὐαγγελίου. "The Gospel's progress," rather than its "furtherance." Προκοπή (προκόπτειν, to clear the way forward) by usage (see e.g. ver. 25 below) denotes an active advance; the advancing person or cause is given by the related noun or pronoun in the genitive.

ἐλήλυθεν. "Have resulted in," "have come out in," the Gospel's progress. It is difficult to find an exact parallel for this use of ἔρχομαι. Grimm (ed. Thayer) groups it with e.g. ἐλθεῖν εἰς πειρασμόν, εἰς ἀπελεγμόν : but the ideas are not identical. Perhaps the expanded thought here is that events have "come" *to the Apostle*, so as to result in the Gospel's progress.

13. φανεροὺς ἐν Χριστῷ. Certainly connect these words. Briefly, they are as if he had written φανεροὺς ὡς ἐν Χριστῷ ὄντας. What was "manifest" about the captivity was that it was "in Christ"; it was due to no political or social crime, but to his union with his Lord.

γενέσθαι. Literally, "Proved, came to be." But the aorist, as often, asks an English perfect to represent it; our English thought separates the present from the past less rapidly than the Greek's. "Have proved" expresses, for us, the fact of recent incidents felt in a present result.

ἐν ὅλῳ τῷ πραιτωρίῳ. Πραιτώριον occurs in N. T. Matt. xxvii. 27; Mar. xv. 16; Joh. xviii. 28, 33, xix. 9; Acts xxiii. 35; always in the sense of the residence of an official grandee, regarded as a *prætor*, or military commander. (Not that the word, in Latin, always keeps a military reference; it is sometimes the near equivalent of *villa*, though always suggesting a grandiose scale. E.g. Sueton. *Aug.*, 72; Juv. i. 75.) The A.V. rendering here is an inference from these cases; as if St Paul were imprisoned within the precincts of the residence of the supreme Prætor, the Emperor—the *Palatium*, the imperial House on the Hill of Pales, Mons Palatinus. In St Paul's day this was a maze of buildings covering the whole hill, and more; Nero having built as far as the Esquiline (Sueton. *Nero*, 31) in constructing his "Golden House." The rendering of the A.V. is accepted by high authorities, as Merivale (*Hist. Rom.*, ch. liv.), and Lewin (*Life &c. of St Paul*, ii. p. 282). On the other hand Lightfoot, on this verse, and in an extensive detached note (*Philippians*, ed. 8, p. 99), prefers to render "in all the prætorian guard," the Roman life-guards of the Cæsar; and he collects ample evidence for this use of πραιτώριον from both authors and inscriptions[1]. And meanwhile

[1] He (p. 102) quotes from an inscription the words, Τι. Κλαύδιον οὐετρανὸν στρατευσάμενον ἐν πραιτωρίῳ, "a veteran, who served in the Guards."

there is no evidence that the Palace was called *Prætorium* by Romans at Rome. To this however Lewin fairly answers that St Paul, a provincial, might easily apply to the Palace a provincial term for a Residency, especially after his imprisonment in Herod's *Prætorium* (Acts xxiii., xxiv.). But again it is yet more likely that, as Lightfoot suggests, the word πραιτώριον, in the sense of "the Guards," would be often on the lips of the "soldiers who kept" St Paul; and so that this would now be to him the more familiar reference. On the whole we advocate the rendering of Lightfoot (and of R.V. text), "throughout the (whole) Prætorian guard." Warder after warder came to the Apostle's chamber (whose locality, on this theory, is left undefined; it may have been far from "the Palace," or close to it), and carried from it information and often, doubtless, deep impressions, giving his comrades at large some knowledge of the Prisoner's message and of the claims of the Saviour.

Other explanations of πραιτώριον are (*a*) the Barrack within the Palatium where a Prætorian detachment was stationed; (*b*) the great Guards' Camp (*castra prætoriana*) just outside the eastern wall of Rome. But the Barrack was too limited a space to justify the phrase ἐν ὅλῳ κτλ.; and there is no evidence that the Camp was ever called τὸ πραιτώριον.

τοῖς λοιποῖς πᾶσιν. "To all other men"; to "the public" at large, whether through the soldiers, or as civilians of all kinds came and went as visitors to the Apostle. The words intimate a wide personal influence.

14. τοὺς πλείονας. "The majority." There were exceptions, a minority. He has in mind what comes out below, the difference between friendly and unfriendly sections among the Roman Christians. Acts xxviii. 15, and the Epistle to the Romans as a whole, assure us that the friendly were the majority. On the whole we gather from this passage (vers. 14—18) that a new energy was moving the whole Roman mission, but that the motives in it varied; the majority of the converts were stimulated by the Apostle's willing sufferings, a minority by opposition to his influence.

τῶν ἀδελφῶν ἐν κυρίῳ. So connect the words (with A.V. and R.V.), not τῶν ἀδελφῶν, ἐν κ. πεποιθότας κτλ. (with Ellicott and Lightfoot). Such authorities notwithstanding, the construction they decline is an easy one in the Greek of the N. T. In classical Greek no doubt we should have τῶν ἐν κυρίῳ ἀδελφῶν or τῶν ἀ. τῶν ἐν κ. But the law of N. T. usage is certainly looser in such "attributives"; see e.g. 1 Cor. x. 18 (τὸν Ἰσραὴλ κατὰ σάρκα); Col. i. 8 (τὴν...ἀγάπην ἐν πνεύματι). True, Gal. v. 10 (πέποιθα εἰς ὑμᾶς ἐν κυρίῳ) has been compared, to justify the rendering here, "Having in the Lord confidence in my bonds"; but the difference here is that ἐν κυρίῳ, if made to begin a clause, would take an emphasis which seems to be uncalled for. (See generally Winer, *N. T. Grammar*, III. § xx. Winer explains as Ellicott, &c.)—The precise phrase ἀδελφὸς ἐν κυρίῳ is not found elsewhere; but it is self-evidently possible; and see 1 Cor. iv. 15 for a (practical) instance of πατὴρ ἐν Χριστῷ.

πεποιθότας τοῖς δεσμοῖς μου. Πεποιθέναι, with the dative of the person or thing trusted, is common in Greek poetry, and occasional in Hellenistic prose. In N. T. the only parallels are 2 Cor. x. 7; Philem. 2. "Confiding in my bonds" is a singular expression; but the paradox is surely intentional. On St Paul *as imprisoned* they leaned, as men always tend to lean on a leadership proved to be strong by self-sacrifice. So led, they began working with a new assurance of their cause, and of their hope.

περισσοτέρως τολμᾶν. "More abundantly venture"; they are *more lavish* of effort and venture. On the bearing of such a statement on the date of the Epistle, see Introduction, ch. ii.—Περισσός and its cognates are favourite words in the warm style of St Paul.

ἀφόβως. They saw the fearless Apostle teaching Christ ἀκωλύτως (Acts xxviii. 31); why should they not venture?

τὸν λόγον τοῦ θεοῦ. The revealed *account* of the glory and work of the Christ of God; the Gospel. It is observable that he regards the work of "speaking the word" as the work not only of ordained messengers but of all Christians.—On the reading see critical note.

15. τινὲς μὲν καὶ διὰ φθόνον καὶ ἔριν. "Some actually for envy and strife, while others, (as) actually, for goodwill." Here he refers to that Judaistic school within the Church which followed him with persistent opposition, especially since the crisis when, in council, he won a decisive victory over their main principle (Acts xv.). They held that the Gospel was indeed the crown of the Law, but that the Law was also the permanent fence of the Gospel; the blessings of the baptismal covenant could be reached only through that of circumcision. Such a tenet would not *necessarily* preclude a true teaching of the Person and central Work of Christ, however much it might (as in time it did) *tend to* a beclouded view even of His Person (see Appendix D). Thus St Paul could on the one hand rejoice that such teachers were conveying to *pagan* hearers the primary Fact of salvation, Jesus Christ; on the other hand he could urgently warn *Christians* (see the Ep. to the Galatians, and below, iii. 2) against their distinctive teaching, as pregnant with spiritual disaster.

For allusions to this class of opponents see Acts xv. 1—31, xx. 30 (perhaps), xxi. 20—25; and the Ep. to the Galatians at large. The passages where he asserts with a special emphasis his authority, or his veracity, very probably point towards their untiring opposition and ill-will.

Not that the Judaizer of this type was his only adversary within the Church. He had also to face an opposition of a "libertine" type, a distortion of his own doctrine of free grace (Rom. vi. 1, &c., and below, iii. 18, 19); and again, of the mystic or gnostic type (see the Ep. to the Colossians). But iii. 1—9 fixes the reference here to Christians of the type of Acts xv. 1.

δι᾽ εὐδοκίαν. Εὐδοκία in N. T. usually means "good-pleasure," the choice of what "seems good" to the chooser. See Matt. xi. 26; Luke x. 21; Eph. i. 5, 9; below, ii. 13. But the idea of "good-will" occurs

Luke ii. 14; Rom. x. 1; and perhaps 2 Thess. i. 11. Both meanings appear in O. T. Greek (e.g. Ps. li. (LXX., l.) 19; cxlv. (LXX., cxliv.) 17; and see Ecclus xxix. 26).—The "good-will" here was that of loving loyalty to the Lord and His afflicted messenger.

16. οἱ μὲν ἐξ ἀγάπης κτλ. On the order of the clauses here, see critical note.

εἰς ἀπολογίαν...κεῖμαι. *In defensionem...positus sum* (Vulgate).—For ἀπολογία, see note on ver. 7 above.—Κεῖμαι: "I am set." For a similar use of the verb see Luke ii. 34, οὗτος κεῖται εἰς πτῶσιν κτλ.; 1 Thess. iii. 3. The thought is as of a soldier *posted*; (perhaps not without a reference to his "lying" in *the prison* which was his present "post"; but κεῖσθαι is at least very rare in this reference). These loyal and loving Christians were animated to co-operation by the fact of St Paul's plainly providential presence at Rome, to be a witness and expounder of the Gospel. He was to be their centre and *point d'appui*; they, in their freedom of movement, his helpers everywhere.

17. ἐξ ἐριθείας. "Prompted by faction, partizanship." On the spelling ἐριθία see Westcott and Hort, *N. T. in Greek*, ii. Appendix, p. 153.—Ἐριθεία (cp. for this meaning Rom. ii. 8; 2 Cor. xii. 20; Gal. v. 20; below, ii. 3; Jas iii. 14, 16) is the work of an ἔριθος, a day-labourer; so, any work of a "sordid" kind; so, in politics, the trade of a hired canvasser, or the like; and so finally, partizan-work in general, and its spirit. Liddell and Scott call the alleged connexion of the word with ἔριον, "accidental."

It has been suggested to render οἱ ἐξ ἀγάπης...οἱ ἐξ ἐριθείας, "the men of (i.e. siding with) love; the men of (i.e. siding with) faction." But this strains the construction, certainly of ver. 16, and it is needless.

τὸν Χριστὸν καταγγέλλουσιν. "Are proclaiming the Christ." Καταγγέλλω (rare in classical Greek, where it sometimes means "to *de-nounce*"; nowhere in Greek O. T., except two places in Apocrypha) is to announce tidings with emphasis, or publicity.—It is a sorrowful paradox, but abundantly illustrated, that the true CHRIST could be emphatically and in a sense earnestly proclaimed with a wrong motive, οὐχ ἀγνῶς.

οἰόμενοι. The word seems to suggest, with a sort of gentle irony, that this "*thought*" was wide of the *fact*.

θλίψιν ἐγείρειν τοῖς δεσμοῖς μου. Lightfoot suggests the paraphrase "to make my chains *gall me*." But the physical reference of θλίψις (not so of θλίβειν) is extremely rare, and in Biblical Greek otherwise unknown; and the phrase seems forced and unlikely. The R.V. paraphrases well, "Thinking to raise up affliction for me in my bonds." So Alford. Vulgate, *pressuram* (a word familiar for "*trouble*") *suscitare*. These Anti-Paulines would "raise up trouble" for him, so they "thought," by preventing the access of enquirers or converts to the imprisoned Apostle; a severe test to his faith and patience.

18. τί γάρ; "Well, what of that?" Τί γάρ; is common in classical Greek in quick steps of more or less argumentative statement. Lightfoot cites Xen. *Mem.* ii. vi. §§ 2, 3, where τί γάρ; (varied by τί δέ; τί οὖν;) repeatedly thus takes up the thread in dialogue.

πλὴν ὅτι. "Only that." A beautiful modification of the thought, that all this "does not matter." It *does* "matter," in one happy respect; it helps to diffuse the Gospel.—On the reading, see critical note.

προφάσει. With those who preached ἐξ ἐριθείας, the "pretext" (perhaps even to themselves) would be zeal for truth; the truer reason was prejudice against a person.

ἀλλὰ καὶ χαρήσομαι. "Aye, and I shall rejoice." "*Shall*" seems better here than "*will*," an expectation rather than a resolve (so Ellicott, Alford, Lightfoot, but not R.V.), because he at once goes on to *anticipate* a bright future.

No long comment is needed on the noble spiritual lesson of this passage. His Lord's interests are his own, and in that fact, amidst extremely vexatious circumstances, he finds by grace more than resignation, more than equanimity; there is positive and assured happiness. Self has yielded the inner throne to Christ, and the result is a Divine harmony between circumstances and the man, as both are seen equally subject to, and usable by, Him.

19. οἶδα γάρ. He explains *why* he "shall rejoice." Next to the highest reason, that "Christ is being proclaimed," comes in this attendant certainty, that his own spiritual good will be furthered.

τοῦτό μοι ἀποβήσεται. "I shall find this resulting."

σωτηρίαν. The word includes in its widest reference the whole process of saving mercy, from the giving of the Saviour to the final glory of the saved. In the life of the Christian it points now to his first faith in Christ (2 Cor. vi. 2), now to his life-long preservation in Christ (e.g. 2 Tim. ii. 20); more frequently to the heavenly issue of the whole (e.g. Rom. xiii. 11; Heb. ix. 28; 1 Pet. i. 5). The same may be said of σώζειν, only that it refers more often than σωτηρία to the *life-long* "saving." Here the probable reference is to the final glory, to the attainment of which, by way not of merit but of training, all gifts of grace contribute. The lower meaning, that of saving of bodily life (as e.g. Acts xxvii. 34), is excluded here by the reference to "the supply of *the Spirit*" just below.

διὰ τῆς ὑμῶν δεήσεως. For St Paul's estimate of the positive power of intercession, see e.g. Rom. xv. 30; Col. iv. 3.

ἐπιχορηγίας. Χορηγία is properly the work of a χορηγός (Attic, χοραγός), the "leader of a chorus" in the theatre. Χοραγός came, in time, to mean the citizen who paid the costs of the performance, and then χορηγία meant his bounty. Thence χορηγία passed on to mean "supply" in general; and so ἐπιχορηγία means additional or abundant supply. It occurs in N. T. only here and Eph. iv. 16. 'Επιχορηγεῖν occurs 2 Cor. ix. 10; Gal. iii. 5; Col. ii. 19; 2 Pet. i. 5, 11; passages which all illustrate the slightly intensive force of the ἐπι-. In classical Greek the verb is rare and the noun unknown.

τοῦ πνεύματος Ἰησοῦ Χριστοῦ. The genitive (πνεύματος) here denotes the Spirit as not the Supplier but the Supply, or more exactly the Resource, "*of*" which comes the supply. For the thought cp. Gal. iii. 5, ὁ ἐπιχορηγῶν ὑμῖν τὸ πνεῦμα.

What is τὸ πνεῦμα Ἰ. Χ.? Not merely Jesus Christ's principles and temper; such a meaning of πνεῦμα is almost if not quite unknown in Greek, classical, biblical, and ecclesiastical. The analogy of e.g. Rom. viii. 9; Gal. iv. 6; 1 Pet. i. 11, taken along with our Lord's own teaching about the relation between the Paraclete and Himself (Joh. xiv.—xvi.), assures us that "the Spirit of Jesus Christ" is here none other than the Eternal Personal Spirit, "sent" by the Son (Joh. xv. 26), occupied with Him as Revealer and Imparter (Joh. xv. 26, xvi. 14). His whole work for the Church and for the soul is connected always with the glorified Lord, with Whom He is so One that where the Spirit comes Christ is (Joh. xiv. 18; cp. Eph. iii. 16, 17).

St Paul expects, in answer to his converts' prayers, a new effusion of the power of the Spirit, developing in him the presence of Jesus Christ.

20. κατὰ τὴν κτλ. "The supply of the Spirit" will evidence itself in the "magnification of Christ in his body." That the Lord *will* be so "magnified" is his eager expectation. Thus, the "supply of the Spirit" will be "according to," correspondent to, that expectation.

ἀποκαραδοκία. "Longing expectation"; the *outstretched head* of the watcher is almost visible in the word. It is not classical, and occurs elsewhere in N. T. only Rom. viii. 19. Ἀποκαραδοκεῖν occurs in Polybius (cent. iii—ii. B.C.), and in Aquila's version (circ. A.D. 150) of Psal. xxxvii. (LXX., xxxvi. 7).—The hope of bringing glory to Christ was to the Apostle *the* possessing and animating interest of life.

αἰσχυνθήσομαι, i.e. practically, "I shall be disappointed," as one who has reckoned badly, to his own shame. See Psal. xxv. (LXX., xxiv.) 3, πάντες οἱ ὑπομένοντές σε οὐ μὴ καταισχυνθῶσι: Rom. v. 5; 2 Tim. i. 12.

ἐν...παρρησία. Ἐν here, as very frequently in N. T., indicates accompaniment, as of a condition (so here) or of a means; representing thus the Hebrew *bêth* as a prepositional prefix. Such (classically) unlikely phrases as ἐν σάλπιγγι (1 Thess. iv. 16), ἐν μαχαίρᾳ (Matt. xxvi. 52), fall under this description.—Παρρησία. The word here naturally keeps its literal meaning, boldness *of speech,* for he is thinking of his *testimony* to his Lord. It sometimes glides into the meaning of more general security, confidence, openness; e.g. Joh. vii. 4; Heb. x. 19, 35.

ὡς πάντοτε καὶ νῦν. "As always, so now"; with an emphasis on "now." Cp. 1 Joh. ii. 18, καὶ νῦν ἀντίχριστοι πολλοὶ γεγόνασιν.

μεγαλυνθήσεται, i.e. practically, "shall be glorified," shall be so manifested as to be praised. He will be enabled to make his Lord bright and great to eyes which otherwise would see little of Him.

ἐν τῷ σώματί μου. Because the body is the soul's necessary vehicle for all action on others. Through the body alone could others "see" how the man had peace and power in his Master, living or dying; through the words of his lips, the looks of his face, the action or patience of his limbs. Cp. Rom. xii. 1, and 2 Cor. iv. 10.

εἴτε διὰ ζωῆς εἴτε κτλ. We gather that he wrote at a time of suspense regarding the issue of his trial. Wonderfully did his relation to Christ, ὡς πάντοτε καὶ νῦν, make the suspense itself an occasion of peace and joy. See just below.

21—26. THE SAME SUBJECT: THE ALTERNATIVE OF LIFE OR DEATH: EXPECTATION OF LIFE.

21. Ἐμοὶ γάρ. Ἐμοὶ is emphatic, with the force not of self-assertion but of intense personal experience. This passage is linked with the former by explaining the secret of his holy equanimity in this suspense between life and death. Life and death are to him a dilemma of blessings, in Christ.

τὸ ζῆν Χριστός. *Vivere Christus,* Vulgate. Luther renders, *Christus ist mein Leben,* and Tindale, after him, "Christ is to me lyfe." But this would demand rather, in the Greek, ἐμοὶ γὰρ ζωὴ Χριστός: and it destroys the balance of the two clauses; we could not go on to render "Gain is death." He is thinking here not of the secret of "life" but of the interests of "living." "Living," τὸ ζῆν, is for him so full of Christ, so occupied with and for Him, that CHRIST sums it up. Such is meant to be the experience of every Christian; see Col. iii. 17, and cp. Eph. iii. 14—21.

τὸ ἀποθανεῖν. "Dying." The aorist (note the change after the present, τὸ ζῆν, which gives the thought of life as a process) denotes the act of dying, not the process, nor again the state, of death. The dying hour is to St Paul the mere gateway into the "large room" of the presence of Christ.

κέρδος. Not merely "no harm," but positive "gain." "Death *is his*" (1 Cor. iii. 22).—This wonderful saying, uttered without an effort, appropriating as a means of bliss man's awful and seemingly always triumphant enemy, is explained just below.—It is observable that his thought here is, apparently, more distinctly fixed on death as his own experience in prospect than it seems to have been in the earlier Epistles (e.g. 2 Cor. v. 4, οὐ θέλομεν ἐκδύσασθαι, but see ver. 8 there). Meantime the hope of the Saviour's Return is bright as ever; see below, iii. 20.

22. εἰ δὲ τὸ ζῆν ἐν σαρκί, τοῦτο κτλ. His thought, after the avowal that for him "to die is gain," is that the other alternative—to live still in the body—has a charm in it, for it implies so much more time for fruitful toil for Christ; and so he is in suspense between bliss and bliss. We may translate, slightly paraphrasing, "But if it" (my actual lot, in the will of God) "should be to live (on) in flesh," i.e. under the conditions of mortality (cp. Gal. ii. 20), "this I shall find (μοι) to be full of fruit of work." Living will mean working, working will mean fruit-bearing (see Joh. xv. 5, 16) for Christ; and life so lived will indeed be "worth living."

The rendering of R.V. (text) is "But if to live in the flesh—if this be the fruit of my work, then (καὶ) what I shall choose, &c." But the explanation of καὶ by "then" is improbable, and the thought of continued life as a "fruit" of previous efforts is difficult and scarcely in place.

καὶ. Simply "and." The "then" of R.V. and "yet" of A.V. are alike needless. He merely takes another step in the same line of thought.

γνωρίζω. The knowledge of insight, recognition, is suggested. "I do not see clearly" (Ellicott).

23. συνέχομαι δέ. On the reading, see critical note.—Δὲ takes up the last clause, with a slightly differencing addition; "What to choose I do not see, *but* stand in suspense."

ἐκ τῶν δύο. With συνέχομαι, the imagery is of a man "*compressed*" by forces acting "*from* both (ἐκ τῶν δύο) sides" upon him, so as to keep him fixed in the midst.

It is a wonderful and entirely Christian dilemma. "The Apostle asks which is most worth his while, to live or to die. The same question is often presented to ourselves, and perhaps our reply has been the same. But may we not have made it with a far different purport?...Life and death have seemed...like two evils, and we knew not which was the less. To the Apostle they seem like two immense blessings, and he knows not which is the better" (Ad. Monod, *Adieux*, No. II.).

τὴν ἐπιθυμίαν. Almost, "my desire." He distinguishes the ἐπιθυμία, the preference by pleasure, from the preference by principle, the προαίρεσις (if we may use the word) simply to do the will of God for others. "Where his Treasure is, there is *his heart.*"

εἰς τὸ ἀναλῦσαι. The verb occurs elsewhere in N. T. only in Luke xii. 36, πότε ἀναλύσει κτλ., "when he shall *return*" (but we may well explain the word there of "*setting out*" homeward). Ἀνάλυσις occurs 2 Tim. iv. 6, obviously in the sense it bears here. Verb and noun alike can refer, by usage, to either (*a*) the *solution* of a compound (so here the Vulgate, *cupio dissolvi*), or (*b*) the *undoing* of a cable, to set sail, or the *striking* of a tent, to travel. Verb and noun are both absent from LXX., but the verb is not infrequent in the Apocrypha, and there usually means to go away, or, as the other side of that act, to return (Tob. ii. 8; Jud. xiii. 1). This points to (*b*) as the probable thought of the verb here; and this is supported by the comments of the Greek expositors; Chrysostom e.g. paraphrases our text by ἐντεῦθεν πρὸς τὸν οὐρανὸν μεθίστασθαι, καὶ σὺν Χριστῷ εἶναι. St Paul "desires" to leave for home; to strike his camp, to weigh his anchor, for the better country. See the same thought under other phraseology 2 Cor. v. 1—8; the wanderer's "tent is taken down," καταλύεται, that he may "go home to the Lord," ἐνδημῆσαι πρὸς τὸν κύριον.

In Suicer's *Thesaurus* (of the language of the Greek Fathers) ἀναλύω and its noun are treated at length, and the words are shewn to have glided in post-apostolic Greek into an almost synonym for dying (Lucian, *Philops.* c. 14, has ὀκτωκαιδεκάτης ὢν ἀνέλυεν). He tells how Melanchthon, dying (1560), talked to his friend Camerarius, "prince of Greek scholars in his day," about ἀναλύω, dwelling with delight on this passage, criticizing the Vulgate rendering, and vindicating that of departure, migration. Luther here has *abzuscheiden*, "to depart."

καὶ σὺν Χριστῷ εἶναι. Such is the blissful "other side" of the Christian's death. Cp. carefully 2 Cor. v. 7, with its profound intimation that to step at death out of the "walk by faith" is, *ipso facto*, to begin to "walk by Object Seen" (διὰ εἴδους), in the disclosed presence of the Lord. "Christianity...does not [in the presence of death] tell us of the splendours of the invisible world, but it does far better when, in three words, it informs us that (ἀναλῦσαι) to loosen from the shore of mortality is (σὺν Χριστῷ εἶναι) to be with Christ" (Is. Taylor, *Saturday Evening*, ch. xxvi.).

The Christian, in this life, is "with Christ," and Christ with him. But so is the Presence manifested in *that* life that it is as if it had not been known before. Cp. Acts vii. 39; words which St Paul had heard spoken.

πολλῷ γὰρ μᾶλλον κρεῖσσον. On the reading, see critical note.— With μᾶλλον κρεῖσσον cp. ἐλαχιστότερος, Eph. iii. 8. The phrase may well be characteristic of St Paul's vivid feeling. But classical Greek gives parallel examples: e.g. Æsch. *S. c. T.* 673, τίς ἄλλος μᾶλλον ἐνδικώτερος; Soph. *Ant.* 1210, ἔρποντι μᾶλλον ἆσσον. In popular Latin there is a distinct tendency to such double comparatives, e.g. Plaut. *Capt.* 3. 4. 112, *nihil invenies magis hoc certo certius*; Stich. 5. 4. 22, *magis dulcius*. "Much rather better" is a bold accumulation. —Observe that he finds this "betterness," in the unseen bliss, in comparison not with this life's darkest but with its brightest; he has just said that "to live (on earth) is CHRIST."

24. ἐπιμένειν τῇ σαρκί. T. R., ἐπιμ. ἐν τῇ σαρκί. Either reading gives a pertinent meaning, "to hold by the flesh," i.e. to cling to this life (as to the Commander's post of duty: cp. e.g. Acts xiv. 33; Rom. vi. 1, xi. 22, 23, for illustrative cases of ἐπιμένειν c. dat.), or, "to stay on in the flesh." Ἐπι- gives to μένειν the special thought of persistence or adherence.

ἀναγκαιότερον. With the noble ἀνάγκη of recognized duty to the Lord, and now especially to others in Him; δι᾽ ὑμᾶς, "on account of you."

25. οἶδα, ὅτι μενῶ. We have good ground for saying that this οἶδα was verified in the event; see 1 Tim. i. 3 for an intimation of a visit to Macedonia after this date.

παραμενῶ πᾶσιν ὑμῖν. T. R., συμπαραμενῶ, which seems preferable; see critical note. Not only will he "stay" (μενῶ) "in the flesh"; his stay will be "*with and beside*" (συμπαραμενῶ) the Philippians, whether in bodily presence or in other full communication.

προκοπὴν. "Progress"; see on ver. 12.

χαρὰν τῆς πίστεως. "Joy of (i.e. related to, born of) the (i.e. *your*) faith." R.V. renders "joy in *the faith*." But cp. Rom. xv. 13, χαρὰ ...ἐν τῷ πιστεύειν, where joy appears as one of the bright issues of personal faith. Ἡ πίστις in the sense of creed, the truth believed (Jude 3, and perhaps 20), is rarely (at most) to be found in St Paul. 1 Tim. gives the most probable examples of it; cp. iii. 9, iv. 1, 6, v. 8, vi. 10, 21. Even there it is difficult to explain the word as only objective; it may rather mean the believer's apprehension of the revealed truth. See Ellicott on Gal. i. 23.

Connect both προκοπὴν and χαρὰν with πίστεως. He thinks of them as alike *advancing* and *rejoicing* in the believing life.

26. καύχημα. A favourite word with St Paul, and especially in Romans, Corinthians, and Galatians; a fact bearing on the date of this Epistle. See Introduction, ch. ii. Καύχημα is an act of exultation, of *glorying*; or otherwise (see Lightfoot on Gal. vi. 4) a *ground* for exultation, as distinct from καύχησις, the exultation itself. This distinction however must not be over-drawn, as there is a tendency, in later Greek especially, to blend the meanings of nouns in -μα and -σις.

περισσεύῃ. Again a favourite word with St Paul, and in the Epistles named in the last note.

ἐν Χριστῷ Ἰησοῦ. The "glorying," like all the actions of the Christian's spirit, was to be conditioned by his life *in* Christ.

ἐν ἐμοί. Here ἐν doubtless means "in the case of," "on occasion of." Cp. Gal. i. 24, and (a close parallel) 2 Thess. i. 4, ὥστε ἡμᾶς...ἐν ὑμῖν καυχᾶσθαι. This variation in the rendering of ἐν (see last note) is not capricious. The phrase ἐν Χριστῷ was, so to speak, stereotyped in its reference to the mystical Union; *this* phrase was familiar in another reference. St Paul was to be their occasion of "glorying," because his restoration to them would be an example of their Lord's faithful love to them.

διὰ τῆς ἐμῆς παρουσίας πάλιν πρὸς ὑμᾶς. We may paraphrase, "through my return (πάλιν, *rursus*) to you 'and presence with you." R.V., "through my presence with you again." Yet the A.V., "by my coming to you again," is probably better as a short rendering. Παρουσία is literally "presence," but by usage it often denotes *a coming into presence*, so as almost to absorb the thought of "presence" in that of "coming." Cp. e.g. 1 Thess. iv. 16, where the subject is the great παρουσία τοῦ κυρίου, the hope of the Church.

**27—30. ENTREATIES TO CHERISH CONSISTENCY, AND ESPECIALLY
UNITY, MORE THAN EVER NOW IN HIS ABSENCE.**

27. Μόνον. "Only"; a word of corrective caution, as if to say,
"Whether I come to you or not, remember the call to a holy and
united life; let not *that* vary for you with my nearness or distance."
Μόνον is similarly used Gal. v. 13, ἐπ' ἐλευθερίᾳ ἐκλήθητε...μόνον μὴ
τὴν ἐλευθερίαν εἰς ἀφορμὴν τῇ σαρκί: and see 2 Thess. ii. 7.

πολιτεύεσθε. Properly, "live your citizen-life." By usage the verb
sometimes means little more than ἀναστρέφεσθαι, with no articulate
reference to πόλις: e.g. in the "long recension" (dated by Lightfoot
cent. iv.) of the Ignatian Epistles, *ad Trall.* ix., we have the words
ὁ Λόγος σὰρξ ἐγένετο καὶ ἐπολιτεύσατο ἄνευ ἁμαρτίας. (And see other
instances in Suicer.) But in the only two places where it occurs in
Biblical Greek before N. T. (2 Macc. vi. 1, xi. 25) it seems to carry
the notion of a common or corporate course of life; and so perhaps
Acts xxiii. 1, the only other N. T. instance of its use: St Paul there
is speaking, probably, of his "life" not from the individual point only
but as a member of the Church of Israel. Lightfoot here says,
"though πολιτεύεσθαι is used very loosely at a later date, at this time
it seems always to refer to public duties devolving on a man as *a
member of a body.*" Here such a reference is entirely in point; he is
about to speak emphatically of the duty of *common* principles and
action at Philippi. See below the kindred noun πολίτευμα, iii. 20,
and note. The verb occurs in Polycarp's Ep. to the Philippians,
ch. v., ἐὰν πολιτευσώμεθα ἀξίως [τοῦ κυρίου].
The "conversation" of the A.V. here represents the Vulg. *con-
versamini*, and means not mutual speech only, but the whole course
and intercourse of life; a meaning surviving still in *"conversant."*

ἵνα εἴτε ἐλθὼν καὶ ἰδὼν ὑμᾶς εἴτε ἀπὼν ἀκούω κτλ. More
regularly he might have written ἵνα εἴτε ἐλθὼν καὶ ἰδὼν ὑμᾶς, εἴτε ἀπὼν
καὶ ἀκούων τὰ περὶ ὑμῶν, γνῶ ὅτι κτλ. The irregularity of compression
still leaves the thought perfectly clear.—Here, as below (ii. 12) he is
anxious to disengage them from an undue dependence on his personal
and present influence; the last thing he wishes is to be necessary to
them, as only Jesus Christ should and could be.

στήκετε. Στήκω is "a late present, formed from ἕστηκα, perf. of
ἵστημι" (Lidd. and Scott, *s.v.*). It does not appear before N. T., and
Suicer gives no patristic example. It is used by the Byzantine
writers. In N. T. it occurs eight times; here, and iv. 1 below; Mar.
xi. 25; Rom. xiv. 4; 1 Cor. xvi. 13; Gal. v. 1; 1 Thess. iii. 8;
2 Thess. ii. 15. In Mar. (ὅταν στήκητε προσευχόμενοι) it means "to
stand" simply; in all the other cases the meaning "to stand *fast*" is
in point.

ἐν ἑνὶ πνεύματι. For the precise phrase see 1 Cor. xii. 13, ἐν ἑνὶ
πνεύματι...ἐβαπτίσθημεν: Eph. ii. 18, ἔχομεν τὴν προσαγωγὴν οἱ ἀμφό-
τεροι ἐν ἑνὶ πνεύματι. In both these places the reference appears to be
to the Holy Spirit, the Paraclete, "in" whom the saints have been
imbued with new life, "in" whom they approach the Father, as

living members of the Son. We may therefore explain this place
also of Him, as the Divine atmosphere, as it were, of life and power.
In all three places manifestly the point of ἑνί is that the One Agent
must have His counterpart in the oneness of those who are filled
with Him.

μιᾷ ψυχῇ. "With one soul"; so Tindale and 'Cranmer'; Vulg.
unanimes. With the expression cp. ii. 2, σύμψυχοι, τὸ ἓν φρονοῦντες,
and ii. 20, ἰσόψυχον. Cp. Acts iv. 32, τοῦ πλήθους...ἦν...ἡ ψυχὴ μία.
It is possible that the word πνεῦμα here suggested the word
ψυχή to the Apostle, by the law of association (see Isai. lvii. 16;
1 Thess. v. 23; Heb. iv. 12). And if so he probably used the two
words in a significant connexion. Ψυχή in Scripture appears often
to indicate life *embodied*. We have then here first the Life-Giver, the
One Πνεῦμα, and then the result and manifestation of His living
presence, the organization and embodiment of it, as it were, in the
one ψυχή of the believing company.

συναθλοῦντες. So below, iv. 3, and nowhere else in N. T. Ἆθλος
(contracted from the Epic ἄεθλος) is a contest, in sport or battle,
and ἆθλον (ἄεθλον) the victor's prize. The Greek "athletic" games
suggested many metaphors to St Paul; e.g. 1 Cor. ix. 24, 27; 2 Tim.
ii. 5, iv. 7. See Appendix L. And cp. Conybeare and Howson,
Life &c. of St Paul, ch. xx., at the beginning. But here this reference,
if present at all, is quite subordinate to the general one of a close
wrestling with complex obstacles.

τῇ πίστει. Lightfoot renders "in concert with the faith," and compares συγχαίρει τῇ ἀληθείᾳ (1 Cor. xiii. 6); συγκακοπάθησον τῷ εὐαγγελίῳ (2 Tim. i. 8). But such a personification of "the faith" is so
bold as to demand special support from the context. And here the
whole emphasis lies on the Christians' co-operation *with one another.*

τῇ πίστει τοῦ εὐαγγελίου. "For the faith in the Gospel"; the faith
which embraces it. (Cp. πίστις ἀληθείας, 2 Thess. ii. 13.) They were
to "strive together" to promote belief in the message of their Lord.
Τῇ πίστει may otherwise be taken as the instrumental dative; "*with*
the faith," as your weapon with which to confront the foe; cp. 1 Pet.
v. 9, ᾧ ἀντίστητε στερεοὶ τῇ πίστει. For the reasons against explaining τῇ πίστει of the Christian's creed, see above on ver. 25.

28. πτυρόμενοι. "Scared." The verb (akin to πτοέω) appears to
occur here only in the whole range of Biblical Greek. In (later)
classical Greek it is used of the starting or "shying" of frightened
animals, and thence of alarm in general, as in the *Axiochus* (attri-
buted to Plato) 370 A, οὐκ ἄν ποτε πτυρείης τὸν θάνατον. The word
would well suit the situation of the "little flock" in violent Philippi.

ἥτις. The feminine of the pronoun is "attracted" by ἔνδειξις.
The ἔνδειξις would be given by the union and quiet courage of the
saints in face of seemingly hopeless odds. No doubt the followers of
a mistaken idea may be united and resolute. But the Apostle does
not say that the Philippians' conduct would logically prove the truth
of the Gospel, to themselves or others. He says that it would be a

practical "indication," an omen, of the ruin of the foes and the
triumph of the disciples of the Truth. The more the Church acted
in the spirit of calm, united decision, the more the coming issue of
the conflict would be realized on both sides.

ἐστὶν αὐτοῖς ἔνδειξις ἀπωλείας, ὑμῶν δὲ σωτηρίας. So probably
read; see critical note. T. R., αὐτοῖς μέν ἐστιν ἔνδ. ἀπωλ., ὑμῖν
δὲ κτλ., seems to be a transcriber's re-writing of the less balanced
original. Reading ὑμῶν, not ὑμῖν, the ἔνδειξις may be taken on both
hands to affect "the adversaries"—"Which to them is an indication
of destruction, but of your salvation." But the following context (see
notes just below) suggests that the Apostle's thought is rather as the
T. R. interprets it.

ἀπώλεια. In its deepest and most awful sense; the eternal loss and
ruin of all persistent opponents of God and His truth. So below, iii.
19; and always in N. T., except only Matt. xxvi. 8; Mar. xiv. 4,
where the word means waste, spoiling (of the precious oil).

σωτηρία. See on ver. 19 above. The prospect of final glory is
"indicated" the more vividly as the disciples unite more firmly and
lovingly around, and in, the cause of their Lord.

καὶ τοῦτο ἀπὸ θεοῦ. Τοῦτο of course does not refer properly to
σωτηρία, which would require αὕτη (cp. διὰ πίστεως, καὶ τοῦτο οὐκ ἐξ
ὑμῶν, Eph. ii. 8), but to the fact connected with it—the "indication"
of its approach through the disciples' conduct in the Christian conflict. That they were enabled to meet the enemy thus, and that
their heavenly hope was thus reinforced—all this was a gift, a token,
"from God."

29. ὅτι...ἐχαρίσθη. The link of thought (ὅτι) is that their trying
circumstances, and the benefits of them, *were*, as he has just hinted,
no evil, but a gift of love (ἐχαρίσθη) from their Divine Friend.

ὑμῖν. Slightly emphatic by position. As if to say, "Yes, it is *you*
whose 'salvation' is thus 'indicated,' whatever doubts and fears your
trials may suggest." They were to take fully *home* the concealed
token of final blessing.

ἐχαρίσθη. The verb denotes specially a grant of free favour, and
thus often the grant of gratuitous forgiveness, as 2 Cor. ii. 7, 10;
Eph. iv. 32; sometimes the work of free grace and salvation at large,
as Rom. viii. 32; 1 Cor. ii. 12. (In Acts iii. 14, ᾐτήσασθε ἄνδρα
φονέα χαρισθῆναι ὑμῖν, we still have the word used of a grant "free"
in the sense of its being arbitrary, extra-legal.)

τὸ ὑπὲρ Χριστοῦ. The article τὸ is explained when we see that the
sentence rose first in the writer's mind thus:—ὑμῖν ἐχαρίσθη τὸ ὑπὲρ
Χριστοῦ πάσχειν, "To you was given the boon of suffering for Christ."
Then, with characteristic wealth of thought, he brought in also the
boon of *faith in Christ;* and the present somewhat complex grammar
is the result, in which the words οὐ μόνον τὸ εἰς αὐτὸν πιστεύειν ἀλλὰ
καὶ are parenthetical, and ὑπὲρ αὐτοῦ redundant.

εἰς αὐτὸν πιστεύειν. The phrase indicates the directness and intensity of saving faith; not that this explanation is to be pressed everywhere, for see e.g. Joh. ii. 23, where the ἐπίστευσαν εἰς τὸ ὄνομα αὐτοῦ refers to a faith not wholly satisfactory.—Faith in Christ is here incidentally viewed as a gift of Divine grace. See Eph. ii. 8, and note in the *Camb. Bible for Schools.*

ὑπὲρ αὐτοῦ πάσχειν. Alike the call, and the power, to "suffer for Him" were a glorious *boon*; not only because of the coming results in glory (Rom. viii. 17; 1 Pet. iv. 13), but because of the profound communion with the Crucified Lord conveyed in and with the suffering.

30. τὸν αὐτὸν ἀγῶνα ἔχοντες. The participle, with its nominative, is out of construction with the ὑμῖν of ver. 29, and in construction with the πτυρόμενοι of ver. 28. So that, grammatically, the words from ἥτις ἐστὶν to πάσχειν must be reckoned parenthetical. But the *thought* of ver. 29 glides into that of ver. 30 *supra grammaticam.*

ἀγῶνα. The word (originally meaning a *gathering* (ἄγω), as at the Greek sports) slightly suggests the athletic arena, and thus echoes συναθλοῦντες above (ver. 27). It recurs Col. ii. 1; 1 Thess. ii. 2; 1 Tim. vi. 12; 2 Tim. iv. 7; Heb. xii. 1. The word ἀγωνία is used of our blessed Lord's great "Wrestling" in the Garden, Luke xxii. 44. The ἀγών here obviously is the strife of faith and patience against persecuting violence.

ἀγῶνα ἔχοντες. For the phrase see Col. ii. 1, ἡλίκον ἀγῶνα ἔχω ὑπὲρ ὑμῶν. The verb in such a connexion comes nearly to mean "*feeling,*" "*experiencing.*" Cp. 2 Cor. i. 9, ἐν ἑαυτοῖς κατάκριμα τοῦ θανάτου ἐσχήκαμεν for a somewhat similar use of ἔχειν.

εἴδετε. In the streets and court-house at Philippi, Acts xvi.

ἀκούετε. In the Roman prison. He appeals to them with the magic power of a *leader* in suffering.

CHAPTER II.

1. εἴ τις σπλάγχνα. So ℵABCD₂G₂ and all extant uncials. "Of the cursives nearly the same must be said" (Scrivener, *Introd. to Crit. of N. T.*, ii. 386). Three important copies of vulg read *si quid viscera* instead of *si qua viscera*. Basil Chrys (in MS.) τις. A few cursives read εἴ τι. Most copies of vulg favour τινα, and so Clem Alex and other fathers, "as edited" (Tisch). "It may be stated that no MS. whatever has been cited for τινα" (Scrivener, *l.c.*). LTTr Alf Ltft WH εἴ τις, Ell Wordsw τινα. Tisch thinks that the evidence proves τις to have been "tolerable even to Greek ears." Scriv, on the other hand, after a strong statement of the evidence, says (p. 387) "yet we may believe the evidence to be as false as it is intolerable, and to afford us another proof of the early and...wellnigh universal corruption of our copies in some minute particulars.... Probably St Paul wrote τι,... which would readily be corrupted into

τις, by reason of the σ following (ΤΙΣΠΛΑΓΧΝΑ) and the τις which had just preceded."

3. μηδὲ κατὰ κενοδοξίαν. So אABC, 17 31 37, vulg copt arm æth and some fathers. D₂G₂K₂LP, most cursives, goth, some fathers ἢ κενοδοξίαν. Syr (pesh and harkl) ἢ κατὰ κενοδοξίαν.

4. ἕκαστοι (first occurrence). So ABG₂, 17, vulg, Bas Ambr. אCD₂K₂LP, most cursives, goth syr (pesh and harkl), Hilar Victorin ἕκαστος. All recent editors (but Wordsw) ἕκαστοι. But the evidence for ἕκαστος is considerable.

σκοποῦντες. So אABCD₂G₂P, several cursives, vulg goth, Basil and some fathers. L, most cursives, Chrys Theodoret Damasc σκοπεῖτε. K, 73, syr (pesh and harkl), Theophylact and some fathers, σκοπείτω. All editors σκοποῦντες.

ἕκαστοι (second occurrence). So אBCD₂, 17, a few other cursives, Victorin. KL, most cursives, syr (pesh and harkl), Chrys Theodoret Damasc ἕκαστος. All recent editors ἕκαστοι.

5. τοῦτο. Some documents (א*AC, 17 and some other cursives, Cyril Al) connect this with the preceding verse;—τὰ ἑτέρων· ἕκαστοι τοῦτο φρονεῖτε. But there is no doubt of the correctness of the reading preferred here.

τοῦτο γὰρ is read by אᶜD₂G₂K₂LP, most cursives, syr (pesh), Chrys Theodoret Damasc. Γὰρ is om by א*ABC, 17 and two other cursives, copt arm æth. LTTr Alf Ltft WH om γὰρ. Ell Wordsw retain. Ell remarks, "as ver. 5 begins an ecclesiastical lection, and as the...force of the γάρ might not have been fully understood, and have led to the omission..., the [retention of γάρ] seems *slightly* more probable."

φρονεῖτε. So אABCD₂G₂, 17, vulg syr (pesh and harkl) æth, Hilar Cyr Victorin. C³K₂LP, most cursives, copt arm goth, Origen Euseb Ath Bas Chrys φρονείσθω. LTTr Alf Ell Ltft φρονεῖτε. Wordsw φρονείσθω. Ell remarks, "[φρονείσθω] is insufficiently attested by uncial authorities, and, on internal grounds, quite as likely to be a correction of φρονεῖτε (to harmonize with ὃ καὶ ἐν X. 'I.) as vice versâ." Still the all-but unanimity of the cursives, and the Greek patristic evidence, give φρονείσθω a strong case.

9. τὸ ὄνομα. So אABC, 17, Euseb Cyr. D₂G₂K₂LP, most cursives, arm, Origen Euseb (alibi) Ath and many Greek fathers om τό. LTTr Alf (doubtfully) Ltft WH τό. Ell om. The case for omission is strong.

11. ἐξομολογήσεται. So ACD₂G₂K₂LP, several cursives, Origen Ath Chrys (alibi). אB, 17, most cursives, Iren Clem Eus Ath (alibi) Chrys (alibi) Cyr ἐξομολογήσηται. L (margin) T Alf Ell Wordsw Ltft WH ἐξομολογήσεται. Tr ἐξομολογήσηται. The Greek patristic evidence is weighty for this latter.

15. γένησθε. So אBCD₂ᶜK₂LP, all cursives, Chrys and many Greek fathers. AD₂*G₂, vulg, Cypr Origen and some fathers ἦτε. All editors γένησθε.

ἄμωμα. So ℵABC, 17 23, Clem Victorin Cyr. D₂G₂K₂LP, most cursives, Chrys Theodoret and some other Greek fathers ἀμώμητα. LTTr Alf Ltft WH ἄμωμα. Ell Wordsw ἀμώμητα. For ἀμώμητα it may be pointed out that Deut. xxxii. 5 (LXX.), a passage certainly in St Paul's mind here, reads οὐκ αὐτῷ τέκνα, μωμητά, γενεὰ σκολιὰ καὶ διεστραμμένη. But it is of course possible to see in ἀμώμητα a later adjustment to this.

μέσον. So ℵABCD*₂G₂, 17 31 73, Clem. D♭₂ᶜKL, most cursives, Chrys and some other Greek fathers ἐν μέσῳ. Here the less easy reading seems to have adequate support, and is therefore the more probable.

21. τὰ Χριστοῦ Ἰησοῦ. So (without τοῦ before Χ. Ἰ.) all uncials, many cursives, Clem and many other fathers. Many other fathers, Chrys (but not consistently) Theodoret τὰ τοῦ.

Χριστοῦ Ἰησοῦ. So BL, most cursives, a copy of vulg copt syr (pesh), Chrys and some fathers. ℵACD₂G₂P, 17 and several other cursives, some copies of vulg, Clem Chrys (*alibi*) and several other fathers Ἰησοῦ Χριστοῦ. T Χριστοῦ Ἰησοῦ. LTr and all other recent editors Ἰησοῦ Χριστοῦ.

23. ἀφίδω. So ℵAB*D*₂G₂, 17. B³CD£LP, most cursives, all Greek quotations ἀπίδω. Ltft says, "If any weight is to be attached to the agreement of the older MSS., the aspirated form (ἀφίδω for ἀπίδω) must be read here." He collects from MSS. of the LXX. several instances of aspirates in compounds of εἶδον: εφιδων, αφειδη, καθιδε, &c. (εφειδε occurs in an inscription), and gives some such compounds with ἐλπίς: αφελπιζοντες, εφ' ελπιδι. "The aspirates are doubtless to be explained as remnants of the digamma." All recent editors (but Wordsw) ἀφίδω.

24. ἐλεύσομαι. ℵ*ACP, vulg syr (pesh) copt add πρὸς ὑμᾶς. Lightfoot inserts these words, in square brackets.

26. πάντας ὑμᾶς. ℵ*ACD₂, several cursives, syr (pesh and harkl) copt arm æth, several Greek fathers, add ἰδεῖν. All recent editors read text.

30. τὸ ἔργον Χριστοῦ. So BG₂, 73 80. D₂K₂L, most cursives, some Greek fathers τοῦ Χριστοῦ. Vulg *Christi*. ℵAP, 17 31 47, copt syr (pesh) arm æth κυρίου. C simply τὸ ἔργον. LTTr Χριστοῦ. WH Κυρίου (marg Χριστοῦ). Ell Wordsw τοῦ Χριστοῦ. Alf Ltft simply τὸ ἔργον. Ltft says, "the authorities, being very evenly divided, neutralize each other. All alike are insertions to explain τὸ ἔργον." But the evidence for τοῦ Χριστοῦ is surely preponderant. Tisch remarks that X͞T, K͞T, the familiar MS. abbreviations, would easily drop from the text.

παραβολευσάμενος. So ℵABD₂G₂, some cursives. CK₂LP, most cursives, Greek fathers παραβουλευσάμενος. The versions are not decisive. In this case the rule of *durior lectio* fairly supports the evidence of the chief uncials. And Ltft says, "no one who has felt the nervous vigour of St Paul's style will hesitate between παραβολευσάμενος and παραβουλεύσαμενος....Both words alike are very rare." All recent editors παραβολευσάμενος.

Ch. II. 1—4. The subject continued: Appeal for Self-forgetful Unity.

1. οὖν. The connexion of thought with the preceding sentences is close. He has pressed on them the duty and blessing of concord and co-operation, and now enforces this with a special appeal to them to minister happiness to himself, in Christ, by obedience.

παράκλησις. Vulg. *consolatio*; Wyclif, "counforte"; other Eng. versions before R.V., "consolation"; R.V. "comfort." This latter is best. Παράκλησις (with its cognate verb) habitually (not quite invariably; see perhaps Acts xx. 12, παρεκλήθησαν οὐ μετρίως) denotes rather encouragement than the tenderer "consolation," and so "comfort" (*confortatio*) may fairly represent it. Mutual love at Philippi would *strengthen* St Paul at Rome.

ἐν Χριστῷ. The παράκλησις would get its power from the *union with Christ* of the Philippians and the Apostle.

παραμύθιον. Vulg. *solatium.* The word occurs here only in N. T., and once only in O. T. Greek (Wisd. of Sol. iii. 18); παραμυθία occurs 1 Cor. xiv. 3. Παραμύθιον (as also παραμυθία) is classical; e.g. Soph. *El.* 130 (Electra to the Chorus): ἥκετ' ἐμῶν καμάτων παραμύθιον. It means the converse which draws the mind aside (παρα-) from care; the *ægrimoniæ alloquium* of Horace (*Epod.* xiii. 18). Our "solace" fairly represents it.

κοινωνία πνεύματος. Cp. 2 Cor. xiii. 14, ἡ κοινωνία τοῦ ἁγίου πνεύματος. That parallel fairly fixes the reference of πνεῦμα here to "the one and the self-same Spirit" (1 Cor. xii. 11), the promised Paraclete, whom all the saints "share" as their common Life-Giver, Strengthener, and Sanctifier, the One Spirit of the One Body. The article is indeed absent here, and some say that in such cases not the Spirit as Person but His gifts or influences are meant. But such presence or absence of the article is a precarious index of reference when the substantive is a great and familiar word; context or parallels must be brought in.

κοινωνία cum gen. habitually means "participation *in.*" So he appeals here to their and his part together in the Life-Giver as a motive to holy sympathy.

εἴ τις. On the reading see critical note.

σπλάγχνα καὶ οἰκτιρμοί. Vulg. *viscera miserationis*; Wyclif, happily, "inwardnesse of merci doynge"; A.V. "bowels and mercies"; R.V., better, "tender mercies and compassions." On the word σπλάγχνα see above on i. 8. Οἰκτιρμός appears always, with very few exceptions, in the plural in Biblical Greek.—He appeals with pathetic simplicity and directness, last of all, to their human kindness as such.

2. πληρώσατε. His cup of joy for Philippi (i. 4) needed only the certainty that the Philippians were one in holy love, to be full to the brim.

ἵνα τὸ αὐτὸ φρονῆτε. On the construction, see on i. 9. We have here a modification of the *purport*-meaning. He here practically *asks them to be* what he now describes, and their being so is the purport of this implied longing.

τὸ αὐτὸ φρονεῖν. Almost, "to be of the same *feeling*"; see on i. 7. The lack of a full unity of hearts in Christ was clearly the weak point of the mission at Philippi.

τὴν αὐτὴν ἀγάπην. "The same" on all sides; true in its mutuality.

σύμψυχοι. On the spelling see critical note on συγκοινωνούς, i. 7. On the word, see note on μιᾷ ψυχῇ, i. 27.

τὸ ἕν. Τὸ αὐτὸ intensified; "being of *one* feeling." The article defines and so accentuates the idea suggested by ἕν.

3. μηδὲν κτλ. Note the brief energy of the verbless phrase, and also the absoluteness of the prohibition, which is binding on all Christian lives at all times.

κατ' ἐριθείαν. On ἐριθεία, see note on i. 17. We might render the words here, "faction-wise," or "party-wise." But ἐριθεία would cover also the notion of an individual ambition, working by intrigue for merely personal ends.

μηδὲ κατὰ κενοδοξίαν. For the reading see critical note.

τῇ ταπεινοφροσύνῃ. The dative may be rendered (as Vulg., A.V. and R.V.) "in," or somewhat better, "with." The definite article gives the noun a certain concreteness, which might almost be represented by "with *your* lowliness." But this would slightly exaggerate the effect. Ταπεινοφροσύνη is apparently not found in Greek before the N.T.; but ταπεινοφρονέω, ταπεινόφρων, appear in LXX., and in connexions where they denote pious humility. In the classics ταπεινός (used of moral not physical subjects) and its compounds almost invariably carry a tone of blame, as of a defect of proper courage and self-assertion.—The good references of the words in Biblical Greek are deeply instructive. Revealed religion bases its mighty *positive* morality on the profound *negative* of the surrender and dethronement of self before a Redeeming Lord who has had pity on perfectly unworthy objects. The world's "poor spirited" and the Lord's "poor in spirit" are phrases of very different tones.

ἡγούμενοι. Such participles, where the normal grammar would place imperatives, are frequent in N.T. See for a group of examples Rom. xii. 9—19.—This precept must be read in the light of the Holy Spirit's illumination of the individual conscience. Where the man habitually viewed himself in the contrasted glory of the Divine holiness he would respond instinctively to the call to rank *himself* as low as possible in the spiritual scale.

4. ἕκαστοι σκοποῦντες. On the reading, see critical note. The "look" is the look of sympathy, kindly interest, self-forgetful (μὴ τὰ ἑαυτῶν) co-operation. This short verse is a far-reaching lesson in Christian ethics.

ἕκαστοι...ἕκαστοι. The plural suggests the individuality rather of groups than of persons. We may almost render "each *circle*." If the Philippians tended to gather in cliques this phrase would have a special point.

5—11. THE APPEAL ENFORCED BY THE SUPREME EXAMPLE OF THE SAVIOUR IN HIS INCARNATION, OBEDIENCE, AND EXALTATION.

5. Τοῦτο φρονεῖτε. "Be this your mind," your "feeling." On the reading, see critical note. Practically, φρονεῖτε and φρονείσθω give the same thought.

In the great passage which follows we have a suggestive example of Christian moral teaching. A simple element of daily duty is being enforced; and the inmost secrets of the Person and Work of Christ are used to enforce it; the spiritual and eternal, in deep continuity, descends into the practical. This process is characteristic of Christianity all through. To isolate Christian morality from Christian theology is to rend asunder the teaching of the New Testament as to its deepest and most vital elements. See further Appendix E.

ὃ καὶ ἐν Χ. Ἰ. Ἐφρονείτω, or better, ἐφρονήθη, must be mentally supplied after these words. And what *was* His φρόνημα, in that mysterious past, *is* such now and for ever; the Christian feels the power not only of his Lord's *act* of infinite kindness, but of His eternal *character*.

ἐν Χριστῷ Ἰησοῦ. He calls Him Ἰησοῦς, using the human Name, though in view of His glory before Incarnation. But the Person who willed to come down and save us is identically the Person who did so save us. And also, what is decreed in the Eternal Mind is to It already fact. So Rev. xiii. 8, τὸ ἀρνίον τὸ ἐσφαγμένον ἀπὸ καταβολῆς κόσμου.

6. ἐν μορφῇ θεοῦ. What is μορφή? Lightfoot, in a "detached note" to this chapter, traces the use of the word in Greek philosophy, in Philo (the link between the language of Scripture and of Plato), and in the N. T. The conclusion is that it denotes the "form" of a thing in the most ideal sense of form; its specific character, its correspondence with its true notion. Visible shew may or may not enter into it; for invisibles have their μορφή, to pure thought. The μορφὴ θεοῦ is thus in fact His Nature "seen" in its attributes; and to be "in" it is to be invested with them. See Lightfoot as quoted, and Trench *Syn. of N. T.*, under μορφή.

ὑπάρχων. R.V. text, "being," margin, "originally being"; but the American Revisers expressly omit the margin (and give "existing" in the text). Ὑπάρχειν in the classics, meaning first "to begin" (doing or being), then comes to mean "to be there," "to be ready"; e.g. when the Athenians equipped a fleet against the Persians, they had to build some ships, but some ὑπῆρχον αὐτοῖσι (Hdt. vii. 144). Thence apparently the word came to mean simply "to be," though the use was not common. In Biblical Greek the use fluctuates between a mere equivalence to εἶναι and the distinct suggestion of a being *already*; as Acts vii. 55, ὑπάρχων πλήρης πνεύματος: viii. 16, βεβαπτισμένοι ὑπῆρχον. In this passage the context decidedly favours this latter meaning. For though some expositors have referred the whole statement to our Lord's incarnate state, as if it viewed Him as e.g. resolving when on earth to decline a majesty and dominion which He might have exerted, while yet He shewed Himself at least God-*like* in His deeds, this is impossible when the context is fairly remembered. For it is plainly implied (ver. 7) that His voluntary humiliation included His becoming δοῦλος and taking ὁμοίωμα ἀνθρώ-πων. So the will to humble Himself was antecedent to that condition, and so to Incarnation. Thus the tendency of ὑπάρχειν to indicate being *already*, or *beforehand*, has legitimate scope here, and an impressive fitness.

Here then our Redeeming Lord is revealed as so "antecedently being in the form of God" that He was, before He stooped to our life, nothing less than Bearer of Divine Attributes, that is to say, GOD. "Though μορφή is not the same as οὐσία, yet the possession of the μορφή involves participation in the οὐσία also; for μορφή implies not the external accidents but the essential attributes" (Lightfoot).

ἁρπαγμόν. The word occurs only here in Biblical Greek, and only once (Lightfoot) in secular Greek (Plutarch, *Mor.* p. 12 A). Words ending in -μος properly suggest an act or process; in this case, therefore, a "seizing," or "robbery." But in usage they readily get the meaning of the matter or aim of the act; e.g. θεσμός, properly "a setting," is by usage "a thing set," "a *statute*." Ἁρπαγμός may therefore be an equivalent here to ἅρπαγμα, a thing seized, or grasped, as plunder or as prize. And the phrase ἅρπαγμα ἡγεῖσθαί τι is not uncommon in later Greek, in the sense of "highly prizing," "welcoming as an unexpected gain" (ἕρμαιον). So explained, οὐχ ἁρπαγμὸν ἡγήσατο here gives a sense perfectly fitting the context: "Possessed of the Divine Attributes, He did not treat His co-equality as a prize, to be held only for Himself, but rather made it occasion for an infinite act of self-sacrifice for others." Such on the whole is the explanation given by the Greek fathers and by some of the ablest Latins (see Lightfoot's "detached note" on ἁρπαγμός). On the other hand some Latins, and St Augustine in particular, give a different turn to the thought, which appears in our A.V. Taking the Latin rendering, *non rapinam arbitratus est*, they made the meaning to be that the Lord Christ *claimed co-equality*, as not *a usurpation* but a right, *and yet* humbled Himself. To this the objection is that (*a*) it lays a needless stress on the derivation of ἁρπαγμός, for by usage it (or its equivalent ἅρπαγμα) need not mean more than a prize or treasure; (*b*) it makes ἀλλὰ equal to ἀλλὰ ὅμως, which is forced Greek; (*c*) most of all, it dislocates text and context. St Paul is emphasizing not mainly our Lord's majesty but His self-sacrificing mercy. His majesty is sufficiently (for the purpose) given in the words ἐν μορφῇ θεοῦ ὑπάρχων:

the point now is that He made an infinitely generous use of His majesty. This is exactly given, and at the right point, by οὐχ ἁρπαγμὸν κτλ., explained as, "He treated it not as *a treasure for Himself* but as something to lay aside (in a sense) for us."

An intermediate explanation, by St Chrysostom, gives the thought somewhat thus: "He knew that Deity was so truly His by right that He laid it (in a sense) aside, with the generous grace of the rightful owner (who knows he is owner all along), instead of clasping it with the tenacity of the usurper." To this Lightfoot objects, with apparent reason, that "it *understands too much*, requiring links to be supplied which the connexion does not suggest."

R.V. renders ἁρπαγμὸν "a prize," and (margin) "Gr., *a thing to be grasped*"; Ellicott, "a thing to be seized on, or grasped at"; Liddell and Scott, "a matter of robbery."

τὸ εἶναι ἴσα θεῷ. Not ἴσος. The neuter plural perhaps suggests a reference rather to equality of attributes than of Person (Lightfoot). R.V. "to be on an equality with God."

Let us remember that these words occur not in a polytheistic reverie but in the Holy Scriptures, which are everywhere jealous for the prerogative of the Lord GOD; and they come from the pen of a man whose Pharisaic monotheism sympathized with that jealousy to the utmost. May it not then be asked how, in any way other than direct assertion, as in Joh. i. 1, the true and proper Deity of Christ could be more plainly stated?

On the use of the word θεός here, distinctively of the Father, see note above on i. 2. And cp. Joh. i. 1; 2 Cor. xiii. 14; Heb. i. 9; Rev. xx. 6, xxii. 1.

7. ἀλλά. "But"; not "yet," which would require ἀλλ' ὅμως. (See note on ἁρπαγμὸν above.) The word introduces the infinitely gracious action of the Saviour as *not* what He would have done had He "thought His Equality a prize." See Ellicott's careful note here.

ἑαυτὸν ἐκένωσεν. Ἑαυτὸν is slightly emphasized by position, with a stress on the sacred freedom of the Lord's will.

R.V. "emptied himself"; Vulg. *semetipsum exinanivit*, following which the Rhemish (Romanist) Version, 1582, renders, "exinanited Himself"; Wyclif, "lowide him silf."

From the verb, the noun κένωσις has passed into theology, appearing here and there in the Fathers (e.g. Cyril. Alex., *dial. V. de SS. Trin.* p. 571; ἦν γὰρ φύσει καὶ ἀληθῶς Θεὸς καὶ πρὸ τῶν τῆς κενώσεως χρόνων), and in many modern treatises. Of late years much has been said on this great mystery by way of proving or suggesting that "in the days of His Flesh" (Heb. v. 7) our Lord (practically) parted with His Deity, and became the (Incarnate) Son of God only in His glorification after death. In particular it is suggested that He accepted all the limits and defects of humanity as it is in us, moral defects excepted (and this exception is not always adequately made); and so was liable not only to hunger, fatigue, and agitation, but also to mistakes about fact, even in so great a matter as the nature of the O. T. Scriptures. On such inferences it must be enough here (see

further Appendix G.) to say first that they can be connected only re-
motely with this passage, which practically explains the κένωσις to
mean His becoming the truly Human Bondservant of the Father;
and then that they are little in harmony with the whole tone of the
Gospels, which present to us the Lord Jesus on earth as "meek and
lowly" indeed, but always mysteriously majestic; dependent indeed
on the Father, and upheld by the Spirit, but always addressing man
with the manner of absolute knowledge and of sovereign power to
meet his needs.

It is enough for us to know that this κένωσις was for him un-
speakably real; that He was pleased, as to His holy Manhood, to
"live by the Spirit," as we are to do; yet that the inalienable basis of
His Personality was always, eternally, presently, Divine.   The ultimate and reasoned analysis of that unique Phenomenon, God and
Man, One Christ, is HIS matter, not ours.   It is for us to accept
Him in its good and certain results, at once our Brother and our
God.   Lightfoot says here nearly all that can be said with reverent
confidence: "'He divested Himself' not of His Divine nature, for
this was impossible, but of the glories, the prerogatives, of Deity.
This He did by taking upon Him the form of a servant."

μορφὴν δούλου λαβών. Ἐκένωσε λαβών naturally means "He emptied
(Himself) *in taking*"; not as if there were two acts, but two aspects
of one act.   The κενῶσαι lay in the λαβεῖν, not in something before
it, or after it.

μορφὴν δούλου. On μορφή see note on ver. 6 above.   It points to
an essential and manifested reality, not to a mere semblance or
make-believe.   As He was Θεός, essentially and in manifestation, so
He became δοῦλος essentially and in manifestation.   And in what
respect δοῦλος? In that He stooped to serve *men*? Or in that He
undertook, in the act of becoming Man, that essential condition of
humanity—bondservice *to God*? The order of thought is in favour of
the latter.   The Apostle goes on to say that His taking μορφὴν δούλου
was coincident with His coming to be ἐν ὁμοιώματι ἀνθρώπων, "just like
men." But men as men are not each others δοῦλοι, while they *are*, as
men, δοῦλοι Θεοῦ.   To God, as Lord of Man, the Incarnate Christ
ἐδούλευσε, and was in this, as in all things, the Archetype of His
disciples.

True, He made Himself the Helper of all.   And on one occasion
(Joh. xiii.) He literally took a menial's place; a fact to which Chrysostom here alludes.   But at that very moment He took care to
assert Himself Κύριος all the while.   Literal "slavery" to man He
certainly never accepted; royally descended, working as a free
artificer, and speaking always with authority.

ἐν ὁμοιώματι ἀνθρώπων. Two facts are suggested here: (*a*) He
was really *like men*, as He was truly man; accepting a truly human
exterior, with its liabilities to trial and suffering; (*b*) He was also
more than men, without which fact there would be no significance in
the ὁμοίωμα, for there would be simple identity.   See Rom. viii. 3, for

a somewhat similar suggestion in the word; ἐν ὁμοιώματι σαρκὸς ἁμαρτίας.

ἀνθρώπων, not ἀνθρώπου. The thought given is as concrete as
possible; He was like, not abstract Man, but men as we see men.

γενόμενος. "Becoming." Another aorist participle, closely connected, like λαβών just before, with the aorist ἐκένωσε. These aspects
of the Humiliation are given as coincident.

8. καί. Here another movement of thought begins. We have
seen the κένωσις of simple Incarnation. We now pass to the Sacrifice
to which, in Manhood, He descended.

σχήματι. *Habitu*, Lat. Versions. Σχῆμα indicates appearance,
with or *without* underlying reality; and thus is a partial antithesis to
μορφή (see first note on ver. 6 above, and cp. Rom. xii. 1). In itself
it neither affirms nor denies reality; it emphasizes appearance.
Thus here it carries out the suggestion just given by ὁμοίωμα. The
Lord was (*a*) man not only in nature but in look, patent to all; and
He was (*b*) more than met the eye: the true and manifest Manhood
was the veil of Godhead.

The dative (σχήματι) is the not infrequent dative of relation, connexion; cp. 1 Cor. vii. 34, ἁγία σώματι καὶ πνεύματι, and in the
classics such phrases as φύσει κακός (see Eph. ii. 3), γένει Ἕλλην.

εὑρεθείς. He was "found," as one who presented Himself for
scrutiny. Εὑρίσκω in Biblical Greek somewhat tends to less distinctive meanings; e.g. Luke ix. 36, εὑρέθη Ἰησοῦς μόνος, where in
effect we have Him simply "*seen* alone." But the thought of in-
spection, examination, is suggested by association here.

ὡς ἄνθρωπος. Either, "as man," or (A.V., R.V.) "as a man." As
the Second Man, Head of redeemed Manhood, He is rather Man
than a man. Yet we may remember that the point of thought here
is not on His difference from His brethren but on His likeness to
them; He moved among them, in fact, as "a man." So, with
wonderful condescension, He calls Himself (the rendering must
obviously be thus there) "*a man* that hath told you the truth" (Joh.
viii. 40).

ἐταπείνωσεν ἑαυτόν, "under the mighty hand (cp. 1 Pet. v. 6) of"
His Father, in the life of surrender which led to the supreme surrender of the Cross. The following context seems to point the reference in this direction.

γενόμενος ὑπήκοος. The aorist participle, in close contact with the
aorist verb (ἐταπείνωσεν), *brings together* the thoughts of self-humbling
and of obedience; the "humiliation" coincided with, was expressed in,
the "becoming obedient" to the Father's will that He should suffer.

μέχρι θανάτου. "To the length of death." "*Even* unto death,"
R.V. *Usque ad mortem*, Lat. Versions. The A.V., "obedient, unto
death," might seem to mean that He "*obeyed death*." This He never
did; He obeyed His Father in dying, in order to "*abolish* death"
(2 Tim. i. 10); dying as our Sacrifice, to meet the κατάρα τοῦ νόμου

(Gal. iii. 13), by the holy will (Acts ii. 23) of the Lawgiver. Thus He carried His life-long "Patience" "to the length of" His "Passion," seeking not His own will, but the will of the Father in our salvation.

θανάτου δὲ σταυροῦ. The δὲ carries a slight connective force; "nor only death, but *death of cross*."—The Cross (*infelix arbor*) was the death not only of extreme agony but of the utmost degradation; to the Roman, certainly in all but the earliest ages of Rome, it was reserved for the slave and for the basest ruffian. *Mors si proponitur, in libertate moriamur...nomen ipsum crucis absit non modo a corpore civium Romanorum, sed etiam a cogitatione, oculis, auribus* (Cicero, *pro C. Rabirio*, v. § 10). In the case of our Redeemer's Crucifixion, we see combined the Hebrew's dread of any death-penalty by suspension (Deut. xxi. 23) with the Roman's horror of the *servile* cross. Thus the supreme Obedience expressed the Sufferer's willingness both to "become a curse for us" (Gal. iii. 13) as before *God* the Lawgiver, and to be "despised and rejected of *men*" (Isai. liii. 3) as "the outcast of the people." "Who shall fathom the abyss Where Thou plungedst for our love?"

9. διό. The glorification of the crucified Christ Jesus was, from the view-point of this passage, the Father's reward for His supreme "regard for the things of others"; His "pleasing not Himself" (Rom. xv. 2). The application intended is that self-forgetting love, for the disciple as for his Lord, is the way to the true exaltation of his being.

ὑπερύψωσεν. The verb occurs only here in N. T.—St Paul loves compounds with ὑπέρ: e.g. ὑπεραυξάνειν, ὑπερεκπερισσοῦ, ὑπερνικᾶν, ὑπερπερισσεύειν, ὑπερπλεονάζειν. All these occur in his writings only, in Biblical Greek.—Render here, "highly exalted," rather than "hath highly exalted." The aorist refers to the historical moment of the Resurrection crowned by the Ascension. For the action of the Eternal Father in the exaltation, cp. e.g. Acts ii. 23, 24, 32, 33, 36; Eph. i. 20—22.

ἐχαρίσατο. "Bestowed," as a gift of supreme and rejoicing love.

τὸ ὄνομα. For the reading, see critical note. Whether or not τὸ is omitted, we must render "*the* name which," in view of the τὸ ὑπὲρ κτλ. next following.

What is this "Name bestowed"? Is it (*a*) the sacred personal name Ἰησοῦς? (Alford, Ellicott). Or is it (*b*) "Name" in the sense of revealed majesty and glory (Lightfoot), as where the LORD proclaims His "Name" to Moses, Exod. xxxiv. 5? The difficulty of (*a*) is that the personal human name was of course distinctively His before His glorification, and is as a fact less used in Scripture after the Gospel narrative is closed; so that there would be a paradox in the thought of a "bestowal" of it on the glorified Christ. True, its then elevation to the highest associations, in the love and worship of the saints, was as it were a giving of the name as a new name; yet this hardly satisfies the intensity of the Apostle's assertion here.

In favour of (*b*) are the clear cases in the N. T. of the use of ὄνομα to denote recognized dignity or glory; e.g. Eph. i. 21. And the true explanation seems to lie in this direction. "The Name bestowed" is the supreme Name, Κύριος (see ver. 11 below), JEHOVAH. In other words the suffering Jesus was, as the once abased and slain sufferer, now raised to the eternal Throne; recognized there by the universe as He who, for man, and for the Father's will, chose in His pre-existent glory to stoop even to the Cross. As God and Man, one Christ, as at once the co-equal Son and the sacrificed Lamb, He there receives the worship which belongs to the Eternal; Ἰησοῦς is saluted Κύριος, in the supreme sense of that "Name."

On St Paul's view of the unique exaltation of the Lord in comparison with every created being, see Liddon, quoted below, Appendix H.

10. ἐν τῷ ὀνόματι Ἰησοῦ. Here Ἰησοῦ may be either genitive or dative. If dative, we must render "in the name Jesus." But if the note just previous reasons rightly, we must choose the genitive; "the name *of* Jesus," the Name borne by Jesus; the Divine Name, Κύριος, proclaimed as the true name of the once humiliated Jesus. So Lightfoot; and so A.V., R.V.

What is the meaning of ἐν τῷ ὀνόματι κτλ.? That all creation is to bow *to* Him thus glorified? Or that all creation should worship *through* Him (cp. e.g. αἰτεῖν ἐν τῷ ὀνόματί μου, Joh. xiv. 13)? The context seems to decide for the former; dealing as it does not with His mediation but with His personal glorification. So Lightfoot; and he gives examples in evidence from the LXX.; e.g. Psal. lxii. 5 (Heb., lxiii. 4), ἐν τῷ ὀνόματί σου ἀρῶ τὰς χεῖράς μου. We may thus paraphrase here, "that before the revealed majesty of the glorified Jesus all creation should bow."

The ancient custom of bowing at the utterance of the Name Jesus (see Canon xviii. of the Church of England) derives no *direct* sanction from this passage.

πᾶν γόνυ κάμψῃ. An implicit quotation of Isai. xlv. 24, ἐμοὶ κάμψει πᾶν γόνυ. The prophet (see the whole context) speaks there in the name of the Eternal Himself; thus we have here a profoundly significant index of St Paul's view of the Nature of the Lord Jesus Christ.

Observe further that in Isai. xlv. 21 we have the words, "a just God and a Saviour," δίκαιος καὶ σωτήρ (cp. Rom. iii. 26, δίκαιος καὶ δικαιῶν), and in ver. 25 occur the words, "all the seed of Israel shall be justified and shall glory," δικαιωθήσονται…καὶ…ἐνδοξασθήσεται πᾶν τὸ σπέρμα (cp. Rom. viii. 30, οὓς ἐδικαίωσε τούτους καὶ ἐδόξασε). Was not the Apostle of Justification thus specially led to the passage as relating to the Son of God and His work?—The same place in Isaiah is directly quoted Rom. xiv. 11.

ἐπουρανίων καὶ ἐπιγείων καὶ καταχθονίων. The words evidently mean all created existence, in its heights and depths. Cp. Rev. v. 13, πᾶν κτίσμα ὃ ἐν τῷ οὐρανῷ, καὶ ἐπὶ τῆς γῆς, καὶ ὑποκάτω τῆς γῆς, words whose whole context, full of the enthronement of the Lamb, is a

Divine commentary here. We need not elaborately divide the reference here, e.g. between angels, living men, buried men (Alford), or
angels, men, and lost spirits (Chrysostom). Rather we have Creation
in its total before us, animate and inanimate existence alike; the non-
personal and unconscious creation being said to "worship," as obeying,
after its manner, the lordship of the exalted Jesus.

11. πᾶσα γλῶσσα ἐξομολογήσεται. For the reading, see critical
note.—Here again cp. Isai. xlv. 24 (in the Alexandrian Text), ἐξομολογήσεται πᾶσα γλῶσσα τῷ θεῷ.

'Εξομολογεῖσθαι, as Lightfoot points out, has in Biblical Greek
almost resigned its meaning of "open avowal" to take that of praise
and thanksgiving. (It is used thus, Matt. xi. 25; Luke x. 21; ἐξομο-
λογοῦμαί σοι, πάτερ.) So "every tongue" is to "give thanks for His
great glory" to the exalted Jesus.

It may be asked, how shall this be fulfilled in the case of the lost,
ὧν τὸ τέλος ἀπώλεια (iii. 19)? Either they are not explicitly referred to
here at all (see note on Eph. i. 10); or their mysterious state may
admit, beyond our knowledge, such a recognition that even it is the
ordinance of "supremest wisdom and primeval love,"[1] manifested in
Jesus Christ, as shall give them a part in the adoration indicated here.

κύριος 'Ιησοῦς Χριστός. Cp. 1 Cor. xii. 3, where the "Lordship"
is seen to be knowable only by Divine revelation. He who took "the
form of a bondservant, and became obedient," even so as to die on the
cross, is now seen and worshipped as "God, whose throne is for ever"
(Heb. i. 8), while yet He is "Christ Jesus, Man" (1 Tim. ii. 5).

It is observable that the Valentinian heretics (cent. ii.), according to
their contemporary Irenæus, ascribed to Jesus the title Saviour but
denied Him that of Lord.

Assuming κύριος here to represent JEHOVAH (יהוה), it is important to
compare Joh. xii. 41, ταῦτα εἶπεν 'Ησαΐας ὅτε εἶδε τὴν δόξαν αὐτοῦ, with
Isai. vi. 5, the place referred to by the Apostle, "Mine eyes have seen
the King, the LORD of hosts," יהוה צבאות

εἰς δόξαν θεοῦ πατρός. The Father is the ultimate Object of adoration, as He is the eternal Origin of the eternal Godhead of the Son. Cp.
Joh. v. 23, xvii. 1; 1 Pet. i. 21; for this profound relation between
the glory of the Son and the glory of the Father. But no isolated
references can properly represent a subject so deeply woven into the
very texture of the Gospel.

In the light of the revealed truth of His Nature, summarized with
luminous fulness in the "Nicene" Creed, we see the Christ of God as
at once divinely adorable in Himself and the true Medium for our
adoration of the Father.

[1] Giustizia mosse il mio alto Fattore:
    Fecemi la divina potestate,
    La somma sapienza *e il primo amore*.
                                Dante, *Inferno*, III. 4–6.

St Chrysostom has a noble comment here, shewing how the attribution of proper Godhead to the Son can only enhance the Father's glory : ὁρᾷς πανταχοῦ, ὅταν ὁ υἱὸς δοξάζηται, τὸν πατέρα δοξαζόμενον... ὅταν λέγωμεν ὅτι...οὐκ ἐλάττων [ἐστὶ] τοῦ πατρός, τοῦτο δόξα τοῦ πατρός... ὅταν εἴπω...ὅτι [υἱὸν ἐγέννησεν] οὐκ ἐλάττονα κατὰ τὴν οὐσίαν, ἀλλ᾽ ἴσον... καὶ ἐν τούτῳ πάλιν τὸν θεὸν θαυμάζω, ὅτι ἄλλον ἡμῖν τοιοῦτον ἔδειξεν ἐξ αὐτοῦ, πλὴν τοῦ πατέρα εἶναι (Hom. VII. *in Philipp.* c. 4).

Thus closes a passage of the Epistle in which, in the course of practical exhortation, the cardinal truth of the true Godhead and true Manhood of Christ, and the greatness of His Example, are presented all the more forcibly because incidentally. The duty of self-sacrificing mutual love is enforced by considerations on His condescension which are meaningless if He is not pre-existent and Divine, and if the reality of His Manhood does not thus involve a supreme instance of unforced self-abasement for the good of others. All merely humanitarian views of His Person and Work, however refined, are totally at variance with this apostolic passage, written within fresh living memory of His life and death.

A striking commentary on the passage is afforded by the hymn (by the late Prof. Anstice) *Thou the cup of death didst drain* (Lord Selborne's *Book of Praise*, Appendix, no. 11).

12—18. INFERENCES FROM THE FOREGOING PASSAGES : THE GREATNESS OF THE METHODS OF SALVATION: THE CONSEQUENT CALL TO A LIFE REVERENT, SELF-FORGETFUL, FRUITFUL, FAITHFUL, JOYFUL.

12. ῞Ωστε. He has now pressed on them the duty and blessing of self-forgetting love, above all by this supreme Example. Here this is still in view, but subordinately; he is possessed by the thought of "so great salvation," and *through this* views the obligation and joy of Christian humility and harmony.

ἀγαπητοί μου. So again iv. 1. Cp. 1 Cor. x. 14, xv. 58 ; 2 Cor. vii. 1, xii. 19; where this tender term similarly goes with earnest practical appeals.

καθὼς πάντοτε ὑπηκούσατε. "As you always obeyed." The aorist looks back to Philippi and the old days there. Let these be like those.

μὴ. Not οὐ : it is not a statement but an appeal ; they are to " work out their salvation " not only when he is there to help them, but now when he is away.

ὡς ἐν τῇ παρουσίᾳ μου μόνον. ῾Ως suggests the agent's condition, or point of view ; "*influenced* by my presence with you." Μόνον is as if to say, "My presence was good for you in its time, but your 'working out' was never to end with it." "The sentence is a fusion of two ideas, μὴ ὡς ἐν τῇ παρουσίᾳ μου κατεργάζεσθε, and μὴ ἐν τῇ παρουσίᾳ μου μόνον κατεργάζεσθε" (Lightfoot).

πολλῷ μᾶλλον. His absence was to be the occasion for a *far fuller* realization of their own personal obligations, and personal *resources in Christ*, for the spiritual life.

μετὰ φόβου καὶ τρόμου. Cp. 1 Cor. ii. 3; Eph. vi. 5. The thought is not of tormenting misgiving about either present peace with God or final perseverance; it is of a reverent and wakeful conscience in His holy presence.

τὴν ἑαυτῶν σωτηρίαν κατεργάζεσθε. Ἑαυτῶν is strongly emphatic. He appeals to them to "learn to walk alone"—alone not of the Lord, but of Paul; not leaning too much on *his* present influence. "Do not make *me* your proxy in spiritual duties which are *your own*."

Σωτηρία here is our whole "saving" from evil, in union with Christ. This the Christian κατεργάζεται (cp. 2 Cor. iv. 17, an instructive parallel, τὸ παραυτίκα ἐλαφρὸν τῆς θλίψεως κατεργάζεται ἡμῖν ...βάρος δόξης) in the sense of his watchfully applying, and as it were developing,. in temptation and duty, the free Divine gift of peace and strength in Christ. "In this way of diligence we receive daily more and more of 'salvation' itself, by liberty from sin, victory over it, peace and communion with God, and the earnests of heavenly felicity" (T. Scott).

There is no contradiction here to the profound and radiant truth of Justification by Faith only. It is an instance of independent lines of truth converging on one goal. From one point of view, that of justifying merit, man is accepted and finally glorified (Rom. viii. 30) because of Christ's work alone, applied to him through faith alone. From another point, that of qualifying capacity, man is glorified as the issue of a work of training, in which he in a true sense has his operating part, though God (see next verse) is the secret of even this operation.

13. θεὸς γάρ. Here is *the reason* both for "fear and trembling" and for the assurance that their Apostle's absence "leaves them not comfortless": they are indwelt by the eternal Holy One and Loving One Himself; let that fact at once awe them and give them a calm confidence.

ὁ ἐνεργῶν ἐν ὑμῖν. Ἐνεργεῖν (ἐνεργεῖσθαι) carries a certain intensity of meaning, and is used habitually in N.T. of spiritual forces. Cp. Matt. xiv. 2, αἱ δυνάμεις ἐνεργοῦσιν ἐν αὐτῷ: Eph. ii. 2, τοῦ πνεύματος τοῦ νῦν ἐνεργοῦντος ἐν τοῖς υἱοῖς τῆς ἀπειθείας: 2 Thess. iii. 7, τὸ μυστήριον...ἤδη ἐνεργεῖται. Here it is supremely appropriate therefore.

The In-dwelling and In-working of God in His saints is a main doctrine of the Gospel. The manner is perfectly mysterious; the fact is certain. By the Holy Spirit, Christ is "in" the disciple (2 Cor. xiii. 5); and "in Christ dwelleth all the fulness of the Godhead" (Col. ii. 9). See further Eph. iii. 17. In the light of a passage like this we read the deep truth that the "grace" which is in the Christian is not merely an emitted influence from above; it is the living Lord Himself, present and operative at the "first springs of thought and will."

καὶ τὸ θέλειν καὶ τὸ ἐνεργεῖν. Almost, "both your willing and your (spiritual) working." Here, though in passing, we touch one of the deepest mysteries of grace. On the one hand is the Christian's will, real, personal, and powerfully appealed to as such.   On the other hand, beneath it, as cause is beneath result, is the will and work of God ; God Himself the hidden secret of the right action of the true human will.   Let us recognize with equal reverence and simplicity both these great parallels of truth.   "With fear and trembling" let us remember human responsibility; with deep submission let us adore the ways of grace, attributing ultimately to God alone every link in the chain of actual salvation.

ὑπὲρ τῆς εὐδοκίας.   "For the sake of His good pleasure," His sovereign and gracious will.   The Christian, enabled by the Divine power within to will and to do, wills and does, not for himself, but for Him whose implement he is.

14.   πάντα ποιεῖτε κτλ.   He carries now into detail the general principle of holiness in the power of the Divine In-dweller, holding still in view the unselfish love for which he pleaded above (ii. 1—4). Observe the characteristic *totality* of the precept, the πάντα.

χωρὶς γογγυσμῶν καὶ διαλογισμῶν.   With γογγυσμῶν cp. Acts vi. 1, γένετο γογγυσμὸς Ἑλληνιστῶν πρὸς τοὺς Ἑβραίους, and 1 Pet. iv. 9, φιλόξενοι εἰς ἀλλήλους ἄνευ γογγυσμοῦ : and with διαλογισμῶν, Jas ii. 4, ἐγένεσθε κριταὶ διαλογισμῶν πονηρῶν.   The "murmurs" and "debates" are not as towards God, but as towards one another; expressions of personal or connexional alienation and prejudice.   So we gather from the direction of the appeal above, ii. 1—4, and below, iv. 2, 3 ; and other places in the Epistle.   Such things were to die in the air of the love and presence of God in Christ.

15.   γένεσθε.   Not ἦτε.   He gently suggests their need of *becoming* more fully what Christians should be.   On the reading, see critical note.

ἄμεμπτοι.   "Except concerning the law of their God" (Dan. vi. 5).

ἀκέραιοι.   Literally, "unmingled" (κεράννυμι) ; pure in purpose, guileless.   The rendering "harmless" seems to assume a derivation from κέρας, which cannot be sustained ; as if it meant what would not push or strike.   See Trench, *Synonyms*, s.v.
   The word occurs elsewhere in N. T. only Matt. x. 16 ; Rom. xvi. 19.   It is classical.   See e.g. Euripides, *Orest.* 922, where a disinterested citizen is described as ἀκέραιος, ἀνεπίληπτον ἠσκηκὼς βίον.

τέκνα θεοῦ.   The precise phrase recurs Joh. i. 12, ἔδωκεν αὐτοῖς ἐξουσίαν τέκνα θεοῦ γενέσθαι: xi. 52, τὰ τέκνα τοῦ θεοῦ τὰ διεσκορπισμένα: Rom. viii. 16 (of the witness of the Spirit with our spirit), 17, 21, τὴν ἐλευθερίαν τῆς δόξης τῶν τέκνων τοῦ θεοῦ, ix. 8 : 1 Joh. iii. 1, ἴδετε ποταπὴν ἀγάπην κτλ., 2, 10, v. 2.   The τέκνον is emphatically the *born* child, shewing the family likeness; the thought in point here.
   As a rule, Scripture uses the words "Father," "son," "child," as between God and man, to mark the connexion not of creation but of new creation ; as here.

ἄμωμα. On the reading, see critical note. The word (from μῶμος, blame, connected with μέμ-φομαι) occurs in Eph. i. 4, v. 27 ; Col. i. 22 (besides a few other N.T. places)—passages in the same group of Epistles. The Philippians were to become blamelessly *true to their character* as God's children.

The LXX. rendering of Deut. xxxii. 5 was here in the Apostle's mind ; ἡμάρτοσαν, οὐκ αὐτῷ τέκνα, μωμητά, γενεὰ σκολιὰ καὶ διεστραμμένη. The "true Israelites" of Philippi were to be the antithesis of the ancient rebels.

μέσον. On the reading, see critical note. The words of Moses (see last note) are still in his mind ; but "the crooked and distorted generation" are now not the Lord's Israel in rebellion, but the unsubdued outside world. "Amidst" that world, not in selfish or timorous isolation from surrounding life, the saints were to walk ; in it, not of it (Joh. xvii. 15) ; a visible contrast, and an attracting power. The Gospel gives no real sanction to the *anchorite* theory of holiness.

ἐν οἷς. The γενεά is viewed as in its individual members (οἷς).

φαίνεσθε. "Ye appear," rather, perhaps, than "ye shine" (for which φαίνειν is the somewhat commoner word); though "there is very little difference between 'appear' and 'shine' here" (Alford).— Φαίνεσθαι is used of the rising and setting of the stars, as in the famous place, *Il.* viii. 556 :

> ὡς δ' ὅτ' ἐν οὐρανῷ ἄστρα φαεινὴν ἀμφὶ σελήνην
> φαίνετ' ἀριπρεπέα.

Hence τὰ φαινόμενα, the title of one of Aratus' astronomical poems (cent. iii. B.C.). Perhaps such a speciality of meaning is traceable here; the saints, in the beautiful light of holiness, rise star-like on the night of surrounding sin.

φωστῆρες. *Luminaria*, Vulg. See last note. The word occurs in the Greek of e.g. Gen. i. 14, 16, γενηθήτωσαν φωστῆρες ἐν τῷ στερεώματι τοῦ οὐρανοῦ...ἐποίησεν ὁ θεὸς τοὺς δύο φωστῆρας κτλ. In the N.T. it occurs only here and (apparently in the very rare sense of "radiance") in Rev. xxi. 11.

He who is "the Light of the World" (Joh. viii. 12), "the Sun of Righteousness" (Mal. iv. 2), "the Morning Star" (Rev. xxii. 16), can make His servants reflect and in that sense repeat Himself. Cp. Isai. lx. 1 ; Matt. v. 14 ; Eph. v. 8.

16. λόγον ζωῆς. The Gospel, as the revelation and offer of eternal life in Christ. So the Saviour's teachings are ῥήματα ζωῆς αἰωνίου, Joh. vi. 68, and the message of His grace is λόγος ζωῆς, 1 Joh. i. 1 (see Westcott *in loco* against a reference there to the Personal Logos). The essence of the λόγος is (1 Joh. v. 11), ὅτι ζωὴν αἰώνιον ἔδωκεν ἡμῖν ὁ θεός· καὶ αὕτη ἡ ζωὴ ἐν τῷ υἱῷ αὐτοῦ ἐστίν.

ἐπέχοντες. "Holding forth" for notice and acceptance. So Homer, *Od.* xvi. 443:

κρέας ὀπτὸν
ἐν χείρεσσιν ἔθηκεν, ἐπέσχε τε οἶνον ἐρυθρόν.

He drops the metaphor of the luminary, and thinks of the banquet and its provision. Ἐπέχειν occurs in some other N.T. passages, but in the sense of giving attention, or (Acts xix. 22) of lingering.—On the phrase λόγον ἐπέχειν see Appendix I.

εἰς καύχημα ἐμοί. Ἐμοὶ is slightly emphatic ; he thankfully claims *his* part in their work and its fruits, as he had brought the light to them.—For the thought of such καύχημα cp. 1 Thess. ii. 19, τίς ἡμῶν ...στέφανος καυχήσεως ; ἢ οὐχὶ καὶ ὑμεῖς ἔμπροσθεν τοῦ Κυρίου ἡμῶν...ἐν τῇ παρουσίᾳ αὐτοῦ; There as here he looks forward to a personal recognition of his converts at the Lord's Coming, and to a special joy over them.

εἰς ἡμέραν Χριστοῦ. "Unto the day," in view of it. He anticipates the "exultation" to be actually felt ἐν ἡμέρᾳ Χριστοῦ.

εἰς κενόν. A phrase exclusively Pauline in N.T. See 2 Cor. vi. 1, μὴ εἰς κενὸν τὴν χάριν...δέξασθαι ; Gal. ii. 2, μήπως εἰς κενὸν τρέχω, 1 Thess. iii. 5, εἰς κενὸν...κόπος.

ἔδραμον...ἐκοπίασα. "Did run," "did toil." He anticipates his *retrospect* from "the day of Christ," and sees the present race and present toil summed up into recollections. For such an aorist cp. 1 Cor. xiii. 12, τότε ἐπιγνώσομαι καθὼς καὶ ἐπεγνώσθην.

On the metaphor of ἔδραμον, a favourite one with St Paul, giving the thought of both the energy and the goal of life, cp. e.g. Acts xx. 24, τελειῶσαι τὸν δρόμον μου : Gal. ii. 2, μή πως εἰς κενὸν τρέχω ἢ ἔδραμον : 2 Tim. iv. 7, τὸν δρόμον τετέλεκα : and see 1 Cor. ix. 24, 26 ; Rom. ix. 16 ; Heb. xii. 1.

Lightfoot thinks that in ἐκοπίασα we have a probable allusion to the *training* of the athletic *runner* ; he finds μὴ τρέχε, μὴ κοπία, in a connexion suggestive of this (*Anthol.* iii. p. 166). He quotes (as a possible echo of St Paul here) Ignatius (*ad Polyc.* c. 6) συντρέχετε, συγκοπιᾶτε. On St Paul's athletic metaphors see Appendix L.

17. Ἀλλὰ εἰ καί. He takes up the thought suggested by ἐκοπίασα, as if to say, "Toil it is indeed; but it is glad, ungrudging toil; if it involves my shedding my blood for you, it will be only joy to me." "Meanwhile" may thus represent ἀλλά.

σπένδομαι. "I am being outpoured"; "libated," in my life-blood. "The present tense places the hypothesis vividly before the eyes; but it does not...refer to present dangers...comp. e.g. Matt. xii. 26" [εἰ ὁ Σατανᾶς τὸν Σ. ἐκβάλλει] (Lightfoot). But it is at least possible that, in suspense as he was about the issue of his trial, he is here thinking of martyrdom as perhaps at the door.

For the phrase cp. 2 Tim. iv. 6, ἐγὼ γὰρ ἤδη σπένδομαι. Lightfoot compares Ignat. *ad Rom.* c. 2, a close parallel here, μὴ παράσχησθέ (μοι) τοῦ σπονδισθῆναι θεῷ, ὡς ἔτι θυσιαστήριον ἕτοιμόν ἐστιν.

The Vulg. here has *immolor*, and the lexicographer Hesychius (cent. iv.) explains σπένδομαι here by θυσιάζομαι. But the imagery is certainly more precise than this allows.

ἐπὶ τῇ θυσίᾳ. "On," as a libation is shed *on* the altar. He views the Philippians, in their character of consecrated believers (cp. Rom. xii. 1), as a holocaust to God; and upon that sacrifice the drink-offering, the outpoured wine, is his own life-blood, his martyrdom for the Gospel which he has preached to them. Cp. Num. xv. 5 for the Mosaic libation, οἶνον εἰς σπονδὴν...ποιήσετε ἐπὶ τῆς ὁλοκαυτώσεως. Lightfoot thinks that a reference to pagan libations is more likely in a letter to a Gentile mission; but surely St Paul familiarized all his converts with O.T. symbolism; and *his own* mind was of course full of it.

τῇ θυσίᾳ καὶ λειτουργίᾳ τῆς πίστεως ὑμῶν. "The sacrifice and ritual" "of" their faith because vitally connected with it. In faith they were self-surrendered to their Saviour; so they were themselves "a living sacrifice," and their lives were a sacerdotal ordinance. Cp. Rom. xv. 16 (with note in the *Cambridge Bible for Schools*) for an instructive parallel. There the ἔθνη are the προσφορά, and the εὐαγγέλιον is the matter on which the ἱερουργία is exercised. Here the Philippians are both sacrifice and priests, while Paul is their libation.

These are the only two passages where the Apostle connects the language of sacerdotalism with the distinctive work of the Christian ministry; and both passages have the tone of figure and, so to speak, poetry.

χαίρω. With the deep joy of love in self-sacrifice.

συνχαίρω πᾶσιν ὑμῖν. Again the warm and significant *"you all."* Συνχαίρειν can mean "to congratulate"; so Plutarch, *Mor.* 231 B (quoted by Lightfoot), συνχαίρω τῇ πόλει, in a context which leaves no doubt of the meaning. This meaning is in point here. Dying for them, his last thought would be congratulation on *their* faith and obedience.

The Epistle of Polycarp to the Philippians, at the beginning, has συνεχάρην ὑμῖν μεγάλως ἐν Κυρίῳ, words which may be an echo of these.

18. τὸ δὲ αὐτό. "In the same manner" (R.V.). So Matt. xxvii. 44, τὸ δ' αὐτὸ καὶ οἱ λῃσταὶ...ὠνείδιζον αὐτόν. "The accusative [τὸ αὐτό] defines rather the character than the object of the action" (Lightfoot).

χαίρετε καὶ συνχαίρετέ μοι. *Gaudete et congratulamini mihi*, Vulg. The Greek leaves us free to explain it as either imperative (as Vulg.) or indicative. If the latter is chosen, it is little else than the imperative in disguise; he *assumes* their joy and congratulation in order to *enjoin* it. Lightfoot quotes from Plutarch (*Mor.* p. 347 c) the χαίρετε καὶ χαίρομεν of the messenger from Marathon; the χαίρετε there is probably indicative.

He bids them share his martyr-joy, as partners of the martyr-spirit.

19—30. HE PROPOSES SOON TO SEND TIMOTHEUS: HE SENDS WITHOUT
DELAY EPAPHRODITUS.

19. Ἐλπίζω δὲ. "But," amidst these exalted joys and trials, he
hopes soon to take a practical step to obtain fuller information about the
Philippians. He refers back to the words ἐν τῇ ἀπουσίᾳ μου, ver. 12.

ἐν κυρίῳ Ἰησοῦ. See note on ἐν σπλάγχνοις X. Ἰ., i. 8.

Τιμόθεον. See note on Τιμόθεος, i. 1.

κἀγὼ. As well as you; he assumes *their* good courage, and with
noble modesty speaks as one who needs it to kindle his own.

εὐψυχῶ. "Be of good heart." The verb is very rare in Greek;
εὐψυχία, εὔψυχος, are not so. For the meaning see e.g. Eurip. *Med.*
402: ἔρπ᾽ εἰς τὸ δεινόν · νῦν ἀγὼν εὐψυχίας.

20. γὰρ. He gives his reason for sending *Timothy.* There was
no one like him in natural fitness for this task.

ἰσόψυχον. A slight echo perhaps of εὐψυχῶ. "Of equal soul," i.e.
to Timotheus (Lightfoot); no other delegate would have such qualifi-
cations of unselfish sympathy with Philippi. "The word ἰσόψυχος is
extremely rare. It occurs in Æsch. *Agam.* 1470 (1446)" (Lightfoot);
κράτος ἰσόψ. ἐκ γυναικῶν, i.e. "a strength of soul, shewn by women, equal"
to that of men. The word occurs elsewhere in the Greek Scriptures
only Psal. liv. 13 (Heb., lv. 14, "It was thou, mine equal"), as a
rendering of the Hebrew "*after my scale*, or *standard*," בערכי.

γνησίως. "Genuinely"; with quite unaffected devotion.

μεριμνήσει. "Shall take anxious thought." Μέριμνα and its verb
are commonly connected with μερίζω, and explained of the *divisions*
in the anxious mind. More recently a connexion has been advocated
with "a root meaning to be thoughtful, and akin to μάρτυς, memor,
&c." (Grimm, ed. Thayer, s.v.). Usage anywise leaves the meaning of
anxiety unmistakable.—See the verb again below, iv. 6, and the note
there. The two passages are not discordant. Timothy's μέριμνα *here*
would be intense thought for others (so 1 Cor. vii. 32, 34, xii. 2, 5;
2 Cor. xi. 28). The μέριμνα forbidden *there* would be, in effect, the
failure to pass on our burthens to the Lord for His care and aid.
This is the ordinary reference of the word in N.T.

21. οἱ πάντες. Slightly more definite than πάντες: it is *the*
πάντες in question; "all of them."

τὰ ἑαυτῶν. Their own ease or safety, or their personal preferences
in toil or duty.

οὐ τὰ X. Ἰ. The whole verse indicates some bitter disappointments
felt by St Paul; Demas (2 Tim. iv. 10) had his precursors. Still we
must not understand St Paul to condemn these disciples without
reserve; like Mark (Acts xiii. 13) they may have been true men found
off their guard. And again common sense bids us explain the πάντες
with caution. He must mean not simply all the Christians around

him, many of whom would not be free agents for this mission; it must be all who could have gone if they would.

Let us not fail to remember that to the true disciple in his true condition τὰ Χριστοῦ Ἰησοῦ are, as such, the supreme interest.

22. τὴν δοκιμήν. "The test" through which he passed, before your eyes, when we were both at Philippi.—Or perhaps δοκιμή here means the result of the test, "proved fitness." In Greek, as in English, abstract nouns are constantly passing from "process" to "result" (e.g. οἰκοδομή), and becoming more concrete.

ὡς πατρὶ τέκνον. "As child with father"; supplying σὺν in idea from the next words. Observe τέκνον, the tender word, of the *born* child; see on ver. 15 above. For St Paul's fatherly love for Timothy see 2 Tim. i. 2, and that whole Epistle.

σὺν ἐμοί. Slightly emphatic by position; as if to say, you saw his devotion of course, for it was shewn in connexion with me, your own Apostle.

ἐδούλευσεν. "He did bondservice"; almost, "he slaved." The aorist gathers up Timothy's toil at Philippi into one thought. This is better than to render it, "He *entered on* bondservice"; for the reference is plainly not to his first Christian work, but to his labours *at Philippi.*

εἰς τὸ εὐαγγέλιον. Well paraphrased by R.V., "in furtherance of the gospel." See note on i. 5 above. For εὐαγγέλιον in the sense of missionary work, see below, iv. 3.

23. τοῦτον μὲν οὖν. "So *him*," with a slight emphasis; he is about to speak of others too, himself and Epaphroditus.

ὡς ἄν...ἐξαυτῆς. "At once when" (Lightfoot). "For ὡς ἄν temporal, comp. Rom. xv. 24 [ὡς ἂν πορεύωμαι εἰς τὴν Σπανίαν], 1 Cor. xi. 34 [τὰ λοιπὰ, ὡς ἂν ἔλθω, διατάξομαι]" (Lightfoot).

ἀφίδω. "Get a view of," as from a point of observation. Cp. Jonah iv. 5, ἕως οὗ ἀπίδῃ τί ἔσται τῇ πόλει.—On the form ἀφίδω here, see above, introductory notes to ch. ii.

τὰ περὶ ἐμέ. "My circumstances," "my position."

24. πέποιθα. See above on πεποιθώς, i. 6; and cp. on οἶδα, i. 25.

ἐν κυρίῳ. See above, on i. 8.

ταχέως. The word is elastic; it may refer to weeks or to months. What he is "sure of" is that he will follow promptly in Timothy's track.—Lightfoot compares the closely parallel language of 1 Cor. iv. 17, 19: ἔπεμψα ὑμῖν Τιμόθεον, ὅς ἐστίν μου τέκνον...ἐλεύσομαι δὲ ταχέως πρὸς ὑμᾶς, ἐὰν ὁ Κύριος θελήσῃ.

25. Ἀναγκαῖον δὲ. As against the less obligatory call for Timothy's journey. There was *a duty*, to Epaphroditus and to Philippi, and it must not be postponed.

ἡγησάμην. Render, in English idiom, "I have counted," or "I count." The aorist is "epistolary," and gives the writer's present thought as it will appear when the reader gets the letter. (Cp. e.g. ἀνέπεμψα, Philem. 11.)

Ἐπαφρόδιτον. He has been identified with Epaphras (Col. i. 7, iv. 12; Philem. 23); and the shorter name is an abbreviation of the longer. But Epaphras belonged to Colossæ in Asia Minor, Epaphroditus to Philippi in Europe. Both names were very common.—It is observable that this saint's name embodies that of Aphrodite. Cp. the names Phœbe, Nereus, &c., Rom. xvi. Little scruple seems to have been attached in the early Church to the retention of pre-baptismal idolatrous names.—We know Epaphroditus only from this Epistle; the one brief portrait shews a noble and lovable character.

τὸν ἀδελφὸν καὶ συνεργὸν καὶ συνστρατιώτην μου. A singularly emphatic commendation. Evidently he had toiled and striven "in the Gospel," in no common way, at St Paul's side, whether at Philippi in the past or now recently at Rome, as Lightfoot suggests. For the word συνστρατιώτης cp. Philem. 2, where it is applied to Archippus; and for the imagery of warfare cp. 2 Cor. x. 3; 1 Tim. i. 18; 2 Tim. ii. 3, 4. The Christian is not only a worker, but in his work has to deal, soldier-wise, with "all the power of the enemy" (Luke x. 19).

ὑμῶν δὲ ἀπόστολον. "Your delegated messenger." Cp. 2 Cor. viii. 23; ἀδελφοὶ ἡμῶν, ἀπόστολοι ἐκκλησιῶν. There is no Scripture evidence for giving the word ἀπόστολος in N.T. the meaning of chief pastor of a church or district. Meanwhile, it seems to mean more than merely a messenger; it has gathered a certain sacredness from our Lord's use of it (Luke vi. 13) for His twelve chosen Messengers; it has a religious colour, like our word missionary. May not this word fairly represent it here?—"your missionary to me," with a gracious pleasantry, as if the Philippians were sending a εὐαγγέλιον of pious love to St Paul.

λειτουργὸν τῆς χρείας μου. Group these words, as does R.V., still under the ὑμῶν just above: "Your missionary and minister to (lit., of) my need." The λειτουργία is explained below, iv. 18, where Epaphroditus appears as the conveyer of the Philippian offerings to St Paul.—Λειτουργός is a public servant or minister. At Athens, λειτουργία and λειτουργεῖν (the noun has not yet been found in this use, though it is more than probable that it bore it) denoted the discharge of a public office at the citizen's own cost. Later, the meaning widened, but commonly retaining the idea of publicity and commission. In the Greek Scriptures λειτουργός is used of a king's servant (1 Kings x. 5); of a magistrate, as the minister of God's order (Rom. xiii. 6); of a priest, as minister of the temple (Heb. viii. 2).— Like ἀπόστολος above, λειτουργός here may carry something of its higher meaning; he came publicly commissioned by the Philippians' love.

26. ἐπιποθῶν ἦν. "He was (i.e., as an English letter would run, "he has been," or "he is") in a state of longing"; he feels home-sick for you. See note on i. 8.

πάντας ὑμᾶς. One of the many instances of markedly inclusive reference to the Philippians. See the last note on i. 8. Epaphroditus, St Paul implies, has no partial or partizan thoughts of the Philippians; his love knows *no cliques*. On the reading here see critical notes.

ἀδημονῶν. "Sore troubled"; almost, "bewildered," "distraught." The word is used of our blessed Lord's Agony, Matt. xxvi. 37; Mar. xiv. 33; its only other occurrences in N.T. The derivation is either (Buttmann, *Lexil.* pp. 29, &c.) from a- and δῆμος, "not at home," "uneasy" (Buttmann compares *nicht daheim sein, mir ist unheimlich*), or (Lobeck, quoted and approved by Lightfoot) is connected with ἀδῆσαι, to be sated, to loathe, and so to be restless.

ὅτι ἠσθένησεν. "That he fell ill," or (if the aorist presents the illness as a point in thought) "that he was ill," or, as an English letter would have it, "that he has been ill." Perhaps he had taken Roman fever.

27. ὁ θεὸς ἠλέησεν αὐτόν. For Epaphroditus, as for St Paul, death would be κέρδος (i. 21, and cp. 1 Cor. iii. 23) from one supreme point of view. Yet death *in itself* is not the Christian's choice; see Joh. xxi. 18 (ὅπου οὐ θέλεις), and 2 Cor. v. 4 (οὐ θέλομεν ἐκδύσασθαι). And it closes the joys of cross-bearing service. As Chrysostom says, discussing the problem of "mercy" here, τὸ κερδᾶναι ψυχὰς οὐκ ἔνι λοιπὸν ἀπελθόντας ἐκεῖ. To Epaphroditus death would have been withdrawal from his beloved work for Philippi; and this pang was spared him.

ἀλλὰ καὶ ἐμέ. Characteristically, he loves to emphasize the value of his friends to him. Cp. e.g. Rom. xvi. 4.

λύπην ἐπὶ λύπην. Bereavement would have been added to great and much-including trial of captivity.—Observe the perfect naturalness and candour of his thought and feeling. He has "the peace of God," and "strength for all things" (iv. 7, 13). But this means no torpor, and no hardening. He is released from embitterment and from murmurs, but by the same process every sensibility is deepened. So it was with his Lord; Joh. xi. 33, 35, 38.

Observe that the χάρισμα ἰαμάτων, exercised by St Paul at Melita (Acts xxviii. 8), was evidently not at his absolute disposal. He could not *command* his friend's recovery; it was mere mercy.

σχῶ. "Get," not merely "have." "That I might not incur an accumulation of griefs."

28. ἔπεμψα. Anglicé, "I have sent," "I am sending."

ἀλυπότερος. Again with perfect candour of heart he does not say "glad," but "less sorrowful." The separation from Epaphroditus would be a human sorrow, which would temper the happiness with which he would restore him to the Philippians; and he does not disguise it.

29. προσδέχεσθε...αὐτόν. "Receive him"; words which *perhaps* suggest that to some among them, affected by their small internal divisions, Epaphroditus would be not quite acceptable. But we may

explain the Greek rather, "*Accept* him," as *my gift* to you; in which
sense no *appeal* would be implied. Cp. Heb. xi. 35, οὐ προσδεξά-
μενοι τὴν ἀπολύτρωσιν.

μετὰ πάσης χαρᾶς. His own "sorrow" hinders not in the least his
sympathy with their joy.

ἐντίμους ἔχετε. "Hold in high value." The adjective is used of
the centurion's "valuable" slave (Luke vii. 2), and of the "costly"
Stone (1 Pet. ii. 4, 6).—Epaphroditus was perhaps a little under-
valued at Philippi, in proportion to St Paul's estimate of him.

30. **διὰ τὸ ἔργον Χριστοῦ.** On the reading, see critical notes.

μέχρι θανάτου ἤγγισεν. Θανάτῳ, or εἰς θάνατον, would be the usual
construction. It is as if he were about to write μέχρι θ. ἠσθένησεν,
and then varied the expression.

παραβολευσάμενος τῇ ψυχῇ. For the reading, see critical notes.
If we read παραβουλευσάμενος, we must render, "taking bad counsel for
his life," i.e. acting with no regard for it. The text may be rendered
"playing the gambler with his life" (as Lightfoot), or "hazarding
his life" (R.V.). Παραβολεύεσθαι is a verb known only through this
passage. Παραβάλλεσθαι is to cast a die, to venture; hence the
adjective παράβολος, reckless; on which apparently this verb is formed.
Lightfoot compares ἀσωτεύεσθαι, to play the spendthrift.—Connected
with παράβολος is the ecclesiastical term παραβολάνος, *parabolanus*, a
member of a "minor order" devoted to nursing the infected, and
other *hazardous* duties. The order probably originated in Constan-
tine's time. It acquired later a bad reputation as a turbulent body,
troublesome to magistrates for riotous interruption of public business.
At the council called the *Latrocinium*, at Ephesus, A.D. 449, "six
hundred of them appeared as the tools of the brutal Barsumas, to
coerce malcontents to support his measures" (*Dict. Chr. Ant.*, s.v.).

ἵνα ἀναπληρώσῃ κτλ. Cp. 1 Cor. xvi. 17: τὸ ὑμέτερον ὑστέρημα
αὐτοὶ ἀνεπλήρωσαν, and Col. i. 24: ἀνταναπληρῶ τὰ ὑστερήματα τῶν
θλίψεων τοῦ Χριστοῦ, that is, the "tribulations" involved in evangelization, which the Lord had as it were left unfinished, to be completed
by his followers.

St Paul here means no blame to the Philippians. Epaphroditus
had come forward to do what they, as a community, could not do—
travel to Rome to help St Paul in his needs, carrying with him the
collection they had so lovingly made.

τῆς πρός με λειτουργίας. "Of the ministration designed for me."

CHAPTER III.

3. **θεοῦ.** So ℵ*ABCD₂ᶜ, 17 37, and many other cursives, copt, Amb
Aug. St Augustine says (*de Trin.* i. 13) that *Græci codices omnes,
aut pæne omnes*, are for this reading, while *in nonnullis...Latinis* he
finds *spiritu Deo.* ℵᶜD₂*, syr (pesh) vulg goth arm æth, Orig Chr Vict
read θεῷ. All modern Editors θεοῦ.

6. ζῆλος. So אּ*ABD₂*. אּᶜD₂.° and the cursives read ζῆλον, the classical form. In Clem. Rom. *Ep. ad Cor.* both forms are freely used: e.g. διὰ ζῆλος, § 4, διὰ ζῆλον, § 5.

7. ἀλλά. So (or ἀλλ') אּᶜBD₂*, the mass of cursives, vulg syrr copt, Aug. אּAG, 17, Cyr Al₆ om ἀλλά.

8. μενοῦνγε. אּA, 17 37, and many other cursives, Bas (in one place) Cyr. μὲν οὖν γε. BD₂G, many cursives, Bas (in one place) Chrys read μὲν οὖν only. LTr Ell μὲν οὖν: Tisch μενοῦνγε: WH μὲν οὖν γε.

σκύβαλα. So (without εἶναι) אּ*BD₂*G₂, 17, vulg syr (pesh) arm æth, Orig. אּᶜAD₂°, 37 47, and most other cursives, Bas Chrys Cyr add εἶναι after σκύβαλα.

10. παθημάτων. So אּ*B. אּᶜD₂G₂K₂L, all cursives, prefix τῶν. This seems preferable, though Tisch Treg omit.

συνμορφιζόμενος. אּ*ᵃⁿᵈᶜD₂* συνμ-. ABP, 17, Orig. Bas. συμμ-. אּᶜD₂ᶜK₂L, the mass of cursives, Chrys Theodoret read συμμορφούμενος. Recent editors all prefer συμμορφιζόμενος, as the less usual form, and so less likely to be an emendation. Another reading is found in G, συνφορτειζόμενος, rendered *cooneratus* in the Latin of the MS.: "bearing with Him the burthen of His death." But this, though there is other Latin evidence for it, is not to be considered.

11. τὴν ἐκ νεκρῶν. So אּABD₂, 17 73 80, vulg goth syr (pesh and harkl), Bas Chrys Orig (Lat. transl.) Tert. So all recent Editors. K₂L, most cursives, copt, Theodoret Theophyl read τῶν νεκρῶν.

12. ὑπὸ Χριστοῦ Ἰησοῦ. So אּA, 47 73 80, vulg copt arm, Chrys Aug. BD₂*G₂, 17, goth, Clem Or (Lat. transl.) Tert Hilar read ὑπὸ Χριστοῦ. The evidence is well balanced. Tisch Χριστοῦ Ἰησοῦ, WH Χριστοῦ [Ἰησοῦ], Lachm Treg Wordsw Ell Alf Ltft read Χριστοῦ.

13. οὔπω. So אּAD₂*, 17 47 73 80 and many other cursives, copt syr (harkl*) æth, Clem Bas. BD₂ᶜG₂, 37 and most other cursives, vulg syr (pesh and philox text) goth arm, Orig Tert read οὔ. Tisch WH [text: marg οὔ] οὔπω. Treg Ell Alf Ltft οὔ.

16. στοιχεῖν. So the sentence ends אּ*AB, 17, copt sah, Hil Aug. אּᶜKL, the mass of cursives, syrr æth add the words κανόνι, τὸ αὐτὸ φρονεῖν. So Wordsw., alone among recent editors. Lightfoot writes *ad loc.*, "the words after στοιχεῖν in the received text (κανόνι, τὸ αὐτὸ φρονεῖν) are interpolated from Gal. vi. 16, Phil. ii. 2. Of these κανόνι is a correct gloss, while τὸ αὐτὸ φρονεῖν expresses an idea alien to the context."

21. σύμμορφον (σύνμ- אּD₂*G). Before this word D₂ᵇK₂L, 17 37 47 and the mass of cursives, syrr, Epiph Chrys Aug Jer read εἰς τὸ γενέσθαι αὐτό. The text is read by אּABD₂*G₂, vulg goth copt arm æth, Iren Euseb Ath Cyr Tert Cyp Hilar. All recent editors read text. The additional words are almost certainly a grammatical gloss.

αὐτῷ. So אּ*ABD₂*, many cursives, Eus Epiph Cyr Chrys (in one place). אּᶜD₂ᶜL, most cursives, Chrys (in two places) Hil Amb read ἑαυτῷ. So Wordsw alone of recent editors. WH αὐτῷ.

Ch. III. 1—3. Let them cultivate joy in the Lord as the true
preservative from Judaistic error.

1. Τὸ λοιπόν. "For the rest"; "For what remains." So below,
iv. 8; and Eph. vi. 10: τὸ λοιπὸν...ἐνδυναμοῦσθε, κτλ. For St Paul's
use of the phrase see also (λοιπὸν) 1 Cor. i. 16; (ὃ δὲ λοιπὸν) 1 Cor. iv. 2;
2 Cor. xiii. 1; 2 Thess. iii. 1, and (τοῦ λοιποῦ) Gal. vi. 17. On the whole
it seems not so much to introduce an immediate conclusion (as
"*finally*" would do) as to mark a transition on the way to it. It
"signifies *for the rest, besides, moreover*,...forming a transition to
other things to which the attention of the...reader is directed"
(Grimm, ed. Thayer, s.v. λοιπός).

Here the Apostle is *approaching* the end of his Epistle, entering on
its last large topic, the difference between a true Gospel and a false.
Hitherto, on the whole, with much accessory matter, he has been
dealing with the blessedness of unity. Now he will deliver a definite
message about saving truth in view of particular errors; and then he
will close. Τὸ λοιπόν fitly introduces this.

The connexion of the passage has been debated; particularly the
bearing of the words τὰ αὐτὰ γράφειν ὑμῖν, following on χαίρετε ἐν
κυρίῳ. No previous injunction *to rejoice* appears in this Epistle; and
there is no trace of a previous Epistle, which might have spoken so.
Bp Lightfoot's solution is as follows: "The same things" are the
exhortations *to unity*, often made already, and which St Paul was
now *just about to reinforce.* But he was interrupted, and did not
dictate again till, perhaps, some days had intervened. He then dropped
the intended appeal, and turned instead to the subject of doctrinal
error. Lightfoot accordingly, in his edition, breaks the text at
the close of ver. 1, and regards ver. 2 as the opening of a new para-
graph or chapter.

But can we think it likely that St Paul, with his scribe beside him,
would have let the Epistle go forth in a state so disjointed?

The following seems a more probable theory: St Paul sees at
Philippi the risk of doctrinal error; error which in one way or another
would undervalue "Christ, and Him crucified." The true antidote
would be a developed and rejoicing insight into Christ and His work,
such as had been given to himself. This shall now be his theme.
And this, in a sense, *he has touched on already*, by his frequent allusions
to the Saviour's union with His people, and above all by such passages
as i. 20—23, ii. 5—18. So in treating now of Christ as their
righteousness, life, peace, and glory, and of "rejoicing in Him" as
such, he is "writing the same things" as before, only in a more
explicit way. All "other gospels," whatever their details, were alike
in this, that they beclouded that great joy. Thus the special injunction to "rejoice" affects both the past context and the following;
particularly it leads on to ver. 3 below, καυχώμενοι ἐν Χ. Ἰ.

"*From the loss of our glory in Thee*, preserve us" (Litany of the
Unitas Fratrum, the "Moravian" Church).

χαίρετε. The R.V. margin has "Or, *farewell.*" But the rendering
"rejoice" (A.V. and text of R.V.) is supported by iv. 3, which seems to

take up this phrase, and adds παντότε. And already in ii. 18 we have had χαίρειν in (obviously) the sense of rejoicing. The Latin Versions read *gaudete in Domino.* Chrysostom writes *in loc.* αἱ θλίψεις...αἱ κατὰ Χριστὸν ἔχουσι χαράν.

τὰ αὐτά. See the notes above, on the connexion of the passage.

ἐμοὶ μὲν οὐκ ὀκνηρόν, ὑμῖν δὲ ἀσφαλές. The words form an iambic trimeter[1] of a rhythm frequent in the Comedians. They may be a quotation. In 1 Cor. xv. 33 we have almost certainly such a quotation: φθείρουσιν ἤθη χρήσθ' (or χρηστὰ) ὁμιλίαι κακαί: " Ill converse cankers fair morality[2]." For similar apparent verse-quotations in the N.T. see Acts xvii. 28, ἐκ τοῦ γὰρ γένος ἐσμέν: Tit. i. 12, Κρῆτες ἀεὶ ψεῦσται κτλ.: and perhaps Jas i. 17, πᾶσα δόσις ἀγαθὴ καὶ πᾶν δώρημα τέλειον.

We may render here, rhythmically, " To me not irksome, it is safe for you."

2. βλέπετε. "Comp. Mark iv. 24, βλέπετε τί ἀκούετε: 2 Joh. 8, βλέπετε ἑαυτούς : so frequently βλέπετε ἀπὸ (e.g. Mark viii. 15) and βλέπετε μὴ (e.g. Luke xxi. 8)" (Lightfoot).—Latin Versions, *videte.*

τοὺς κύνας. "The dogs"; a known class or party; evidently the Judaistic teachers within the Church, to whom he has referred already in another tone and connexion (i. 15) as active at Rome. These Pharisee-Christians perhaps called the uncircumcised converts κύνες, as the Pharisees proper called all Gentiles. See e.g. Joh. Lightfoot (*Hor. Hebr.* on Matt. xv. 26): "By this title the Jews disgraced the Gentiles... אומות עולם נמשלו ככלבים. *The nations of the world* [that is *the heathen*] *are likened to dogs* [Midr. Tillin, fol. 6. 3]." The habits of the dog suggest ideas of uncleanness ; and its half-wild condition in Eastern towns makes it a simile for an outcast. In Scripture, the "dog" appears in connexions almost always of either contempt or dread; e.g. 1 Sam. xxiv. 14; 2 Ki. viii. 13 ; Psal. xxii. 16, 20 ; Matt. vii. 6 ; Rev. xxii. 15. St Paul here "turns the tables" on the Judaistic rigorist. The Judaist, and not the simple believer who comes direct from paganism to Messiah, is the real outcast from Messiah's covenant. The same view is expressed more fully, Gal. v. 2—4: κατηργήθητε ἀπὸ Χριστοῦ, οἵτινες ἐν νόμῳ δικαιοῦσθε.

τοὺς κακοὺς ἐργάτας. "The evil workers" (R.V.). Or possibly, "the bad," i.e. unskilful, "workmen." These are the same persons under another view. Possibly, by a sort of verbal play, he alludes to their doctrine of salvation by "works," ἔργα, not by faith (see e.g. Rom. iii. 27, xi. 6; Gal. ii. 16, iii. 2); as if to say, "They are all for *working,* to win merit. But they are bungling workmen, spoiling the

---

[1] I owe this remark to a friend.

[2] The words occur in a fragment of the *Thais* of Menander; but Socrates (the historian) adduces (iii. 16, *ad fin.*) the verse as proof that St Paul was not ἀνήκοος τοῦ Εὐριπίδου δραμάτων. (And cp. Clem. Alex. *Strom.* i. 14, 59.) "Perhaps Menander borrowed...from Euripides" (Alford). Socrates (*ibid.*) quotes Tit. i. 12; Acts xvii. 28; as proofs of St Paul's acquaintance with Epimenides and Aratus respectively.

fabric of the Gospel." See 2 Cor. xi. 13 for the same apparent double meaning of this word; ψευδαπόστολοι, ἐργάται δόλιοι.

See ii. 12 above for the precept to *work* in the right sense and direction.

τὴν κατατομήν. Latin Versions, *concisionem.* "The mutilation"; i.e. the persons who teach it. By this harsh word, kindred to περιτομή, he condemns the Judaist's rigid zeal for bodily circumcision. In the light of the Gospel, to demand circumcision as a saving ordinance was to demand a mere maltreatment of the body, no better than that of the Baal-priests (1 Ki. xviii. 28, κατετέμνοντο κατὰ τὸν ἐθισμὸν αὐτῶν, LXX.).

See Lightfoot on Gal. v. 12 (ὄφελον καὶ ἀποκόψονται) for a somewhat similar use of words in a kindred connexion. Lightfoot's interesting note here gives other instances of St Paul's play on words; e.g. 2 Thess. iii. 11, ἐργαζόμενος, περιεργαζομένους; Rom. xii. 3, φρονεῖν, ὑπερφρονεῖν, σωφρονεῖν. Cp. Acts viii. 30, γινώσκεις ἃ ἀναγινώσκεις;

Wyclif curiously renders, "se yᵉ dyuysioun"; Tindale and 'Cranmer,' "Beware of dissencion (dissensyon)."

3. ἡμεῖς γάρ ἐσμεν ἡ περιτομή. Cp. esp. Gal. iii. 7, 29, εἰ ὑμεῖς Χριστοῦ, ἄρα τοῦ Ἀβραὰμ σπέρμα ἐστέ, κατ' ἐπαγγελίαν κληρόνομοι, and Eph. ii. 11, 19, οἱ λεγόμενοι ἀκροβυστία ὑπὸ τῆς λεγομένης περιτομῆς... συμπολῖται [ἐστὲ] τῶν ἁγίων, κτλ.

οἱ πνεύματι θεοῦ λατρεύοντες. "Who worship by the Spirit of God" (R.V.). On the reading, see critical note. In this reading λατρεύειν is used without an expressed object, as in e.g. Luke ii. 37, λατρεύουσα νύκτα καὶ ἡμέραν. The verb originally means any sort of service (λάτρις, *ancilla*), domestic or otherwise; but in Biblical Greek usage gives it an almost invariable connexion (see Deut. xxviii. 48 for an exception) with the service of *worship*, and occasionally (e.g. Heb. viii. 5, xiii. 10) with the worship of *priestly ritual.* Probably this use is in view here. The Apostle claims the spiritual believer as the true priest of the true rite.

πνεύματι θεοῦ. For this phrase (πνεῦμα θεοῦ) in St Paul see Rom. viii. 9, 14; 1 Cor. vii. 40, xii. 3; 2 Cor. iii. 3. See 2 Cor. iii. at large for the supremely significant place given by St Paul in the Gospel message to the gift and work of the Holy Spirit.

καυχώμενοι. "Exulting," "glorying." The verb occurs here only in the Epistle; καύχημα occurs i. 26, ii. 16. The idea is a joy emphatically triumphant, the travesty of which would be *boastfulness.* Cp. Gal. vi. 13, ἐμοὶ...μὴ γένοιτο καυχᾶσθαι εἰ μὴ ἐν τῷ σταυρῷ, κτλ.

What national and ritual privilege seemed to the Judaist, that Christ Jesus was to the Christian; pedestal and crown, righteousness and glory.

καὶ οὐκ ἐν σαρκὶ πεποιθότες. Lit., "and not in flesh confiding." The words suggest, by their arrangement, that we Christians *have* a "confidence," but that it is in something better than "the flesh."

Σάρξ : the word has occurred twice already, i. 22, 24, obviously in
the sense of bodily conditions of life. Here, in a moral context, it has
to be illustrated by e.g. Rom. vii. 5, ὅτε ἦμεν ἐν τῇ σαρκί : viii. 9, οὐκ
ἐστὲ ἐν σαρκί, ἀλλὰ ἐν πνεύματι : Gal. iii. 3, ἐναρξάμενοι πνεύματι, νῦν
σαρκὶ ἐπιτελεῖσθε : v. 19, τὰ ἔργα τῆς σαρκός : vi. 12, εὐπροσωπῆσαι ἐν
σαρκί. Reviewing these and other like places in St Paul, we find that
a fair practical equivalent for the word here is "self," as used e.g. in
the English of Lavater's hymn (*O Jesus Christus, wachs in mir*) :

> " Make this poor *self* grow less and less,
>   Be Thou my life and aim."

It denotes man as *apart from* God, and then *at discord with* God.
Accordingly it often comes to stand for whatever in man is not
subject to the Holy Spirit ; and so reaches what is its practical meaning here—anything, other than God, taken by man for his trust and
strength, e.g. religious observances, traditional privilege and position,
personal religious reputation. From this whole region the Christian's
πεποίθησις is transferred to Christ and His Spirit.

4—11. St Paul's own experience as a converted Pharisee, and its Lessons.

4. καίπερ ἐγὼ ἔχων. The nominative is practically absolute; he
might have written καίπερ ἐμοῦ ἔχοντος, as nothing in the previous
context stands in apposition with ἐγώ. But the meaning is luminous.
Strictly, the Apostle asserts that he *has*, not merely might have,
this "confidence." But the whole context of this passage, and of
St Paul's entire Gospel, assures us that this is only "a way of
speaking." He is looking from the Judaist's view point, and speaks
so. Granted those premisses, he *has*, in an eminent degree, what his
adversary claims to have. R.V. rightly paraphrases, "though I
myself might have confidence even in the flesh."—Καὶ ἐν σαρκί : *on
the Judaist's principles*, he is so good a legalist that he might rest his
salvation *even* on "the flesh," should Christ be not enough !

δοκεῖ. "Thinketh." So R.V. text, and A.V. R.V. margin,
"seemeth." But the other is right in this context. For this (frequent) use of δοκεῖν see e.g. Luke xxiv. 37, ἐδόκουν πνεῦμα θεωρεῖν :
Acts xii. 9, ἐδόκει ὅραμα βλέπειν. A still closer parallel here is Matt.
iii. 9, μὴ δόξητε λέγειν ἐν ἑαυτοῖς, where we are compelled to paraphrase,
"Do not think in yourselves that you may say." So here, "Thinketh
that he may have confidence."

ἐγὼ μᾶλλον. Cp. 2 Cor. xi. 21, 22 for a series of similar assertions.

5. περιτομῇ. "As to circumcision." For the dative of reference
cp. e.g. Rom. xii. 10, τῇ φιλαδελφίᾳ φιλόστοργοι, τῇ σπουδῇ μὴ ὀκνηροί.

ὀκταήμερος. He was a born child of the covenant, and so received
its seal as early as possible ; no proselyte, circumcised as an adult ;
no Ishmaelite, waiting till he was thirteen (Gen. xvii. 25) ; cf. Joseph.
Antt. i. 13 § 1, Ἄραβες μετὰ ἔτος τρισκαιδέκατον [ποιοῦνται τὰς περι-
τομάς].

ἐκ γένους Ἰσραήλ. "Descended from Israel's race." "Israel" here may either be Israel collective, the chosen Nation, or Israel individual, the Patriarch who became "a prince with God" (Gen. xxxii. 28). The latter reference gives the more vivid emphasis, and so seems the more probable here.

See Trench, *N.T. Synonyms*, § xxxix, and Lightfoot on Gal. vi. 16, for the idea proper to the words Israel, Israelite. Lightfoot says, "Israel is the sacred name for the Jews, as the nation of the Theocracy, the people under God's covenant. Compare Ephes. ii. 12 ἀπηλλο-τριωμένοι τῆς πολιτείας τοῦ Ἰσραήλ : Rom. ix. 4 οἵτινές εἰσιν Ἰσραηλῖται, ὧν ἡ υἱοθεσία κ.τ.λ....Joh. i. 48 ἴδε ἀληθῶς Ἰσραηλίτης."

Βενιαμείν. So Rom. xi. 1; and cp. Acts xiii. 21. His tribe might give him special occasion for πεποίθησις. Its head was Jacob's much-loved son; it gave Israel its first lawful king (whose name the Apostle bore); and it had proved "faithful among the faithless" when, under Rehoboam, the Ten Tribes forsook the Davidic crown (1 Ki. xii. 21). Ehud (Judg. iii.) and Mordecai (Esth. ii. 5) were Benjamites. St Paul's character nobly illustrates the courage and the fidelity of his tribe.— See further Conybeare and Howson, *Life &c. of St Paul*, ch. ii.

Ἑβραῖος ἐξ Ἑβραίων. "Hebrew, and of Hebrew parentage." Cp. again 2 Cor. xi. 22.—In the O.T. and Apocrypha the word "Hebrew" (occurring about 40 times altogether) is the distinctive national term, by which an Israelite would describe himself, or be described, as against such similar terms as Philistine &c. But in the N.T. (not in later Christian writers, or in Jewish or pagan literature) it denotes the Jew who cherished his national language and manners, as distinguished from the "Hellenist," who usually spoke Greek and largely conformed to Gentile customs. See Acts vi. 1. The "Hebrew" would thus pose as one of an inner national circle. See further Trench, *ut supra*, and Conyb. and Howson, ch. ii.

κατὰ νόμον. "*The* law," in the sense of the Mosaic ordinances, is obviously intended. Here, as often, the article is omitted, because the word is otherwise sufficiently defined.

Φαρισαῖος. So Acts xxiii. 6, xxvi. 5; cp. Gal. i. 14. In rabbinic Hebrew the word is פְּרוּשִׁין, *Pᵉrûshîn*, from פָּרַשׁ, "to separate, to define." "Suidas s.v. quotes Cedrenus as follows, Φαρισαῖοι, οἱ ἑρμηνευόμενοι ἀφωρισμένοι· παρὰ τὸ μερίζειν καὶ ἀφορίζειν ἑαυτοὺς τῶν ἄλλων ἁπάντων εἴς τε τὸ καθαρώτατον τοῦ βίου καὶ ἀκριβέστατον, καὶ εἰς τὰ τοῦ νόμου ἐντάλματα" (Grimm, ed. Thayer, s.v.). See Josephus, *Antt.* xiii. 18, 23, xvii. 3, xviii. 2, for accounts of the Pharisees by a Pharisee of the Apostolic age. "The Pharisees were the enthusiasts of the later Judaism" (Conyb. and Howson, as above); the votaries of religious precision, elaborate devotion, vigorous proselytism, exclusive privilege, and the most intense nationalism. They were in high esteem with the common people, according to Josephus. He gives their numbers as about 6000 (*Antt.* xvii. 3); when an oath of allegiance to Herod I. was demanded, οἴδε οἱ ἄνδρες οὐκ ὤμοσαν, ὄντες ὑπὲρ ἑξακισχίλιοι.

St Paul was "son of a Pharisee" (Acts xxiii. 6; though Lightfoot here suggests that this means "a Pharisee's disciple"); and the student and follower (Acts xxii. 3) of the Pharisee (Acts v. 34) Gamaliel, probably "Rabban" Gamaliel, grandson of Hillel.

6. κατὰ ζῆλος. Here in the sense of ardour, earnestness; sincere, though sinfully conditioned by moral blindness. (See Acts xxvi. 9 ἐγὼ...ἔδοξα ἐμαυτῷ πρὸς τὸ ὄνομα...δεῖν πολλὰ ἐναντία πρᾶξαι.)—Ζῆλος sometimes takes the meaning of jealousy, rancour; e.g. Rom. xiii. 13, μὴ ἔριδι καὶ ζήλῳ. But this would be out of place here.

διώκων τὴν ἐκκλησίαν. See his own words, Acts xxvi. 11, περισσῶς ἐμμαινόμενος αὐτοῖς ἐδίωκον, κτλ.: 1 Cor. xv. 9, ἐδίωξα τὴν ἐκκλ. τοῦ θεοῦ: Gal. i. 13, καθ' ὑπερβολὴν ἐδίωκον τὴν ἐκκλ. τοῦ θεοῦ καὶ ἐπόρθουν αὐτήν.

κατὰ δικαιοσύνην τὴν ἐν νόμῳ. Literally, "as to law-included righteousness." He means evidently completeness of legal observance, with its supposed claims to merit. No inquisitor could have found him defective here.

γενόμενος ἄμεμπτος. Almost, "*turning out* blameless." R.V. well, "*found* blameless."

On the Pharisaic theory, his position was perfect, his title to "confidence in the flesh" complete.

7. ἀλλὰ ἅτινα. Almost, "But the kind of things which." Ἅτινα is just more than ἅ. He thinks not only of the things as things, but of their class and character.—On the reading ἀλλὰ, see critical note.

κέρδη. Observe the plural. He had counted over his items of privilege and pride, like a miser with his bags of gold.

ἥγημαι. "I have accounted"; we may say, "I have come to reckon."

διὰ τὸν Χριστόν. "On account of the" (almost, "our") "Christ"; not "for His sake" (ὑπὲρ τοῦ X.) but "because of the fact of Him"; because of the discovery, in Him, of the infinitely more than equivalent of the κέρδη of the past. MESSIAH, found out in His true glory, was *cause* enough for the change of view.

ζημίαν. Observe the singular. The κέρδη are all fused now into one undistinguished ζημία. And ζημία imports not only "no gain," but a positive detriment. True, some of the κέρδη at least were in themselves good things; pedigree, covenant-connexion, zeal, exactitude, self-discipline. But as a fact, viewed as he had viewed them, they had been shutting out Christ from his soul, and so every day of reliance on them was a day of deprivation of the supreme Blessing.

8. ἀλλὰ μενοῦνγε καί. Μὲν οὖν corrects by emphasis; its common use in dialogue and discussion. "Nay rather, I even, &c."

ἡγοῦμαι. The present tense emphasizes the present consciousness; the ἥγημαι is carried full into the present moment of thought.

πάντα. He has enumerated many things, but he will sweep *every-thing* into the scale which CHRIST has over-weighed. All that goes under the head of personal ambition, for example, must go; his prospects of national and Church distinction; all, all is ζημία, as against Christ.

διὰ τὸ ὑπερέχον. "On account of the surpassing(ness)." See on ii. 9 for St Paul's love of superlative and accumulative words.

τῆς γνώσεως. For αὕτη ἐστὶν ἡ αἰώνιος ζωή, ἵνα γινώσκωσι, κτλ. (Joh. xvii. 3). On the conditions and bliss of such knowledge see e.g. Joh. i. 10—12, xiv. 7, xvii. 25; Eph. iii. 19.—St Paul sometimes depreciates γνῶσις (e.g. 1 Cor. viii. 1, xiii. 2, 8). But there he means a knowledge separable from Divine light and life, a knowledge of mere theory, or of mere wonder, not of God in Christ. The γνῶσις here is the recognition of the glory of the Son of the Father, a knowledge inseparable from love; see the great paradox of Eph. iii. 19, γνῶναι τὴν ὑπερβάλλουσαν τῆς γνώσεως ἀγάπην τοῦ Χριστοῦ. Note the implicit witness of the language before us to the Deity of Christ. In Him this man had found the ultimate repose of his whole mental and moral nature.

Χριστοῦ Ἰησοῦ τοῦ κυρίου μου. Observe the solemnity and fulness of the terms; a "final cadence" of faith, as its glorious Object is viewed anew. See too the characteristic μου (cp. note on i. 3 above). The Gospel has an *individualism*, perfectly harmonious with its *communism*, but never to be merged in it. The individual "comes to" Christ (Joh. vi. 35, 37); and has Christ for Head (1 Cor. xi. 3); and lives by faith in Him who has loved and redeemed the individual (Gal. ii. 20). And such individual contact with the Lord is the secret of all true diffusion and communication of blessing through the individual.

δι' ὅν. Again, "on account of whom"; because of the fact of His glory.

τὰ πάντα ἐζημιώθην. "I was deprived of my all." He echoes the ζημίαν twice uttered above. His *estimate* was rudely verified, as it were, by circumstances. The treasures he inwardly surrendered were, as far as could be done, torn from him by man, when he deserted the Sanhedrin for Jesus Christ.

Deeply moving is this passing reference to his tremendous sacrifice, a sacrifice which has of course a weighty bearing on the solidity of the reasons for St Paul's change, and so on the evidences of our Faith. On this last point see the deservedly classical *Observations on the Character &c. of St Paul*, by George, first Lord Lyttelton, 1747.

τὰ πάντα. Rendered above, "*my* all." This may be just too much as a translation for the τὰ, but fairly indicates its reference.

σκύβαλα. *Stercora*, Vulg. "Refuse," R.V. marg. In the medieval Lexicon of Suidas the word is explained by κύων and βάλλειν: Κυσίβαλόν τι ὄν, τὸ τοῖς κυσὶ βαλλόμενον. Others "connect it with σκώρ (cp. scoria, Lat. *stercus*), al. with a root meaning 'to shiver,' 'shred'" (Grimm, ed. Thayer, s.v.). "The word seems to signify generally 'refuse,' being applied most frequently in one sense or other to food, as in Plut. *Mor.* p. 352 D περίττωμα δὲ τροφῆς καὶ σκύβαλον οὐδὲν ἀγνόν ...ἐστι [κ.τ.λ.]. The two significations most common are (1) 'Excrement...' This sense is frequent in medical writers. (2) 'The... leavings of a feast...' So again σκυβάλισμα, Pseudo-Phocyl. 144... σκυβάλισμα τραπέζης" (Lightfoot). "The Judaizers spoke of themselves as banqueters...at the Father's table, of Gentile Christians as dogs... snatching up the refuse meat... St Paul has reversed the image" (Lightfoot).

ἵνα Χριστὸν κερδήσω. The verb echoes the κέρδη of ver. 7. The repudiation of those "gains" was the condition for the reception of the supreme "gain," Christ Himself, received by faith. *In a sense* he paid them down in exchange for Christ, and so "gained" Him; *Christum lucri fecit* (Vulg.). Cp. the language of Rev. iii. 18, συμβουλεύω σοι ἀγοράσαι παρ' ἐμοῦ. True, they were worse than nothing, and Christ was all; but the imagery only enforces this by its paradox. Ἵνα κερδήσω. We might expect the optative here, as he is dealing with a past experience; and so with εὑρεθῶ just below. The conjunctive may be explained as expressing, in present terms, a past crisis, vividly realized. But besides, the subtle distinction between conjunctive and optative was not kept up in the popular language; so that the conjunctive was as a rule used for both "may" and "might." Cp. 1 Tim. i. 16, ἠλεήθην...ἵνα ἐν ἐμοί...ἐνδείξηται 'I. X., κτλ., and Acts v. 26, ἐφοβοῦντο τὸν λαόν, [ἵνα] μὴ λιθάσθωσιν.

Possibly the clause καὶ ἡγ. σκ. is parenthetic; the passage would thus present a vivid antithesis: "I suffered *the loss* of my all (and mere refuse I now see it to be) that I might make Christ *my gain*."

9. εὑρεθῶ. "Found," at any moment of *scrutiny*, here or hereafter. Lightfoot (on Gal. ii. 17, and here) remarks that εὑρίσκειν is very frequent in Aramaized Greek, and has somewhat lost its distinctive meaning. In the N.T. however it is seldom if ever used where that meaning has no point. Such a passage as 2 Pet. iii. 14 is a parallel here; σπουδάσατε...ἀμώμητοι αὐτῷ εὑρεθῆναι ἐν εἰρήνῃ, where the reference is to the Lord's Coming.

ἐν αὐτῷ. Here the Christian's incorporation with his Lord, for acceptance and spiritual life, is full in view. In the Epistles to the Ephesians and Colossians, written from the same chamber as this Epistle, we have this truth fully developed. See further above on i. 1, 8.

μὴ ἔχων ἐμὴν δικαιοσύνην. "Not having a righteousness of mine own" (R.V.). The ἐμὴν is slightly emphatic by position.

Δικαιοσύνη is a word characteristic, and often of special meaning, in St Paul. In numerous passages (see esp. Rom. iii. 5—26, iv. 3, 5, 6, 9, 11, 13; 1 Cor. i. 30; 2 Cor. iii. 10; Gal. ii. 21, with context) its leading idea is of satisfactoriness to law, to legal judgment. "A righteousness of mine own" is thus a title to acceptance before God, on my own merits, supposed to satisfy the legal standard. See further, Appendix K.

τὴν ἐκ νόμου. "The (righteousness) which is derived from the law," on the Pharisaic theory of law and law-keeping, or any theory akin to it. For though he has the Pharisee proper, and the Christian Judaist, first in view, he looks beyond them to the whole principle they represent; this we may surely affirm in the light of the Epistles to the Romans and the Galatians. From the special Mosaic code he rises to the larger fact of the whole Divine preceptive code, taken as a covenant of "righteousness," of acceptance: "Do this, perfectly, and live; do this, and claim your acceptance." Against this whole idea he places in its radiant simplicity the idea of "faith"; an acceptance procured for us by the Redeeming Lord, and appropriated by us by the single means of faith, that is to say, acceptance of Him as our all, on the warrant of His promise. Such "faith" unites us to Christ, in the spiritual order; and in that union, by no "fiction" but in fact, we receive His merits for our acceptance, and His power for our life and service. See further, Appendix K.

Here we infer (from the general line of Pauline teaching) that the primary thought is that of an acceptance for Christ's sake, as against acceptance for any personal merits of the man. Then comes in the spiritual development of the accepted person, as he receives the Christ who has died *for* him to live *in* him.

τὴν διὰ πίστεως Χριστοῦ. "That which is through faith in Christ." For the construction πίστις Χριστοῦ, with Χριστός for object not subject, cp. Mar. xi. 22, ἔχετε πίστιν θεοῦ: Acts iii. 16, ἐπὶ τῇ πίστει τοῦ ὀνόματος αὐτοῦ: Gal. ii. 20, ἐν πίστει ζῶ τῇ τοῦ υἱοῦ τοῦ θεοῦ. In such cases the genitive gives the idea of cohesion, *nexus*; it presents the Object as clasped by πίστις.

Here again, as with νόμος and δικαιοσύνη, St Paul's writings are the best commentary; see esp. Rom. iii. 21—28, χωρὶς νόμου δικαιοσύνη... δικ. δὲ Θεοῦ διὰ πίστεως Ἰησοῦ Χριστοῦ...εἰς τὸ εἶναι αὐτὸν δίκαιον καὶ δικαιοῦντα τὸν ἐκ πίστεως Ἰησοῦ, κτλ. In that passage there comes out, what is only latent here, the thought that the "faith" has reference specially to Christ in His propitiation, and that the blessing which it immediately receives is the justification (acceptance) of the believer. See further Rom. iv., v., viii. 33, 34; Gal. iii. 1—14, 21—24; Eph. ii. 8, 9. As to the πίστις itself, at least its leading idea is personal trust in a promise, or, better, in a Promiser. Setting aside Jas ii. 14—26, where the argument takes up and uses an inadequate notion of πίστις, namely *correct creed* (see Lightfoot, *Gal.*, detached notes following ch. iii.), the word constantly conveys in Scripture the thought of personal reliance, trustful acceptance[1]. The essence of such reliance is that it goes forth from self to God, bringing nothing that it may receive all. Thus it has a moral *fitness* (quite different from *deservingness*) to be the recipient of Divine gifts. In faith, man forgets himself, to embrace his Redeemer.

τὴν ἐκ θεοῦ δικαιοσύνην. "The righteousness," the way of accept-

---

[1] *Fides est fiducia*, Luther. See this admirably developed by J. C. Hare, *Victory of Faith*, pp. 15—22 (ed. 1847). Below, Appendix K.

ance, "which has its origin in God." Its source is the pure Divine love, flowing out in the line of Divine holiness.

ἐπὶ τῇ πίστει. "On terms of faith." Cp. Acts iii. 16, ἐπὶ τῇ πίστει τοῦ ὀνόματος αὐτοῦ.

On the doctrine of this verse see Appendix K.

10. τοῦ γνῶναι αὐτόν. "In order to know Him." This construction is very common in the LXX. In the N.T. it is used especially by St Luke and St Paul; cp. Luke xxiv. 29, εἰσῆλθε τοῦ μεῖναι σὺν αὐτοῖς: 1 Cor. x. 13, ποιήσει...ἔκβασιν, τοῦ δύνασθαι ὑμᾶς ὑπενεγκεῖν. It is not peculiar to Hellenistic Greek; it appears in classical prose, particularly after Demosthenes' time (Winer, *Grammar*, iii. § xliv.).—Note the sequence of thought: he embraces the Divine "righteousness," and renounces his own, *in order to the end* here stated—the true knowledge of Christ, communion with Him, and so assimilation to Him. Accepting Christ as his one ground of peace with God (Rom. v. 1), he now gets such a view of himself and his Redeemer as to affect profoundly his whole conscious relations with Him, and the effect of those relations on his being. Thus ver. 10 is no mere echo of ver. 9; it gives another range of truth, which yet is in the deepest connexion with the previous thought. To use a convenient classification, ver. 9 deals with Justification, ver. 10 with Sanctification in relation to it.

Τοῦ γνῶναι. The aorist suggests a *crisis* of knowledge. From such a crisis a *process* of growing knowledge is sure to issue; for the Object of the γνῶναι "passeth knowledge" (Eph. iii. 19). But it is the crisis which is in immediate view here.

τὴν δύναμιν τῆς ἀναστάσεως αὐτοῦ. His Resurrection has manifold "power." It evidences justification (e.g. Rom. iv. 24, 25, and esp. 1 Cor. xv. 14, 17, 18). It assures the Christian of his own future resurrection (1 Cor. xv. 20; 1 Thess. iv. 14). Yet more, it is that by which (completed in the Ascension) the Lord became actually the Giver of the Spirit which unites us to our Head. See Joh. vii. 39, οὔπω ἦν πνεῦμα ἅγιον, ὅτι Ἰησοῦς οὔπω ἐδοξάσθη: cp. Acts ii. 33. This aspect of truth is prominent in the Epistles to Ephesus and Colossæ, nearly contemporary with this Epistle; we have here a passing hint of what is developed there.

The thought of the Lord's Resurrection is probably suggested by the implied reference just above to the atoning Death on which it followed. The whole passage indicates that while our acceptance rests always on the propitiatory work of Christ for us, our power for holy service and suffering lies in our union with Him as the Risen One, to whom we are joined by the Spirit.

Cp. Rom. v. 10, καταλλαγέντες [διὰ τοῦ θανάτου τοῦ Χριστοῦ] σωθησόμεθα ἐν τῇ ζωῇ αὐτοῦ: and 2 Cor. iv. 10; Col. iii. 1—4; Heb. xiii. 20, 21.

κοινωνίαν (τῶν) παθημάτων αὐτοῦ. A share in His experience as the Sufferer. The Lord who has redeemed us has done it, as a fact, at an awful cost of pain, physical and spiritual; so a moral necessity calls His redeemed ones, united as they are to Him, to "carry the cross" after Him, in His Spirit's strength, and for His sake. And this will prove a deep secret of fuller spiritual sympathy and fellowship with Him. Cp. 2 Cor. i. 5, καθὼς περισσεύει τὰ παθήματα τοῦ Χριστοῦ εἰς ἡμᾶς, οὕτως διὰ τοῦ Χριστοῦ περισσεύει ἡ παράκλησις ἡμῶν: xii. 10, εὐδοκῶ ἐν ἀσθενείαις κτλ. ὑπὲρ Χριστοῦ· ὅταν γὰρ ἀσθενῶ τότε δυνατός εἰμι.

συνμορφιζόμενος. On the reading, see critical note.—*Configuratus*, Vulg. But the Latin, with its lack of a present pass. part., misses the point of the Greek—a *process* of conformation; R.V., "becoming conformed."

The immediate thought is that of spiritual harmony with the suffering Lord's state of will. His Death, as the supreme expression of His holy love and surrender, draws the Apostle as with a spiritual magnet to seek assimilation of character to Him who died. The Atoning Work is not forgotten; for the full glory of Christ's Death as Model is never wholly seen apart from a view of its propitiatory purpose; but that purpose is not the first thought here.—Cp. 2 Cor. iv. 10, πάντοτε τὴν νέκρωσιν τοῦ Ἰησοῦ ἐν τῷ σώματι περιφέροντες, ἵνα καὶ ἡ ζωὴ τοῦ Ἰ. ἐν τῷ σώματι ἡμῶν φανερωθῇ.

11. εἴπως καταντήσω κτλ. "If by any means I may arrive." Observe the (unusual) use of the conjunctive with εἰ. Cp. 1 Cor. xiv. 5, ἐκτὸς εἰ μή τις διερμηνεύῃ, and the reading εἰ...θερίσωμεν in some MSS. of 1 Cor. ix. 11. The construction is found in e.g. the Greek tragedians, and in Greek of the Roman period it is not unfrequent.—Note the strong language of *contingency*; cp. 1 Cor. ix. 27, μή πως...ἀδόκιμος γένωμαι. Contrast the exulting assurance of Rom. viii. 35, τίς ἡμᾶς χωρίσει; κτλ.: and cp. ibid. ver. 30; Joh. x. 27—29; &c.; and indeed the whole tone of "joy and peace in believing" so largely pervading the Scriptures. The two classes of expression represent as it were parallel lines, each of which is necessary to convey the idea of salvation. One line is the omnipotent grace, "made perfect in our weakness" (2 Cor. xii. 9). The other is the unalterable fact of our duty, to watch and pray. As one line or the other is brought into prominence (and there are times when one, or the other, *must* be stated alone), the language of assurance or of contingency is appropriate; till the parallel lines (as to us they seem and practically are) prove at last, in the love of God, to converge in glory.

εἰς τὴν ἐξανάστασιν τὴν ἐκ νεκρῶν. On the reading, see critical note. "At the resurrection which is from the dead." The phrase is peculiar and forcible, both by the use of the rare ἐξανάστασις, found here only in Biblical Greek (but ἐξανίστημι, with no special emphasis of meaning, is not uncommon in O. T. Greek), and by the τὴν ἐκ νεκρῶν. The double compound ἐξανα- must not be pressed; such forms are a characteristic of later classical Greek, in which (Polybius, Strabo) ἐξανάστασις occurs; ἐξανίστημι being familiar earlier, in e.g. the Tragedians, Thucydides, and Plato, and often without emphasis on the ἐξ. But in the phrase here as a whole there is assuredly a fulness and force of its own. Accordingly it has been held that St Paul refers to a special resurrection, and that this is the mysterious "first resurrection" of Rev. xx. 5, 6, a rising of either all saints only, or of a special class of saints only; a resurrection "up from among the dead," leaving the multitude behind. But St Paul nowhere else makes any *certain* reference to such a prospect (1 Cor. xv. 23, 24, is not decisive, and 1 Thess. iv. 16 has another bearing). This surely makes it unlikely that he should refer to it here, where he is plainly dealing with plain and ruling truths and hopes. It seems best then to explain these words of the glorious prospect of the resurrection of believers in general, as it is seen in 1 Cor. xv.; and the force of the phrase may be due to the energy and climax of the passage; he throws his whole soul into the thought of leaving behind for ever the state of death, which state he denotes (on this hypothesis) by the concrete phrase, οἱ νεκροί.

It is observable that he here implies his expectation of death, to be followed by resurrection; not of survival till the Lord's Return.

12—16.   His spiritual Condition is one of Progress, not Perfection.

12.   Οὐχ ὅτι κτλ. This passage of caution and reserve, following out the εἴπως καταντήσω just above, is probably suggested by the thought of the antinomian teaching which he denounces explicitly below, ver. 18, 19. Such teaching would represent the Christian as already at the goal; lifted beyond responsibility, duty, and the call to go forward. No, says St Paul; I have indeed "gained" Christ; I have "the righteousness of God"; I "know" my Lord, and His "power," and am "getting conformed to His death"; but I must be only the humbler and more watchful; the process, the outcome, must be ever moving on; the goal lies, from one great view-point, only at the close of a path of watching and prayer.

Οὐχ ὅτι ἤδη ἔλαβον. *Non quod jam acceperim*, Vulg. "Not that I have already obtained," R.V. The aorist is best represented here by our perfect; with "already" we can hardly do otherwise. Greek tends, more than English, to throw back the past; to treat as in the past what still affects the present.—The verb gives the notion not of "attaining" a height but of "receiving" a gift. What the gift is, is indicated just below, ver. 14, τὸ βραβεῖον κτλ. Cp. 1 Cor. ix. 24, εἰς λαμβάνει τὸ βραβεῖον.

τετελείωμαι. He would be τέλειος, in the absolute sense, only when he joined the πνεύματα δικαίων τετελειωμένων (Heb. xii. 23). Indeed, as to his whole being, he would be τέλειος only when the ἀπολύτρωσις τοῦ σώματος was achieved in resurrection (Rom. viii. 23). Only when "we see Him as He is" shall we be altogether ὅμοιοι αὐτῷ. And nothing short of that can be an absolute "perfection," the goal of the συμμορφίζεσθαι (ver. 10).

Τελειόω, τελείωσις, were used in later church-Greek as special terms for the death of martyrs; in the Menologium it is the regular phrase: ξίφει τελειοῦται, ποντισθεὶς τελειοῦται, and the like. Chrysostom (Hom. xiv. on 1 Tim.), in a passage on the monastic life, says that the monks never speak of a brother's "end," but of his "perfecting":

κἂν ἀπαγγελθῇ ὅτι ὁ δεῖνα τετελεύτηκε, πολλὴ ἡ εὐφροσύνη, πολλὴ ἡ ἡδονή· μᾶλλον δὲ οὐδὲ τολμᾷ τις εἰπεῖν ὅτι ὁ δεῖνα τετελεύτηκε, ἀλλ᾽ ὁ δεῖνα τετελείωται.　In Scripture this bright ideal is intended to be realized by all believers, as they enter on the heavenly rest.

διώκω δέ.　"But I press on," R.V.　He thinks of the race, with its goal and crown; cp. Acts xx. 24, ὡς τελειῶσαι τὸν δρόμον μου : 2 Tim. iv. 7, τὸν δρόμον τετέλεκα.　Cp. 1 Cor. ix. 24—27 ; 2 Tim. ii. 5, iv. 7 ; Heb. xii. 1.

εἰ καταλάβω.　"If I may grasp."　Again the conjunctive with εἰ. See note on εἴπως καταντήσω above.—Cp. for the phrase 1 Cor. ix. 24, οὕτως τρέχετε ἵνα καταλάβητε.—The ἔλαβον just above is intensified into καταλάβω here ; he thinks of the crown, till in thought he not only "receives " but "grasps " it.

Lightfoot quotes διώκοντες οὐ κατέλαβον from Lucian, *Hermot.* 77.

ἐφ᾽ ᾧ καὶ κατελήμφθην.　Either, "Inasmuch as I was actually grasped" (cp. 2 Cor. v. 4, στενάζομεν, ἐφ᾽ ᾧ οὐ θέλομεν, κτλ.: and cp. Rom. v. 12) or, "That, with a view to which I was actually grasped." St Paul's usage (as quoted) inclines to the former rendering ; the phraseology and context somewhat recommend the latter, which is adopted by A.V., R.V. (text; margin, "*seeing that* I was apprehended"), Ellicott, Alford, and (on the whole) Lightfoot.—He presses on to "grasp," with the animating thought that Christ had "grasped" him, in the hour of conversion, on purpose that he, through the path of faith and obedience, might at length reach the goal and prize of glory.　The remembrance of the Divine energy of that "grasp" energizes here all his thought and language.

13.　ἀδελφοί.　A personal address, to bring home and enforce the truth.

ἐγὼ ἐμαυτὸν κτλ.　Whatever *others* may think of *them*selves.　He has the antinomians of ver. 18, 19 in his mind.

14.　ἓν δέ.　The concentration of purpose makes all thought and action one.　Cp. Joh. ix. 25, ἓν οἶδα, ὅτι τυφλὸς ὤν, κτλ.

ἐπιλανθανόμενος.　As to complacency, not as to gratitude.

ἐπεκτεινόμενος.　The compound presents the runner as stretching *out* his head and body *towards* the goal.—C. Simeon, of Cambridge, says in one of his last letters, alluding to his still abundant toils, " I am so near the goal that I cannot help running with all my might." St Chrysostom writes here, ὁ δρομεὺς οὐχ ὅσους ἤνυσεν ἀναλογίζεται διαύλους ("laps "), ἀλλ᾽ ὅσους λείπεται [ἀνύσαι].—"To abound more and more " (1 Thess. iv. 1, 10) was St Paul's ideal of Christian life for others, and above all for himself.

κατὰ σκοπὸν διώκω.　"I press on goal-ward."　Cp. 1 Cor. ix. 26, οὕτως τρέχω ὡς οὐκ ἀδήλως, "as not in the dark " ; as with my goal clear in view.　The word σκοπός is used in the classics rather of a target than a goal ; but the context here is decisive.

εἰς τὸ βραβεῖον. "Unto the prize" (R.V.); εἰς leads the thought up to the attainment itself.

Βραβεῖον. The word occurs (in N.T.) only here and 1 Cor. ix. 24, πάντες μὲν τρέχουσιν, εἷς δὲ λαμβάνει τὸ βραβεῖον. The word βραβεῖον is late and scarce in classical Greek, though βραβεύς (an umpire, arbiter, and then, more widely, a leader) is familiar in the Tragedians, and βραβεία (an umpire's office) occurs in Euripides. In patristic Greek βραβεῖον, naturally, is often found. E.g. Clement of Rome (1 Ep. Cor. v. 5) writes of St Paul that ὑπομονῆς βραβεῖον ὑπέδειξεν. The word is transliterated in Latin *brabeum, brabium, bravium;* so in the Lat. Versions here.—The "prize" is "the crown," "the wreath," στέφανος, glory everlasting as the issue and triumph of the life of grace. Cp. Rev. ii. 10, and esp. 2 Tim. iv. 7, 8.

On St Paul's use of athletic metaphors, see Appendix L.

τῆς ἄνω κλήσεως. Vulg., *supernæ vocationis.*—Cp. Joh. viii. 23, ἐγὼ ἐκ τῶν ἄνω εἰμί: Gal. iv. 26, ἡ ἄνω Ἰερουσαλήμ: Col. iii. 1, 2, τὰ ἄνω ζητεῖτε, φρονεῖτε.—The κλῆσις was ἄνω alike in its origin, its influence, and its issue.

κλῆσις τοῦ θεοῦ ἐν Χριστῷ Ἰησοῦ. Καλεῖν, κλῆσις, κλητός, in the Epistles, refer not merely to the external invitations of the Gospel but to the internal attraction and victory of grace. See e.g. 1 Cor. i. 23, 24, where the κλητοί are differenced from those who have heard the message of Christ but who find only σκάνδαλον or μωρία in it.—Τοῦ θεοῦ. The Father. He is the ultimate "Caller" (so Rom. viii. 29, οὓς ἐκάλεσε, κτλ., and cp. Gal. i. 15; 2 Tim. i. 9); and the "call" is ἐν Χρ. Ἰ. as it comes *through* the Son and leads to union *with* Him. Cp. for the phrase 1 Cor. vii. 22, ὁ ἐν κυρίῳ κληθεὶς δοῦλος, κτλ.

15. τέλειοι. Here is an apparent discrepancy with his rejection of the thought of his being "perfected," just above. But he seems to be taking up here, with a sort of loving irony, a word used by those who favoured some form of "perfectionism." It is as if he would say, "Are we really *perfect* Christians, all that Christians should be, in thought and life? Then among the things which *should be* in us is a holy discontent with our actual holiness. The man in this sense *perfect* will be the very man to think himself not yet *perfected.*" We may notice also that τέλειος is an elastic word; it often means "full-grown" as against "infantine"; cp. Heb. v. 13, 14, νήπιός…ἐστιν· τελείων δέ ἐστιν ἡ στερεὰ τροφή. The τέλειος in this respect would have mature *faculty,* but would not therefore claim ideal *character.* The Apostle may thus be using the word with reference at once to a *misuse* of it, and to a legitimate use.

φρονῶμεν. See notes on φρονεῖν above, i. 7, ii. 2, 5.

ὁ θεὸς ὑμῖν ἀποκαλύψει. By the action of His Spirit, amidst the discipline of life, shewing more and more the correspondence of the inspired Message with the facts of the soul.—Such words, while they breathe a deep tolerance and patience, imply the Apostle's commission as a supernaturally inspired messenger of Christ; otherwise he would

make an undue claim. Cp. Gal. i. 6—12, where the strong assertions of
the absolute and unique truth of "his Gospel" are expressly based on
its direct conveyance to him δι' ἀποκαλύψεως Ἰησοῦ Χριστοῦ.

16. πλήν. "Only." He qualifies the thought of certain present
differences of view, by a plea for all the agreement possible.

εἰς ὃ ἐφθάσαμεν. "(As regards) the point we have reached."
Φθάνειν, in classical Greek, implies properly arrival *beforehand*, out-
stripping; and so 1 Thess. iv. 15, οὐ μὴ φθάσωμεν τοὺς κοιμηθέντας.
Later, and ordinarily in N.T., it loses much of this speciality, and
means little but "to arrive." Yet in most places a shadow of its
proper meaning can be traced; the arrival is usually either sudden
or difficult. Cp. Matt. xii. 28, ἄρα ἔφθασεν ἐφ' ὑμᾶς ἡ βασιλεία τοῦ
θεοῦ: Rom. ix. 31, εἰς νόμον δικαιοσύνης οὐκ ἔφθασε. Here we may
trace a hint of *difficulty;* the thought of the toilsome race is still
present; as if to say, "as regards the point we have *succeeded in*
reaching."—On the rendering of ἐφθάσαμεν by an English perfect, see
above, note on ἔλαβον, ver. 12.

τῷ αὐτῷ στοιχεῖν. "Take your steps on the same (principle)."
Στοιχεῖν, more than περιπατεῖν, suggests the step, the detail. Cp.
Rom. iv. 12, τοῖς στοιχοῦσι τοῖς ἴχνεσι, κτλ.—The use of "the
infinitive for the imperative" is familiar in classical Greek, especially
in the earlier writers; e.g. Soph. *O.T.* 462, κἂν λάβῃς μ' ἐψευσμένον
φάσκειν ἔμ' ἤδη μαντικῇ μηδὲ φρονεῖν. The construction is regularly
used in address *to others* (see Alford here), not in appeals to self; we
render here therefore, "Take *your* steps, &c."

Here, as in so many places, the Apostle makes a sidelong reference
to the need of the spirit of unity at Philippi. "As regards the point
they have reached," they are besought to cultivate a conscious
harmony in principle and practice.

On the reading of this verse, see critical note.

**17—21.   APPLICATION OF THE THOUGHT OF PROGRESS: WARNING
AGAINST UNHOLY MISUSE OF THE TRUTH OF GRACE: THE COMING
GLORY OF THE BODY, A MOTIVE TO PURITY.**

17. Συμμιμηταί μου γίνεσθε. Literally, "Become my co-imitators";
"join in copying my example." In this case, the example is that
of the renunciation of self-righteousness and of the dream of an
attained perfection. St Paul often thus invites "imitation"; see
below, iv. 9, ἅ...εἴδετε ἐν ἐμοί...πράσσετε : 1 Cor. iv. 16, παρακαλῶ ὑμᾶς,
μιμηταί μου γίνεσθε : xi. 1, μιμηταί μου γίνεσθε, καθὼς κἀγὼ Χριστοῦ :
2 Thess. iii. 7, οἴδατε πῶς δεῖ μιμεῖσθαι ἡμᾶς : 9, ἵνα ἑαυτοὺς τύπον δῶμεν
ὑμῖν εἰς τὸ μ. ἡμᾶς : and Acts xx. 18—21, 30—35. This is not egotism,
but a mark of entire confidence in his message and its principles, and
a clear conscience as to the power of them on his own life.

σκοπεῖτε. *Observate,* Vulg.—Σκοπεῖν usually implies the need of
caution and avoidance; cp. Rom. xvi. 17, σκοπεῖν τοὺς τὰς διχοστασίας
..ποιοῦντας, καὶ ἐκκλίνετε ἀπ' αὐτῶν. Here context gives the opposite

reference; to *see* St Paul's example, for daily practice, let them watch
its reflection in his attached followers among themselves.

περιπατοῦντας. The verb occurs here only (with ver. 18) in the
Epistle. Elsewhere it is a favourite with St Paul, to denote life in its
action and intercourse; e.g. Rom. vi. 4, ἐν καινότητι ζωῆς περιπατήσωμεν: xiii. 13, εὐσχημόνως περιπατήσωμεν: Gal. v. 16, πνεύματι περιπα-
τεῖτε: Eph. ii. 2, 10, iv. 1, 17, v. 2, 8, 15; and many other places.

τύπον ἡμᾶς. "Shrinking from the egotism of dwelling on his own
personal example, St Paul passes at once from the singular (μου) to
the plural (ἡμᾶς)" (Lightfoot). He similarly uses the plural in
2 Thess. iii. 7, quoted above, and 1 Thess. i. 6.

18. πολλοί. So early did an antinomian travesty of the Gospel of
free grace arise and spread. Similar errors are in view in Rom. xvi.
17, 18, where he denounces the utterers of unwholesome χρηστολογία
καὶ εὐλογία. The moral disorders at Corinth (1 Cor. v., vi.) were
probably defended on such principles. To this class of error Rom.
vi. 1 probably refers, ἐπιμένωμεν τῇ ἁμαρτίᾳ, ἵνα ἡ χάρις πλεονάσῃ: and
Eph. v. 6, μηδεὶς ὑμᾶς ἀπατάτω κενοῖς λόγοις. There were varieties no
doubt under a common moral likeness. Some would hold the tenet
prominent later in "Gnosticism," that matter must be evil, and that
the body therefore can never be holy. Others (and these surely are
in view in the Roman Epistle, and probably here) would push the
truth of free justification into a real isolation from other truth, and
so into deadly error; teaching that the πνευματικός is so accepted in
Christ that his moral actions matter not to God. Every great period
of spiritual upheaval and power is, as by a subtle law, defaced by
some such growths of great misbelief. Such were the phenomena,
cent. xvi., of the Libertines at Geneva, and the Prophets of Zwickau;
and in one degree or another such things are continually felt in
Christian life and history.

At Philippi, this "school" would be broadly, perhaps bitterly,
divided from the Judaists. But the "extremes might meet" so as
to account for the mention of both here in a certain connexion. A
stern formal legalism has a tendency to slight "the weightier matters
of the law," heart-purity among them. Still, the persons here
directly in view (vv. 18, 19) *gloried* in their shame"; this must
mean a positive and reasoned libertinism.

πολλάκις. Sadly echoing πολλοί.

ἔλεγον. "I used to tell you of as...." As if he would write,
πολλάκις ἔλεγον αὐτοὺς τοὺς ἐχθροὺς κτλ. For λέγειν so used cp. e.g.
Æsch. *Eum.* 48, οὗτοι γυναῖκας ἀλλὰ Γοργόνας λέγω.—"I used," in
former days, when among you. So very early was the mischief in the
air.

νῦν δὲ καὶ κλαίων. "But now actually weeping." Years had only
shewn him more clearly the deplorable mischiefs of the delusion.

For St Paul's tears, see Acts xx. 19, δουλεύων τῷ κυρίῳ...μετὰ δακρύων:
31, οὐκ ἐπαυσάμην μετὰ δακρύων νουθετῶν: 2 Cor. ii. 4, ἔγραψα ὑμῖν διὰ
πολλῶν δακρύων.—Κλαίειν implies not tears only but lamentation,

audible grief, and thus gives a peculiar pathos to a passage like this.
—See Appendix M for an extract from a sermon by Adolphe Monod
(in his *Saint Paul, Cinq Discours*), *Son Christianisme, ou ses Larmes.*

τοὺς ἐχθροὺς τοῦ σταυροῦ. "As the personal enemies of the cross";
deluding themselves and their followers into the horrible belief that
the Cross of Atonement, God's own argument and secret for our
holiness, was in effect intended to give security to sin. Possibly the
praise of the Cross was much on their lips; but their doctrine and
practice made them its most formidable enemies, disgracing it in the
world's eyes.

19. τέλος. A word awful and hopeless. Τὸ γὰρ τέλος ἐκείνων,
θάνατος, Rom. vi. 21. Cp. 2 Cor. xi. 15, ὧν τὸ τέλος ἔσται κατὰ τὰ ἔργα:
Heb. vi. 8, ἧς τὸ τέλος εἰς καῦσιν: 1 Pet. iv. 17, τί τὸ τέλος τῶν ἀπειθούν-
των τῷ εὐαγγελίῳ;

ἀπώλεια. "Perdition"; ruin. See above, on i. 28.

ὁ θεὸς. The antinomian boasted probably of a special intimacy
with God.

ἡ κοιλία. "The" (not necessarily "their") "belly." Cp. Rom.
xvi. 18, where probably the same "school" is in view; Χριστῷ οὐ
δουλεύουσιν, ἀλλὰ τῇ ἑαυτῶν κοιλίᾳ. In 1 Cor. vi. 13 the words βρώματα
τῇ κοιλίᾳ καὶ ἡ κ. τοῖς βρώμασιν are probably quoted from a supposed
advocate of this same evil "Gospel."—Κοιλία is not used in classical
Greek in other than its physical meaning (γαστήρ appears for
"gluttony"; e.g. γαστρὶ δουλεύειν, Xen. *Mem.* i. 6. 8); but we have
κοιλιοδαίμων in the fragments of Eupolis (Κόλακ. 4), for "a votary
of the belly." So *venter* in Latin; Lightfoot refers to Seneca, *de
Vita Beata,* IX. 4: *hominis bonum quæro, non ventris.*

ἡ δόξα ἐν τῇ αἰσχύνῃ αὐτῶν. No doubt they claimed a "glory"; a
larger liberty, a deeper insight, a sublimated Christianity. But their
vaunted wisdom was exactly their foulest shame.

οἱ τὰ ἐπίγεια φρονοῦντες. "They whose mind is for the things of
earth." The construction is free but clear.—Contrast Col. iii. 2, τὰ
ἄνω φρονεῖτε, μὴ τὰ ἐπὶ τῆς γῆς: and see the practical precepts in the
context there, ver. 5, &c.: νεκρώσατε οὖν τὰ μέλη ὑμῶν τὰ ἐπὶ τῆς
γῆς, κτλ.—For φρονεῖν see notes above, on i. 7, ii. 2.

The dogmatic libertine would claim to live in an upper region, to be
so conversant with *celestial* principles as to be free of *terrestrial*
restraints. As a fact, his fine-spun theory was a transparent veil over
the bodily lusts which were his real interests.

20. ἡμῶν γὰρ. The link of thought with ver. 18 is easily traced;
"Such thoughts and lives are wholly alien to ours; *for* &c."

"While the earliest MSS. all read γάρ, the earliest citations (with
several versions [e.g. Vulg., *autem*]) have persistently δέ. I have
therefore given δὲ as a possible alternative; although it is probably a
substitution for γάρ, of which the connexion was not very obvious"
(Lightfoot).

τὸ πολίτευμα. R.V. text, "citizenship"; margin, "or, *common-wealth*." A.V., "conversation" (which is the rendering of all our older versions, except Wyclif's, which has "lyvyng"). This represents the *conversatio* of the Vulg.; "the intercourse of life" (see above, note on πολιτεύεσθε, i. 27). The meaning is thus, in effect, "We live and move (on earth) as those who are (spiritually) in heaven."

The word πολίτευμα occurs here alone in Biblical Greek. In classical Greek it denotes (a) an act, or measure, of government; e.g. τῶν τοιούτων πολιτευμάτων οὐδὲν πολιτεύομαι (Demosth., 107. 16); (b) the governing body of a state, a "government"; (c) the constitution of a state, e.g. τὸ τῆς δημοκρατίας πολίτευμα (Æschin., 51. 12). This latter meaning obviously is most in point here. St Paul means that Christians are citizens of the heavenly city or realm, free of its privileges, but therefore also "obliged by their nobility" to live on earth as those who belong to heaven. Ἐπὶ γῆς διατρίβουσιν, ἀλλ' ἐν οὐρανῷ πολιτεύονται, says the writer of the Ep. to Diognetus (v. 9), cent. ii., probably with this passage in his mind. Meanwhile, for reasons to be further given from below (on ἐξ οὗ) it seems at least possible that St Paul's thought, in the use of πολίτευμα here, glided from "citizenship," or "commonwealth," almost to "city"; it at least bordered upon *locality*. The translation "*seat of* citizenship" may thus not unfairly represent it.

ἐν οὐρανοῖς. "In the heavens." (The word is self-defined; the article is not necessary.) A very frequent plural in Biblical Greek; the classics always use the singular.—For the Heavenly City cp. Gal. iv. 26, ἡ ἄνω Ἱερουσαλήμ: Heb. xii. 22, πόλις θεοῦ ζῶντος, Ἱερουσαλὴμ ἐπουράνιος (so Rev. iii. 12; see xxi., xxii.). It is called Οὐρανόπολις (Euseb., *Dem. Ev.* iv. p. 126, οὐρανόπολις, ἡ ἀληθῶς Ἱερουσαλήμ: Clem. Alex. *Pæd.* ii., xii. 119, τὰς δώδεκα τῆς οὐρανοπόλεως πύλας), with its οὐρανοπολῖται (Œcum. *in c.* ix. *ad Hebræos*; οὐρανοπολῖταί εἰσιν οἱ πιστοί, εἰ καὶ ἐπὶ γῆς τέως πολιτεύονται).—St Augustine's great work, *de Civitate Dei* (about A.D. 420), contains a wealth of illustrations of the idea of this passage. To him, at the crisis of the fall of the imperial City, the Christian appears as citizen of a State which is the antithesis, not of civil order, which is of God, but of "the world," which is against Him. This holy State, or City, exists now, and works for good through its citizens, but it is to be completed and revealed only when eternal glory begins. See Smith, *Dict. Chr. Biography*, i. 221.

The thought of the City was dear to St Augustine. The noble medieval lines of Hildebert, *Me receptet Syon illa, Urbs beata, urbs tranquilla* (see Trench, *Sacred Lat. Poetry*, p. 332, with pp. 312–320), quoted at the close of Longfellow's *Golden Legend*, come almost verbatim from Augustine, *de Spiritu et Animâ*, c. LX.: *O civitas sancta, civitas speciosa, de longinquo te saluto, ad te clamo, te requiro.*

ἐξ οὗ. The pronoun cannot refer directly to the plural οὐρανοί. It must either be the mere adverbial equivalent of ὅθεν, or it must refer to πολίτευμα. The first explanation is simple; and it is asserted (see Winer, *Gr. of N. T. Greek*, ed. Moulton, p. 177) that ἐξ οὗ is used for ὅθεν. But the evidence produced is, to say the least, inconclusive. The reference of οὗ to πολίτευμα seems preferable. St Paul seems to use πολίτευμα with, so to speak, a local notion in it.

καὶ σωτῆρα ἀπεκδεχόμεθα. "We are actually waiting for, as our Saviour, &c." Ἀπεκδέχομαι by its form suggests a "waiting" full of persistence and desire. It occurs elsewhere, Rom. viii. 19, ἡ ἀπο-καραδοκία...ἀπεκδέχεται, κτλ.: 23, στενάζομεν, υἱοθεσίαν ἀπεκδεχόμενοι: 25, δι' ὑπομονῆς ἀπεκδεχόμεθα: 1 Cor. i. 7, ἀπεκδεχομένους τὴν ἀποκά-λυψιν τοῦ κ. ἡμῶν Ἰ. Χ.: Gal. v. 5, ἐλπίδα δικαιοσύνης ἀπεκδεχόμεθα: Heb. ix. 28, ὀφθήσεται τοῖς αὐτὸν ἀπεκδεχομένοις: 1 Pet. iii. 20, ἀπεξεδέχετο (so read) ἡ τοῦ Θεοῦ μακροθυμία. Of these passages all but the last (and perhaps Gal. v. 5) refer to the Lord's longed for Return in glory, ἡ μακαρία ἐλπίς (Tit. ii. 13), which everywhere shines out in the N.T. as the Promise of promises to the believer and to the Church.

Σωτῆρα. At His coming He will complete our "salvation" by accomplishing the ἀπολύτρωσις τοῦ σώματος, and so realizing in all its aspects our υἱοθεσία (Rom. viii. 23) in Himself. With σωτήρ here compare Rom. xiii. 1, ἐγγύτερον ἡμῖν ἡ σωτηρία: where "salvation" has the same reference to the Lord's Return.

κύριον Ἰησοῦν Χριστόν. The full designation well accords with the holy hope and joy of the context.

21.   μετασχηματίσει. See the note on σχῆμα, above, ii. 8. Cp. 2 Cor. xi. 13, μετασχηματιζόμενοι εἰς ἀποστόλους Χριστοῦ: 14, μετασχη-ματίζεται εἰς ἄγγελον φωτός: 15, μ. ὡς διάκονοι δικαιοσύνης. There, obviously, *superficial* changes are in view, true to the distinctive meaning of σχῆμα. And so it is here, in a true sense. Already the *essentials* of the "new creation" (2 Cor. v. 17; Gal. vi. 15), which is to be "manifested in glory" (Col. iii. 4), are present in the believer. Where the Holy Spirit "dwells," there already, even for the body, resides the pledge and as it were germ of the heavenly state (Rom. viii. 11). Thus the final transfiguration will be, so to speak, rather of *guise* than of *being*; as with the Lord Himself on the mountain-top. (But observe that in Matt. xvii. 2; Mar. ix. 2, we have μετε-μορφώθη.)

τὸ σῶμα τῆς ταπεινώσεως ἡμῶν. Cp. A.V., "our vile" (i.e. cheap, common) "body" (Beza's *corpus nostrum humile*, and Luther's *unsern nichtigen Leib*). This is a paraphrase of the Greek, involving the reader's loss and possible serious misguidance. No contempt of the body is implied by the Greek; only the body is "connected with our humiliation" as being, in its present state, inseparably connected with the burthens and limitations of earth, and conditioned by mortality.

Observe this peculiar mystery and glory of the Gospel, a promise of heavenly perfectness for *the body* of the Christian. It is no mere prison of the spirit; it is its counterpart, destined to share with it, in deep harmony, the coming bliss. Its stricken *condition*, in the Fall, makes it often the load of the spirit now; hereafter it shall be its wings.

The bearing of all this on the libertine, who sinned εἰς τὸ ἴδιον σῶμα (1 Cor. vi. 18), is manifest.

σύμμορφον. "To be conformed," R.V. See note on μορφή, above, ii. 6. It is implied that the coming likeness to our Blessed Lord's Body shall be in appearance (σχῆμα) *because in reality;* the glorious surface shall but express the glorious substance. Ὅμοιοι αὐτῷ ἐσό-μεθα (1 Joh. iii. 2): to HIM, not only to His "guise."

τῷ σώματι τῆς δόξης αὐτοῦ. His sacred Body, as He resumed it in Resurrection, and carried it up in Ascension, and manifests Himself in it to the Blessed (ὁ υἱὸς τοῦ ἀνθρώπου, ἐκ δεξιῶν...τοῦ Θεοῦ, Acts vii. 56). It is τῆς δόξης αὐτοῦ, as answering perfectly to His personal Exaltation, and being, so far as He pleases, the vehicle of its display. Of it thus conditioned St Paul had a glimpse at his conversion (Acts ix. 3, 17, xxii. 14); cp. 1 Cor. ix. 1, οὐχὶ Ἰησοῦν τὸν κ. ἡμῶν ἑώρακα; xv. 8, ἔσχατον πάντων, ὤφθη κἀμοί.

Our future likeness *in body to His body* is alone in direct view here, because the Apostle is dealing with specially *sensual* forms of error. But it stands in profound implied connexion with moral and spiritual likeness.

From this passage, as from others (see esp. 1 Cor. xv. 42—44, where σπείρεται and ἐγείρεται refer to *the same thing*), we gather that the Christian's body here and hereafter is somehow continuous; not wholly a new thing in subsistence. But when we say this, we have said all we know; the mystery of the nature of matter falls upon our attempts to think the question out. The ἐπουράνιοι (1 Cor. xv. 48) will be "the same"; truly continuous, in their whole being, with the pilgrims of earth. But no one can say that therefore some particle of the body of humiliation must live on in the body of glory; any more than it is necessary to bodily identity now that constituent particles of the body of childhood should continue in the body of old age. However, the next words assure us that we may leave the matter in peace in the hands of "the Saviour, the Lord Jesus Christ." Somehow, in His will and power,

> "Though changed and glorified each face,
>   Not unremembered [we shall] meet,
> For endless ages to embrace."
>   (*The Christian Year*, St Andrew's Day.)

κατὰ τὴν ἐνέργειαν τοῦ δύνασθαι αὐτόν. Literally, "According to the working of His being able." *Secundum operationem qua possit,* Vulg. The A.V., "*mighty* working," aims to represent the special force of ἐνέργεια (see note on ἐνεργεῖν, ii. 13); but it is too strong. The ἐνέργεια is just the putting forth of the δύνασθαι.

καὶ ὑποτάξαι αὐτῷ τὰ πάντα. Καί emphasizes the whole thought.— Elsewhere the FATHER appears as "subduing all things" to the Son, in the final victory. So 1 Cor. xv. 25 (Psal. cx. 1), 27 (Psal. viii. 6), δῆλον ὅτι ἐκτὸς τοῦ ὑποτάξαντος αὐτῷ τὰ πάντα. But the Father and the Son are One in will and power.—Cp. Joh. v. 31, οὕτως καὶ ὁ υἱὸς οὓς θέλει ζωοποιεῖ.

αὐτῷ. On the reading, see critical note.—"To Himself": so we must render, in common sense, whether we read αὐτῷ or αὑτῷ.—We too, in English, sometimes say "*him*" where "*himself*" is meant.— In such cases the thought is from the speaker's or writer's view-point, rather than from that of the subject of the words.

His "subjugation" is thus such that what He subdues shall some-how serve Him. His very enemies shall be "*His footstool*"; and in His glorified saints He shall be glorified (2 Thess. i. 10). Through this great conquest of the Son the Father will be supremely magnified; see 1 Cor. xv. 28, αὐτὸς ὁ υἱὸς ὑποταγήσεται, κτλ.; a prophecy beyond our full understanding, but pointing to an infinitely developed mani-festation in eternity of the glory of the Father in the Son. But the immediate thought of this passage is the almighty grace and power of the incarnate, glorified, returning SAVIOUR of His people.

τὰ πάντα. The expression differs just so far from πάντα that it sums up "all things" and presents them together.

CHAPTER IV.

2. Εὐοδίαν. So certainly, not Εὐωδίαν, which appears in a very few MSS. not of high authority.

3. γνήσιε σύνζυγε (the MSS. are divided between συνζ- and συζ-). So ℵABD, 17 27 47 73 and some other cursives, vulg (*germane compar*) copt goth æth, Orig Victorin. KL, most cursives, syrr, Chr Thdt, read σύζυγε γνήσιε. WH print Σύνζυγε (as a proper name) in the margin.

13. ἐν τῷ ἐνδυναμοῦντί με. So ℵ*ABD₂*, 17, vulg copt arm æth, Clem Victorin Amb. So all recent Editors. ℵᶜD₂ᶜG₂K₂L, almost all cursives, Orig Ath Cyr Chrys add Χριστῷ, and a few fathers Χριστῷ Ἰησοῦ (or Ἰ. Χ., or Χ. Ἰ. τῷ κυρίῳ ἡμῶν).

19. πληρώσει. So ℵABD₂ᶜKL, most cursives, copt arm æth, Chr (twice). D₂*G₂, 17 37, and several other cursives, vulg, Chrys (twice) Cyr Victorin and other fathers read πληρώσαι. All recent Editors -σει. In such a case it is the more likely alternative that the assertion would be softened, in copies or quotations, into an aspiration.

τὸ πλοῦτος. So ℵ*ABD₂*G₂, 17. Most cursives and quotations read the masc. form, τὸν πλοῦτον.

23. τοῦ κ. Ἰ. Χ. So ℵABG₂K₂L, most cursives, arm. D₂, some cursives, syr (pesh) copt æth and some fathers add ἡμῶν.

τοῦ πνεύματος ὑμῶν. So ℵ*ABD₂G₂, 6 17 31 47 73 80 and some other cursives, copt arm æth, Damasc Victorin. So all recent Editors. ℵᶜKL, most cursives, syrr, Chrys Thdrt Thphyl read μετὰ πάντων ὑμῶν.

Ἀμήν is added by ℵAD₂K₂L, almost all cursives, vulg copt syrr arm æth. Wordsw alone of recent Editors retains it. The evidence for it is strong.

Subscription. This is omitted in the present edition, with Lachm Tisch Wordsw Ell WH. Treg Alf give πρὸς Φιλιππησίους, with ℵAB,

17. Some other forms given by Treg are πρὸς Φιλιππηνσίους ἐπληρώθη (D₂, 1 Thess. following), ἐτελέσθη πρὸς Φιλιππησίους (G, Col. following), τοῦ ἁγίου ἀποστόλου Παύλου ἐπιστολὴ πρὸς Φιλιππισίους ἐγράφη ἀπὸ Ῥώμης δι᾽ Ἐπαφροδίτου (L).

CH. IV. 1—7. WITH SUCH A HOPE, AND SUCH A LORD, LET THEM BE
    STEADFAST, UNITED, JOYFUL, SELF-FORGETFUL, RESTFUL, PRAYERFUL;
    THE PEACE OF GOD SHALL BE THEIRS.

1. Ὥστε. The word is frequent in St Paul to introduce an inference. He has now to infer much from the glorious *data* just stated.

ἀγαπητοί. A word characteristic of the Gospel of love, and used by all the apostolic writers. St Paul has it 27 times.

ἐπιπόθητοι. The word is found here only in N.T. Ἐπιποθεῖν is used not seldom in LXX. In this Epistle it occurs i. 6, ii. 26; and ἐπιποθία, Rom. xv. 23, ἐπιποθίαν ἔχων τοῦ ἐλθεῖν πρὸς ὑμᾶς : and ἐπιπόθησις, 2 Cor. vii. 7, 11.

χαρὰ καὶ στέφανός μου. Cp. 1 Thess. ii. 19, 20, τίς γὰρ ἡμῶν...χαρὰ ἢ στέφανος καυχήσεως ;...ὑμεῖς ἐστε ἡ δόξα ἡμῶν καὶ ἡ χαρά : words addressed to the sister Macedonian Church. Here, as there, he is looking forward to the Lord's Return, and to a joyful recognition of his converts then.

οὕτως. In the faith and in the practice just expounded.

στήκετε. For this verb see above, note on i. 27. Cp. 1 Cor. xvi. 13, στήκετε ἐν τῇ πίστει : 1 Thess. iii. 8, νῦν ζῶμεν, ἐὰν ὑμεῖς στήκετε ἐν κυρίῳ : and see Gal. v. 1.

ἐν κυρίῳ. In recollection and use of your vital union with Him, as your righteousness and your hope.

ἀγαπητοί. He can hardly say the last word of love.

2. Εὐοδίαν...Συντυχήν. Both are feminine names (the bearers are referred to as *women* just below, ver. 3), and both are known in the inscriptions. Lightfoot quotes (from the collections of Gruter and Muratori) e.g. Euhodia, Euodia, Syntyche, Suntyche, Syntiche. In Tindale and 'Cranmer' the second name appears as "Sintiches," intended (like Euo*dias*, shortened from Euodianus) to be masculine. But the inscriptions give neither Euodias nor Syntyches; this last would be at best a very doubtful variant for (the regular) Syntychus.

We know nothing of Euodia and Syntyche outside this passage. They may have been διάκονοι τῆς ἐκκλησίας (Rom. xvi. 1); they had certainly given St Paul active help. Perhaps their high reputation had ensnared them in self-esteem and so led to mutual jealousy.— Lightfoot (*Phil.*, pp. 55—57) points out that "the active zeal of the women [in the Macedonian missions] is a remarkable fact, without a parallel in the Apostle's history elsewhere, and only to be compared with their prominence at an earlier date in the personal ministry of our Lord"; and that "the extant Macedonian inscriptions seem to assign to the sex a higher social influence than is common among the civilized nations of antiquity." See above, Introduction, ch. i.

As a curiosity of interpretation Ellicott (see also Lightfoot, p. 170) mentions the conjectures of Schwegler (developed by Volkmar) that the two names are really designations of *Church-parties,* and were devised with a meaning: "Euodia," "right-path," is orthodoxy, i.e. *Petrinism;* Syntyche, "partner," symbolizes the incorporation of the Gentiles, *Paulinism.* Of course this theory views the Epistle as a fabricated *eirenicon,* belonging to an after-generation.

3. ἐρωτῶ. "I beg"; as in our polite use of that word. In secular writers (and often in Biblical Greek) ἐρωτάω regularly means "to enquire," "to question." The meaning "to request" is very rare in secular Greek; occasional in LXX., and somewhat frequent in N.T., e.g. Luke xiv. 18, ἐρωτῶ σε, ἔχε με παρῃτημένον (the construction used here): John xiv. 16, ἐρωτήσω τὸν πατέρα: 1 Thess. v. 12, ἐρωτῶμεν ὑμᾶς εἰδέναι κτλ.

καὶ σέ. "Thee *also,*" as co-operating with St Paul.

γνήσιε σύνζυγε. "True yoke-fellow." Vulg., *te, germane compar,* which Wyclif renders, "the german felowe," i.e. "thee, genuine (germane) comrade."—For the metaphor (σύζυγος) cp. 2 Cor. vi. 14, μὴ γίνεσθε ἑτεροζυγοῦντες ἀπίστοις.—Who was this person? One curious explanation is, St Paul's wife[1]. So Clem. Alex., *Strom.* iii. p. 535 (Potter): ὁ Παῦλος οὐκ ὀκνεῖ ἔν τινι ἐπιστολῇ τὴν αὑτοῦ προσαγορεύειν σύζυγον, ἣν οὐ περιεκόμιζε κτλ. This is not only unlikely in itself, but γνήσιε is against it; "the uncertain gender of σύνζ. would cause γνήσιος to revert to three terminations" (Ellicott). Another suggestion is that σύνζ. is in fact a proper name, Σύνζυγος, belonging to some Philippian leader, and that St Paul describes him as "true to his name" (γνήσιε). Such a play on Ὀνήσιμος occurs Philem. 11. But Syzygus does not occur as a name in inscriptions. Chrysostom suggests a husband or brother of one of the women; others, Timothy. Lightfoot advocates Epaphroditus, who would thus have this friendly commission given him in writing as well as orally. This is at least probable.

συνλαμβάνου αὐταῖς. "Help them"; obviously, the two Christian women. The word "help" happily suggests that they would themselves do their best for peace.—This open mention of a personal difficulty seems to indicate the modest and, so to speak, domestic scale of the Philippian community.

αἵτινες. Just more than αἵ: see above on ἅτινα, iii. 7. R.V., well, "for they."

συνήθλησάν μοι. So above, i. 27, συναθλοῦντες, where see the note. These two women had given earnest and energetic aid in St Paul's work at Philippi; perhaps with special χαρίσματα (see Acts xxi. 9;

---

[1] Renan translates the words here, *ma chère épouse* (*Saint Paul,* p. 148). See Salmon, *Intr. to N.T.,* p. 465 note.

cp. 1 Cor. xi. 5), or simply as instructors of other women, or in practical labours of love.

ἐν τῷ εὐαγγελίῳ. Cp. i. 5, ii. 22, and below on ver. 15.

μετὰ καὶ Κλήμεντος, κτλ. I.e., probably, Clement &c. were
associated with them in the special "wrestling" to which St Paul
refers. The words may of course mean that Clement &c. are asked
to join the "yokefellow" in "helping" the two women (a view preferred in the note here in the *Camb. Bible for Schools*) ; but it
seems less likely that St Paul would thus call in help from many
quarters in a personal matter than that he should (with happy tact)
pass from his allusion to the disagreement to expand his allusion to
past labours in which the two persons at variance had joined.

Κλήμης. We cannot be sure of his identity ; the name was common. Origen (*in Joann.* i. 29) identifies him with St Clement of
Rome, whom he names as ὁ πιστὸς Κλ. ὑπὸ Παύλου μαρτυρούμενος,
quoting this passage. So Eusebius (*H. E.* iii. 4), Κλήμης τῆς Ῥωμαίων
...ἐκκλησίας τρίτος ἐπίσκοπος...Παύλου...συναθλητὴς γεγονέναι πρὸς αὐτοῦ
μαρτυρεῖται. So Jerome (*Scriptt. Eccl.*) ; not Chrysostom here. There
is nothing impossible in this. But the dates of St Clement's life and
work are obscure in detail, and some evidence makes him survive till
quite 120, more than half a century later than this. In his Ep. to the
Corinthians (cp. xlvii.) he makes most reverent mention of St Paul,
but does not claim him as his personal chief.—See Lightfoot, *Phil.*,
p. 168.

τῶν λοιπῶν συνεργῶν μου. "The rest of my fellow workers," at the
time and in the circumstances here recalled.

ὧν τὰ ὀνόματα ἐν βίβλῳ ζωῆς. A βίβλος which God has written
appears Exod. xxxii. 31, 33 ; a βίβλος ζώντων, Psal. lxviii. (Heb., lxix.)
33 ; ἡ βίβλος simply, Dan. ix. 12 ; ἡ β. τῆς ζωῆς, Rev. iii. 5, xx. 15 ;
τὸ βιβλίον τῆς ζ., Rev. xiii 8, xvii. 8, xxi. 27. Cp. Isai. iv. 3 ; Ezek.
xiii. 9 ; Dan. xii. 1. On the whole, in the light of these passages,
St Paul seems here to refer to "the Lord's knowledge of them that
are His" (2 Tim. ii. 19 ; cp. Joh. x. 27, 28), for time and eternity.
All the passages in the Revelation, save iii. 5, connect the phrase with
the ultimate preservation of the saints ; especially xiii. 8, xvii. 8 ;
cp. Dan. xii. 1 and Luke x. 20. Rev. iii. 5 (οὐ μὴ ἐξαλείψω τὸ ὄνομα,
κτλ.) seems to point another way (see Trench here, *Seven Epistles*).
But compared with other passages, that sentence may be only
a vivid assurance that the name *shall be found* in the (indelible)
register. Exod. xxxii. and Psal. lxix. may well refer to a register of
"the living" in respect of life temporal, not eternal.—Practically,
Clement and "the rest" are referred to as having fully evidenced by
their works their part in that "life eternal" which is to know God
and Christ (Joh. xvii. 3).—The word ὀνόματα powerfully suggests the
individual incidence of Divine love. Cp. Luke x. 20, τὰ ὀνόματα
ὑμῶν ἐγγέγραπται ἐν τοῖς οὐρανοῖς.

4. Χαίρετε ἐν κυρίῳ πάντοτε. *Gaudete in Domino semper*, Vulg.—
See above iii. 1, and notes, where the evidence of πάντοτε in favour of

rendering χαίρετε by "rejoice" is pointed out.—Cp. 1 Thess. v. 16, 17, πάντοτε χαίρετε, ἀδιαλείπτως προσεύχεσθε.

He leads them above all lower reasons for joy, and away from all variations of events and feelings, direct to HIM (ἐν κυρίῳ) who is the supreme and unalterable gladness of the believer. And now, in deep sequence, he draws in detail the ideal of the life upon which Christ thus shines.

5. τὸ ἐπιεικὲς ὑμῶν. Vulg., *Modestia vestra;* A.V., "your moderation"; Wyclif, "youre pacience"; Tindale and 'Cranmer,' "youre softenes"; Geneva, "your patient mynde"; Rheims, "your modestie"; Luther, *Eure Lindigkeit;* R.V. text, "your forbearance," marg. "your gentleness." "Forbearance" is best, though scarcely adequate. Ἐπιεικής, ἐπιείκεια, are connected either with εἴκω, "to yield," or, more probably, with τὸ εἰκός (ἔοικα), "the equitable." Aristotle (*Eth. N.,* v. 10. 6) contrasts the ἐπιεικής with the ἀκριβοδίκαιος, the stickler for his full rights; the ἐπιεικής will rather take sides against himself, look from the other's point of view, remember his own duties and the other's rights. Ἐπιείκεια is, so to speak, πραότης applied in action. In the N.T. we have it (or ἐπιεικής) in e.g. 2 Cor. x. 1, παρακαλῶ ὑμᾶς διὰ τῆς πραότητος καὶ ἐπιεικείας τοῦ Χριστοῦ: 1 Tim. iii. 2, 3, δεῖ...ἐπίσκοπον...εἶναι...ἐπιεικῆ, ἄμαχον (so Tit. iii. 2): Jas iii. 17, σοφία... ἐπιεικής, εὐπειθής.—The ἐπιεικὲς ὑμῶν of this passage is the spirit which will yield like air in matters of personal feeling or interest, while it will stand like rock in respect of moral principle. See Trench's careful discussion, *N.T. Synonyms,* § xliii.

γνωσθήτω πᾶσιν ἀνθρώποις. For τὸ ἐπιεικὲς is essentially practical and operative. Estius (quoted by Trench) says that " ἐπιείκεια magis [quam πραότης] ad exteriorem conversationem pertinet."

ὁ κύριος ἐγγύς. Perhaps rather in the sense of *presence* than of *coming;* cp. Psal. cxviii. (Heb., cxix.) 151, ἐγγὺς εἶ, κύριε. "In the secret of His presence" (בְּסֵתֶר פָּנֶיךָ), ἐν ἀποκρύφῳ τοῦ προσώπου αὐτοῦ, Psal. xxxi. (xxx.) 19) they were to be "hid" from the vexations of life around them. Yet the deeply calming thought of the Lord's Return may well be latent in the words too. In the *Teaching of the Twelve Apostles* (probably cent. i.), the final Eucharistic prayer closes with the words Μαρὰν ἀθὰ ("The Lord cometh," 1 Cor. xvi. 21) ἀμήν.

6. μηδὲν μεριμνᾶτε. "In nothing be anxious," R.V. *Nihil solliciti sitis,* Vulg. *Sorget nichts,* Luther. On the etymology of μεριμνᾶν, and on the thought here, see above on ii. 20. The mental action here blamed is there (in Timothy) commended; a discrepancy harmonized by the different conditions contemplated in the two places. Here the saints are enjoined never to forget their Lord's attention and loving power, and in that spirit to meet every trial to inward peace. Cp. Psal. lv. (LXX., liv.) 22, ἐπίρριψον ἐπὶ κύριον τὴν μέριμνάν σου (יְהָבְךָ): 1 Pet. v. 7, πᾶσαν τὴν μέριμναν ὑμῶν ἐπιρρίψαντες ἐπ᾽ αὐτόν, ὅτι κτλ.: 1 Cor. vii. 32, θέλω ὑμᾶς ἀμερίμνους εἶναι. See the warnings against μέριμναι τοῦ αἰῶνος, μ. βιωτικαί, Mar. iv, 19; Luke xxi. 34.

ἀλλ' ἐν παντί. The all-inclusive positive exactly answers the all-inclusive negative, μηδέν. Cp. πᾶσαν τὴν μέριμναν, κτλ., 1 Pet. v. 7.

τῇ προσευχῇ καὶ τῇ δεήσει. Προσευχή and δέησις occur together, in LXX., e.g. Psal. vi. 9, εἰσήκουσε κύριος τῆς δ. μου, κύριος τὴν π. μου προσεδέξατο: in N.T., Eph. vi. 18, διὰ πάσης π. καὶ δ. προσευχόμενοι: here: 1 Tim. ii. 1, παρακαλῶ ποιεῖσθαι δεήσεις, προσευχάς: v. 5, προσμένει ταῖς δεήσεσι καὶ ταῖς π. Προσευχή is the larger word, and always sacred; it includes all varieties of worship; our "prayer" thus nearly corresponds to it, though we occasionally use "prayer," "pray," in mundane connexions. Δέησις has no limitation to religious uses, and is the narrower word ; "request," petition for desired benefits. (See Trench, N.T. Syn., s.v. προσευχή.) Not that the distinction is to be much pressed in an accumulation like this; practically he means to emphasize the one thought of a reverent approach to God about our needs.

μετὰ εὐχαριστίας. Cp. Col. ii. 7, περισσεύοντες ἐν εὐχαριστίᾳ: iii. 15, ἡ εἰρήνη τοῦ θεοῦ βραβευέτω ἐν ταῖς καρδίαις ὑμῶν...καὶ εὐχάριστοι γίνεσθε: iv. 2, τῇ προσευχῇ προσκαρτερεῖτε, γρηγοροῦντες ἐν αὐτῇ ἐν εὐχαριστίᾳ: 1 Tim. ii. 1, παρακαλῶ...ποιεῖσθαι δεήσεις, προσευχάς...εὐχαριστίας. "The temper of the Christian should always be one of thanksgiving...The Psalms, in Hebrew, are the Praises (תְּהִלִּים). All prayer ought to include the element of thanksgiving, for mercies temporal and spiritual" (Bp Perowne).—The privilege of access to God is itself an abiding theme of praise.

γνωριζέσθω. Exactly as if He needed information. He, not we, must reconcile such action on our part with His Infinity. True faith will rest (and act) on such a precept, with little anxiety about the rationale; and Scripture is full of illustrations and encouragements, from the prayers of the patriarchal saints (e.g. Gen. xviii., xxiv.) onwards.

7. καί. An important link here. Prayerfulness and the Divine peace are in profound connexion.

ἡ εἰρήνη τοῦ θεοῦ. The inward serenity, caused by the known presence of ὁ θεὸς τῆς εἰρήνης (ver. 9), as His Spirit calms our spirit. Cp. Col. iii. 15, [ἐνδύσασθε...τὴν ἀγάπην...], καὶ ἡ εἰρήνη τοῦ χριστοῦ βραβευέτω ἐν ταῖς καρδίαις ὑμῶν: and see Joh. xiv. 27, εἰρήνην τὴν ἐμὴν δίδωμι ὑμῖν.

πάντα νοῦν. "All mind," all mere thinking power. "It passes the mind of man," to analyse or describe. Lightfoot renders " 'surpassing every device or counsel' of man, i.e. [producing] a higher satisfaction than all anxious forethought." But this seems scarcely to harmonize with the lofty tone of the words. Lightfoot himself quotes as in favour of the ordinary rendering Eph. iii. 20, τῷ δυναμένῳ ὑπὲρ πάντα ποιῆσαι...ὧν...νοοῦμεν.—Vulg., not happily, omnem sensum.

φρουρήσει. "Shall guard," R.V. Geneva, "shall defend." Vulg., custodiat, missing the point of the future tense, with its strong positive promise, far different from an aspiration. For the verb cp. 2 Cor. xi.

32, ἐφρούρει τὴν Δαμασκηνῶν πόλιν: 1 Pet. i. 5, τοὺς ἐν δυνάμει θεοῦ φρου-
ρουμένους διὰ πίστεως εἰς σωτηρίαν.

καρδίας...νοήματα. "Heart" in Scripture includes the whole inner
world, with its contents of understanding (a frequent special reference), affections, and will.—Νοήματα are the actions of the νοῦς. Cp.
2 Cor. ii. 11, οὐ γὰρ αὐτοῦ τὰ νοήματα ἀγνοοῦμεν (the word is confined
to this Ep. and 2 Cor. in the whole range of Biblical Greek).—Even
the details of our mental action, as we plan, reason, judge, and the
like, shall be shielded from evil by the peace of God.

ἐν Χριστῷ Ἰησοῦ. "*In*," not (A.V.) "through." The Lord is
the Place of peace.

**8—9.   A LAST SPIRITUAL APPEAL : LET THEIR MINDS BE TRUE TO
ALL THAT IS GOOD: LET THEM FOLLOW PAUL'S TEACHING AND
PRACTICE.**

8. Τὸ λοιπόν. See above, on iii. 1. Once more he gathers up the
thought towards a close.—Are their "hearts and thoughts" thus
"sentinelled," in Christ, by the peace of God? Then let them, in
their safe Castle, "in the Secret of the Presence," not sleep, but give
their minds all possible pure material to work upon, with a view to
holy practice. Let them reckon up, think over, estimate aright
(λογίζεσθε), all things true and good; perhaps specially in contrast
to the subtle "reckonings" of the teachers denounced above (iii. 18,
19), who would divorce the "spiritual" and the moral.

ὅσα ἐστὶν ἀληθῆ. "All things which are true." Truthfulness of
word and act, sincerity of character, is utterly indispensable to the
holiness of the Gospel.

σεμνά. "Honourable," R.V.; almost, "dignified"); like the old
English use of "solemn."—Vulg., *pudica*.—Cp. 1 Tim. iii. 8, where
the children of the ἐπίσκοπος are to be ruled μετὰ πάσης σεμνότητος:
11, where the γυναῖκες of the διάκονοι are to be σεμναί: Tit. ii. 2, πρεσβύ-
τας...εἶναι σεμνούς. The word points to seriousness of purpose and to
self-respect in conduct.

δίκαια. As between man and man. The Christian will be a model
of dutifulness.

ἀγνά. Probably in the special respect of true bodily chastity, in
thought and act. "'Αγνός and καθαρός differ from ἅγιος in that they
admit the thought or the fact of temptation or pollution; while ἅγιος
describes that which is holy absolutely, either in itself or in idea"
(Westcott, on 1 Joh. iii. 3). See also Trench, *Syn.* ii., xxxviii.

προσφιλῆ. "Pleasing," "amiable." The Christian must remember
manner. Grace must make him gracious; he is to "*adorn* (κοσμεῖν)
the doctrine of God his Saviour" (Tit. ii. 10).

εὔφημα. "Sweet spoken"; προσφιλῆ in a special respect. "Not
'well-spoken of, well-reputed,' for the word seems never to have this
passive meaning; but with its usual active sense, 'fair-speaking,' and
so 'winning, attractive'" (Lightfoot). In the classics a frequent

meaning is "auspicious," the opposite of δύσφημος: so εὔφημον ἧμαρ,
Æsch. *Ag.* 636; and it thus glides into the meaning "silent," with
the silence which precludes δυσφημία. But such aspects of the word
can hardly be supposed present here. Ellicott explains, "fair-sound-
ing," "high-*toned*." R.V. (with A.V.) renders, "of good report";
margin, "or, *gracious*."

εἴ τις ἀρετή. "Whatever virtue there is." "St Paul seems studi-
ously to avoid this common heathen term for moral excellence....[It is
not] found elsewhere in the N.T. except in 1 Pet. ii. 9 [τὰς ἀρετάς,
"the excellencies," of God], 2 Pet. i. 3 [τοῦ καλέσαντος ἡμᾶς ἰδίᾳ...
ἀρετῇ], 5 [ἐπιχορηγήσατε ἐν τῇ πίστει ὑμῶν τὴν ἀ.], in all which passages
it seems to have some special sense. In the O.T. it always signifies
'glory, praise'...In the Apocrypha it has its ordinary classical sense.
Some [e.g. Alford] treat εἴ τις ἀ., εἴ τις ἔπαινος, as comprehensive
expressions, recapitulating the previous subjects under two general
heads, the intrinsic character and the subjective estimation. The
strangeness of the word, however, combined with the change of expression εἴ τις, will suggest another explanation; 'Whatever value may
reside in your old heathen conception of virtue, whatever considera-
tion is due to the praise of men'; as if the Apostle were anxious not
to omit any possible ground of appeal. Thus Beza's remark on
ἀρετή seems to be just; 'Verbum nimis humile, si cum donis Spiritus
Sancti comparetur'" (Lightfoot). By origin and usage ἀρετή is connected with thoughts of manhood and self-reliance. In the Gospel,
the basis of goodness is self-renunciation, in order to the reception of
χάρις, the undeserved gift of God.

ἔπαινος. It is not right to do good for the selfish pleasure of praise.
But to praise good deeds is right, and so may give the recipient of
the praise a pure moral pleasure. St Paul appeals to the fact of such
desert of praise, and uses it to attract thought in right directions.
"Make right praise an index of the things on which you should spend
thought."

λογίζεσθε. "Reckon up," "calculate." To illustrate negatively,
ἀγάπη οὐ λογίζεται τὸ κακόν (1 Cor. xiii. 5), "does not reckon up the
evil" done against her; does not dwell on it, brooding over it,
counting up the elements of the grievance.

9. ἃ καὶ ἐμάθετε...ἐν ἐμοί. On the apparent egotism, see above on
iii. 17.—The aorists refer to the past days at Philippi.

παρελάβετε. In the sense of receiving a truth passed on by a
teacher, who on his part παραδίδωσιν. See e.g. 1 Cor. xi. 23, ἐγὼ
παρέλαβον ἀπὸ τοῦ κυρίου ὃ καὶ παρέδωκα ὑμῖν. Cp. Gal. i. 9, εἴ τις ὑμᾶς
εὐαγγελίζεται παρ' ὃ παρελάβετε, ἀνάθεμα ἔστω: and 1 Thess. iv. 1.
Παραλαμβάνειν thus comes very nearly to mean "to learn" and παρα-
διδόναι (παράδοσις) "to teach."

ἐν ἐμοί. Strictly, the words attach themselves to εἴδετε only. It
is as if he had written ἃ ἐμάθετε κτλ. παρ' ἐμοῦ καὶ εἴδ. ἐν ἐμοί.

πράσσετε. "Practise." "Roughly speaking, ποιεῖν may be said to
...designate performance, πράσσειν intentional...habitual performance;

π. to point to an actual result, πρ. to the scope and character of the result" (Grimm, ed. Thayer, s.v. ποιεῖν).

καὶ. See above on the καὶ which introduces ver. 7.

ὁ θεὸς τῆς εἰρήνης. Author and Giver of "The peace of God." The phrase occurs Rom. xv. 33, xvi. 20, ὁ θ. τῆς εἰρ. συντρίψει τὸν σατανᾶν : 2 Cor. xiii. 11, ὁ θ. τῆς ἀγάπης καὶ τῆς εἰρ. ἔσται μεθ' ὑμῶν : 1 Thess. v. 23, αὐτὸς ὁ θ. τῆς εἰρ. ἁγιάσαι ὑμᾶς κτλ. : Heb. xiii. 20, ὁ δὲ θ. τῆς εἰρ., ὁ ἀναγαγὼν κτλ. And cp. 2 Thess. iii. 16, ὁ κύριος τῆς εἰρ.: and 1 Cor. xiv. 33, οὐ γὰρ ἀκαταστασίας ὁ θ. ἀλλὰ εἰρήνης. In the last case the peace is plainly *social* peace rather than internal, personal peace. But the two are closely connected ; the peace of God in the individual tends always to the peace of the society, for it means the banishment of the self-spirit. Here very possibly St Paul has in side-view the Philippians' need of peace in their community, and of a higher tone of Christian thought and feeling as an aid towards it. But the whole context is so full of the inward aspects of Christian experience that it seems best to take this phrase as referring *primarily* to the sabbath of the soul, the peace of God in the man.

10—20.　Loving Thanks for their Alms, brought by Epaphroditus.

10. Ἐχάρην δὲ. The thought now finally turns from the didactic to the personal.—R.V., "But I rejoice" ; the present ; taking ἐχάρην as an epistolary aorist. See on ii. 25. The time reference, however, may be to the day when the gift arrived, now probably some while ago.

ἐν κυρίῳ. The persons and the act were all bound up with Him.

ἤδη ποτὲ. "At length," R.V., a milder phrase than the "at the last" of A.V. No reproach, we may be sure, underlies the allusion to the interval ; see the loving words of the next sentence. He may even mean to emphasize the thought of the Philippians' persistence and fidelity.

ἀνεθάλετε τὸ ὑπὲρ ἐμοῦ φρονεῖν. "You have burgeoned into thought on my behalf." The poetic boldness of the phrase is unmistakable. It is an almost *pleasantry* of expression, full of courteous affectionateness.—Ἀναθάλλειν occurs here only in N.T. In the classics it is always intransitive ; in Biblical Greek it is transitive as well, e.g. Ezek. xvii. 24, ἀναθάλλων ξύλον ξηρόν : Ecclus i. 15, φόβος κυρίου ἀναθάλλων εἰρήνην. Here either construction is intelligible.—Φρονεῖν (ἐφρονεῖτε) in this verse comes very near φροντίζειν in meaning ; a rare phenomenon.

ἐφ' ᾧ. "As to which" ; i.e. as to St Paul's condition and interests, implied in the ὑπὲρ ἐμοῦ just before.

ἠκαιρεῖσθε. "You lacked the καιρός," not having, at the moment the *needed bearer* for the subsidy.

11. καθ' ὑστέρησιν. "In terms of need." Vulg., *propter penuriam.*
See Mar. xii. 44 for the only other occurrence of the noun in Biblical
Greek ; ἐκ τῆς ὑστερήσεως αὐτῆς πάντα...ἔβαλεν (*de penuria sua,* Vulg.).

ἐγὼ γὰρ ἔμαθον. "For *I*" (with a slight emphasis) "have learned."
Here the English perfect (A.V. and R.V.) well represents the Greek
aorist.

ἐν οἷς εἰμί. "In the position in which I am placed" (Lightfoot).
It is obviously a contracted construction, for ἐν ἐκείνοις ἐν κτλ.

αὐτάρκης. Literally, "self-sufficing"; i.e. independent of circumstances. *Omnia sua secum portat.* The adjective occurs here only in
N.T.; rarely in LXX.—For αὐτάρκεια see 2 Cor. ix. 8, πᾶσαν ἀ. ἔχοντες
(through fulness of grace): 1 Tim. vi. 6, πορισμὸς μέγας ἡ εὐσέβεια
μετ' αὐταρκείας. Aristotle defines τὸ αὐταρκες as τὰ πάντα ὑπάρχειν καὶ
δεῖσθαι μηθενός (*Polit.* vii. 5 *init.*). And this is just the Apostle's consciousness, in his possession of Christ under all circumstances.

12. οἶδα καὶ ταπεινοῦσθαι. Apparently he would have written οἶδα
καὶ τ. καὶ περισσεύειν: but a second οἶδα is thrown in for emphasis.
See Lightfoot's note.—"I know both how to be abased." For this
use of 'εἰδέναι, *callere*, "to know how," cp. e.g. Matt. vii. 11, οἴδατε
δόματα ἀγαθὰ διδόναι : 1 Thess. iv. 4, εἰδέναι ἕκαστον ὑμῶν τὸ ἑαυτοῦ
σκεῦος κτᾶσθαι. For ταπεινοῦσθαι in the sense of "running low," cp.
Diodorus I. 36, of the fall of the Nile: καθ' ἡμέραν...ταπεινοῦται. The
same word is used of other rivers in the context.

οἶδα καὶ περισσεύειν. As I do now, thanks to the Philippians.—"I
know how to abound"; for plenty as well as want needs grace if it is
to be borne aright.

ἐν παντὶ καὶ ἐν πᾶσιν. In the detail and in the aggregate of experience. Lightfoot compares 2 Cor. xi. 6, ἐν παντὶ φανερώσαντες ἐν
πᾶσιν εἰς ὑμᾶς.

μεμύημαι. "I have been initiated." R.V., "I have learned the
secret." The word is the perf. pass. of μυέω, "to initiate"; connected with μύω, "to shut the eyes." Hence μύστης, μυστικός, μυστήριον, κτλ.—The μυστήρια, or secret religious rites, were a great
phenomenon in classical paganism, frequently mentioned from
Herodotus downwards. The most famous were those of Demeter,
at Eleusis in Attica; but every considerable Greek city had its
"mysteries." The secrecy of these rites perhaps originated in the
desire of the votaries of pre-Hellenic religion to protect their belief
and worship by concealment. "The mysteries probably were...
scenic representations of mythical legends" (Liddell and Scott, s.v.).
The celebration was always secret; but initiation was granted to even
slaves, while it was sought by the most cultured and dignified, including Roman Emperors; with the hope apparently of a special
immunity from evil in this life and the next. See Smith, *Dict. of Gr.
and R. Ant.*, s.v. Mysteries.—Freemasonry familiarly illustrates such a
system of concealment; and we now often borrow its name, somewhat
as St Paul here borrows μυεῖν (and μυστήριον itself, e.g. Rom. xi. 25, xvi.

25, and about twenty times altogether; and cp. e.g. Matt. xiii. 11;
Rev. i. 20, x. 7, xvii. 5, 7), when we speak of "the freemasonry of the
Gospel," meaning the intimate sympathy of hearts in Christ.

χορτάζεσθαι. "To be filled," "full fed." St Paul uses the word
here only. Its first meaning was to give fodder to cattle; but it lost
this lower (as a distinctive) meaning in later and Biblical Greek. Cp.
Psal. cvi. (Heb., cvii.) 9, ἐχόρτασε ψυχὴν κενήν : Matt. v. 6, οἱ πεινῶντες
..τὴν δικαιοσύνην...χορτασθήσονται.

πεινᾶν. No doubt often in stern literality; cp. 1 Cor. iv. 11, πεινῶ-
μεν καὶ διψῶμεν καὶ γυμνητεύομεν : 2 Cor. xi. 27 ἐν λιμῷ καὶ δίψει.

13. πάντα ἰσχύω. "For all things I have strength"; to do or to
bear. Ἰσχύς tends to denote *physical* strength; the idea here passes
into metaphor; his spiritual *frame* is strong.—Vulg., beautifully,
omnia possum.—Πάντα is not, of course, "all things" absolutely. It
is "all things" in the actual path of duty and suffering allotted by
his Master. Along that path (let us note the word and its message)
not only *some* things but *all* can be met in peace and strength.

ἐν τῷ ἐνδυναμοῦντί με. "In Him who enableth me," who gives me
δύναμις, ability.—For the reading, see critical note.—Ἐνδυναμόω in the
active occurs 1 Tim. i. 12, χάριν ἔχω τῷ ἐνδυναμώσαντί με : 2 Tim. iv.
17, ὁ κύριος ἐνεδυνάμωσέ με : and in the middle or passive, Acts ix. 22,
Σαῦλος ἐνεδυναμοῦτο : Rom. iv. 20, ἐνεδυναμώθη τῇ πίστει : Eph. vi. 10;
2 Tim. ii. 1; Heb. xi. 34.

Observe ἐν τῷ ἐνδ. It is only in vital union with the Head that the
member is thus "able" (Joh. xv. 5, χωρὶς ἐμοῦ οὐ δύνασθε : cp. 2 Cor.
ix. 8, xii. 9, 10).

14. πλὴν καλῶς ἐποιήσατε. He is lovingly anxious lest his
"ability in Christ" should even seem to blunt his gratitude to his
friends, whose "deep poverty had abounded to the riches of their
liberality" (2 Cor. viii. 1, 2).

ἐποιήσατε. "Ye did"; when you sent your alms.

συνκοινωνήσαντες. "Unitedly sharing in."—See above, i. 7.—
Their practical sympathy, with its self-denial, *blent* their experience
and that of the afflicted Apostle into one; and they were all of one
mind (συν-) in so acting.

15. οἴδατε δὲ. The δὲ suggests, with the same delicacy of love,
that their earlier gifts would have sufficed to assure him of their fellowship with him. "You have now done well; but indeed you had
repeatedly, and to a rare degree, shewn your sympathy before."

καὶ ὑμεῖς. You as well as I.

Φιλιππήσιοι. This form of the civic adjective appears also in
"Titles" of the Epistle, and in "Subscriptions." Other forms (in
secular Greek) are Φιλιππεῖς, Φιλιππηνοί. Probably the Latin "colonists" called themselves *Philippenses*, which is the word used here in
the Vulg. So *Corinthienses, Romanenses, Sicilienses*, were foreign
residents in Corinth, &c. (See Facciolati, Lexicon, s.v. *Corinthiensis*.)

And this word may have grown out of that, for Greek tends to represent the Latin *-ens-* by *-ησ-*: so *Clemens*, Κλήμης.

ἐν ἀρχῇ τοῦ εὐαγγελίου. In the beginning of his Gospel-work in their region. For this use of the word εὐαγγέλιον see above i. 5, 7, 12, iv. 3. Cp. 2 Cor. x. 14, ἄχρι καὶ ὑμῶν ἐφθάσαμεν ἐν τῷ εὐ. τοῦ χριστοῦ.

ὅτε ἐξῆλθον ἀπὸ Μακεδονίας. "On my leaving Macedonia"; not "when I *had* left," for he proceeds to refer to an incident at Thessalonica, in Macedonia. He means the general period of his removal from Macedonia (Roman Northern Greece) into Achaia (Roman Southern Greece). For the narrative, see Acts xvii. 1—15. He is looking back now over some ten years.

οὐδεμία...ἐκκλησία. We gather that thus early the Gospel had taken root in more than one or two spots in Macedonia, not counting Philippi and Thessalonica. Acts xvi. (and xvii. 1) evidently gives only the leading specimen of the first work of the evangelists.

εἰς λόγον. "As regards"; literally, "to the account of." Lightfoot quotes Thucyd., iii. 46, ἐς χρημάτων λόγον ἰσχυούσαις (πόλεσι), "states strong in regard to wealth"; and Demosth. (*de F. L.*, p. 385), εἰς ἀρετῆς λόγον.

δόσεως καὶ λήμψεως. A recognized formula for money transactions, where one gives and another takes. Chrysostom explains the words as meaning εἰς δόσεως τῶν σαρκικῶν καὶ λήψ. τῶν πνευματικῶν—the Philippians gaining blessing in return for their alms. But this misses the point; St Paul is speaking exclusively of practical liberality. See Lightfoot here.

16. καὶ ἐν Θεσσαλονίκῃ. That is, even when I was no further away from you than Thessalonica; so prompt and generous were you. —See Acts xvii. 1—9.—Thessalonica was just 100 Roman (about 92 English) miles from Philippi, on the Via Egnatia. Amphipolis and Apollonia were the two intermediate stations, each about 30 miles from the other and from one of the two other towns. Apparently Paul and Silas, leaving Philippi and hastening to Thessalonica, passed only a night at each intermediate place, and remained at least some weeks at Thessalonica. See Conybeare and H., ch. ix.; and Lewin, *L. and E. of St Paul*, vol. I. ch. xi. Thessalonica was thus St Paul's first long pause; and it lay comparatively near Philippi.

καὶ ἅπαξ καὶ δίς. Within no very long time. In Acts xvii. 2 we read of σάββατα τρία before the disturbances began. No certain note of time is given afterwards; but the withdrawal to Berœa was not long delayed. Short as the stay was, it was long enough to produce profound impressions, as the Thessalonian Epistles testify.

εἰς τὴν χρείαν μοι. At Thessalonica he refused to take support from the converts, and worked for his living. See 1 Thess. ii. 9, νυκτὸς καὶ ἡμέρας ἐργαζόμενοι, πρὸς τὸ μὴ ἐπιβαρῆσαί τινα ὑμῶν, ἐκηρύξαμεν εἰς ὑμᾶς τὸ εὐ. τοῦ θεοῦ.

17. οὐχ ὅτι κτλ. Here again see the sensitive delicacy of love. He fears lest this allusion to the cherished past, made only to shew

that he needs no present proof of sympathy, might after all read like
" thanks for future favours."

ἐπιζητῶ. Almost "am hunting for." Cp. Matt. xx. 39, γενεὰ
πονηρά...σημεῖον ἐπιζητεῖ: Rom. xi. 7, ὃ ἐπιζ. Ἰσραήλ, τοῦτο οὐκ ἐπέ-
τυχε.

τὸ δόμα. "*The* gift"; the mere money, for myself.

τὸν καρπὸν τὸν πλεονάζοντα κτλ. "The fruit which is abounding
to your account." Chrysostom writes here, ὁ καρπὸς ἐκείνοις τίκτεται.
(Cp. Æsch. *S. c. T.* 437, τῷδε κέρδει κέρδος ἄλλο τίκτεται.) Τόκος is regularly used in the sense of interest on money; and it is probable that
Chrysostom's τίκτεται implies that he, a Greek, took St Paul to be
using here the language of the money market; so that καρπός, πλεονάζειν, λόγος, might all be metaphorical; "The *interest* which *is accruing*
to your *credit.*" The objection is that καρπός and πλεονάζειν do not
appear elsewhere as technical financial words; but such an application of them here is at least possible.

Observe τὸν πλεονάζοντα. He takes it as certain that the καρπός "*is*
abounding," not only "*may* abound."

18. ἀπέχω δὲ. The δὲ carries on the correction, begun in ver. 17,
of any possible mistake of his warm words. He is well supplied; he
must not be suspected of suggesting more gifts in the future.

ἀπέχω. "I have received in full." Cp. Matt. vi. 2, 5, 16, ἀπέ-
χουσι τὸν μισθὸν αὐτῶν: Luke vi. 24, ἀπέχετε τὴν παράκλησιν ὑμῶν:
Philem. 15, ἵνα αἰώνιον αὐτὸν ἀπέχῃς. So in classical Greek, Callim.,
Epigr. 57, τὸ χρέος ὡς ἀπέχεις, Ἀσκληπιέ, κτλ. If the Philippians
did owe him anything, they have amply paid!

παρὰ Ἐπαφροδίτου. See on ii. 25—30. Here we learn explicitly
what is implied there (ver. 25, 30), that he was the bringer of the
collection to St Paul.

τὰ παρ' ὑμῶν. He will not say τὰ παρ' ὑ. χρήματα: it was more
than money; the money was but the symbol of their hearts.

ὀσμὴν εὐωδίας. "Odour of fragrancy" (εὖ, ὄζω). So Eph. v. 2, of
the Saviour's atoning Sacrifice. The phrase is common in LXX. for
the Hebrew רֵיחַ הַנִּיחֹחַ, " savour of rest" (e.g. Gen. viii. 21); the fume
of the altar, recognized by the Deity as a token of allegiance or propitiation. Here the ὀσμὴ εὐωδίας is either that of the "burnt-offering"
of self-dedication, embodied in self-denying giving, or that of the
"peace-offering" of thanksgiving, similarly embodied (cp. Lev. i. 9,
iii. 5), or that of both, as both are combined in our Liturgy of the
Holy Communion.

θυσίαν δεκτὴν εὐάρεστον. Cp. Heb. xiii. 16, τῆς εὐποιΐας καὶ
κοινωνίας μὴ ἐπιλανθάνεσθε, τοιαύταις γὰρ θυσίαις εὐαρεστεῖται ὁ θεός.

19. ὁ δὲ θεός μου. "And my God," R.V. But there is surely a
slight implied contrast, or correction; as if he said, "I would requite
you if I could; *but* my God will do so."

ὁ θεός μου. Words deeply characteristic of St Paul; see on i. 3 above. Lightfoot well remarks that they are specially in point here; the Apostle is thinking of what God will do for others *on his behalf*.

πληρώσει. The future of the certainty of faith. For πληροῦν χρείαν cp. Psal. cxxvi. (Heb., cxxvii.) 6, μακάριος ὃς πληρώσει τὴν ἐπιθυμίαν αὐτοῦ.

πᾶσαν χρείαν ὑμῶν. "Your every need." See again 2 Cor. viii. 2 for the exceptional poverty (ἡ κατὰ βάθους πτωχεία) of the Macedonian converts. The main reference here is, surely, to temporal "need"; such need as the Philippians had so lovingly "filled" for St Paul. See 2 Cor. ix. 8, 9, δυνατεῖ ὁ θεὸς πᾶσαν χάριν περισσεῦσαι εἰς ὑμᾶς, ἵνα κτλ.: where the *first* thought seems to be of God's ability to give His self-denying servants the means for yet further bounties for His work. But neither here nor there are we to shut out the widest and deepest applications of the promise.

κατὰ τὸ πλοῦτος αὐτοῦ ἐν δόξῃ. According to, on the scale of, those resources which reside in the δόξα of His manifested power and love; in fact, in His revealed Self. Cp. Rom. vi. 4 for such a use of δόξα : ἠγέρθη Χριστὸς...διὰ τῆς δόξης τοῦ πατρός.
Lightfoot explains the thought to be, "He shall supply your need by placing you in glory," the glory of His heavenly presence. But this seems to be somewhat far-fetched, and indeed to be out of place if the explanation of χρεία given above is right.
St Paul loves the word πλοῦτος, and its cognates, in spiritual connexions. Cp. Rom. ii. 4, ix. 23, x. 12, xi. 12, 33; 1 Cor. i. 5; 2 Cor. viii. 9, ix. 11; Eph. i. 7, 18, ii. 4, 7, iii. 8, 16; Col. i. 27, ii. 2.

ἐν Χριστῷ ᾽Ιησοῦ. Cp. Col. ii. 9, 10, ἐστὲ ἐν αὐτῷ πεπληρωμένοι: and 1 Cor. i. 5, ἐν παντὶ ἐπλουτίσθητε ἐν αὐτῷ. The "glory" of both grace and providence is lodged *in Him* for His people.

20. τῷ δὲ θεῷ κτλ. "Now to our God and Father &c."; the ultimate Source of all blessing for the members of His Son.

ἡμῶν. "It is no longer μου, for the reference is now not to himself as distinguished from the Philippians, but as united to them" (Lightfoot).

ἡ δόξα. "The adoring praise" due in view of all fruits of His grace and promises of His blessing.

ἡ δ. εἰς τοὺς αἰῶνας τῶν αἰώνων. For this phrase in Ascriptions cp. Gal. i. 5; 2 Tim. iv. 18; Heb. xiii. 21. The "for ever and ever" of A.V. and R.V. is a true paraphrase. The idea conveyed by the Greek is of cycles consisting of, embracing, other cycles, *ad infinitum;* the ever-developing "ages" of heavenly life.

ἀμήν. Properly a Hebrew adverb, אָמֵן, "surely"; repeatedly used as here in O.T. See e.g. Deut. xxvii. 15, &c., where "all the people" affirm the sentences against sin with their אָמֵן.

21—23. SALUTATIONS AND FAREWELL.

21. Ἀσπάσασθε. Cp. Rom. xvi. 3—16 for such ἀσπασμοί in detail.

πάντα ἅγιον ἐν Χριστῷ Ἰησοῦ. "Every saint" (see on i. 1) "in Christ Jesus." We might explain the clause, as Lightfoot inclines to do, "Salute in Christ Jesus every saint"; cp. 1 Cor. xvi. 19, ἀσπάζονται ὑμᾶς ἐν κυρίῳ πολλὰ Ἀκύλας καὶ Πρίσκα (Rom. xvi. 22 is not clear). But on the whole the other connexion seems preferable, looking at i. 1, πᾶσι τοῖς ἁγ. ἐν Χρ. Ἰ.

οἱ σὺν ἐμοὶ ἀδελφοί. "Apparently the Apostle's personal companions, as distinguished from the Christians resident at Rome, who are described in the following verse" (Lightfoot).

22. μάλιστα δέ. There was something marked and emphatic about this message.

οἱ ἐκ τῆς Καίσαρος οἰκίας. "Probably slaves and freedmen attached to the palace" (Lightfoot). It has been thought, on the other hand, that these persons were members of the imperial family, or at least grandees of the court; and this has been used either to prove a remarkable advance of the Gospel in the highest circles during St Paul's imprisonment (and incidentally to evidence a late date for the Epistle in that imprisonment), or to indicate the spuriousness of the Epistle. Lightfoot (*Phil.*, pp. 171—178) has fully shewn that "the Household of Cæsar" was a term embracing a vast number of persons, not only in Rome but in the provinces, all of them either actual or former imperial slaves, filling every description of more or less domestic office. He illustrates his statements from the numerous epitaphs of members of the *Domus Cæsaris* found within the last 175 years near Rome, most of them of the Julian and Claudian times. It is remarkable that the names in these epitaphs afford curiously many coincidences with *the names in Rom. xvi.;* among them are Amplias, Urbanus, Stachys, Apelles, Tryphæna, Tryphosa, Rufus, Hermes, Hermas, Patrobas, Philologus, Julius, Nereis (a name which might possibly be that of the sister (Rom. xvi. 15) of a man Nereus). It appears by the way very likely that both Aristobulus' and Narcissus' "households" (Rom. xvi. 10, 11) were in fact the slave-establishments respectively of the son of Herod the Great and of the favourite freedman of Claudius—transferred to the possession of the Emperor. Lightfoot infers a high probability that the "saints" greeted in Rom. xvi., as resident at Rome, were on the whole identical with "the saints of the Household" who here send greeting from Rome. Various as no doubt were their functions, and their nationalities, the members of the Household, as such, must have had an *esprit de corps* which made it likely, humanly speaking, that a powerful influence like that of the Gospel would be felt widely among them, if felt at all; and that it would be intensified by the difficulties of their surroundings; and that so that they would be in the way to make a united and emphatic expression of their faith and love on occasion.

This view of "the saints" here mentioned, as to their associations and duties, not only in the age of Nero but in the precincts of his court, and probably (for many of them) within the chambers of his palace, gives a noble passing illustration of the power of grace to triumph over circumstances, and to transfigure life where it seems most impossible. "Dieu laisse quelquefois ses serviteurs au milieu du monde, pour montrer la souveraineté de sa grace" (Quesnel on this verse).

A certain parallel to the *Domus Cæsaris* appears in the vast *Maison du Roy* of the French monarchy. But the *Maison* was for the nobility alone.

23. Ἡ χάρις τοῦ κ. Ἰ. Χ. So, or nearly so, every Epistle of St Paul's closes, or almost closes. In the Ep. to the Romans the "grace" occurs twice; xvi. 20, 24. The exact form here used (τοῦ πνεύματος ὑμῶν) occurs Gal. vi. 16; Philem. 25.

Observe the implied testimony to the Divine glory of the Saviour, named thus alone, and in conclusion, as the Fountain of grace.

μετὰ τοῦ πνεύματος ὑμῶν. On the reading, see critical note.—The πνεῦμα is the inmost basis of the life and will of man. It is not absorbed, or annulled, by the Divine χάρις, which is "with" it. Cp. 1 Cor. xv. 10, οὐκ ἐγώ, ἀλλὰ ἡ χάρις τοῦ θεοῦ σὺν ἐμοί.

On ἀμήν (here in T.R.) and on the Subscription, see critical note.

APPENDICES.

A. ST PAUL'S RESIDENCE AT ROME.
(Introduction, Ch. i.)

"ST PAUL arrived in Rome, from Melita, in the spring of A.D. 61, probably early in March. There he spent 'two full years' (Acts xxviii. 30), at the close of which, as we have good reason to believe, he was released.

"In the long delay before his trial[1] he was of course in custody; but this was comparatively lenient. He occupied lodgings of his own (Acts xxviii. 16, 23, 30), probably a storey or flat in one of the lofty houses common in Rome. It is impossible to determine for certain where in the City this lodging was, but it is likely that it was either in or near the great Camp of the Prætorians, or Imperial Guard, outside the Colline Gate, just N.E. of the City[2]. In this abode the Apostle was attached day and night by a light coupling-chain to a Prætorian sentinel, but was as free, apparently, to invite and maintain general intercourse as if he had been merely confined by illness.

"The company actually found in his rooms at different times was very various. His first visitors (indeed they must have been the providers of his lodging) would be the Roman Christians, including

[1] Due probably to procrastination in the prosecution and to the caprice of the Emperor. See Lewin, vol. II. p. 236, for a parallel case.

[2] See Bp Lightfoot, *Philippians*, pp. 9 &c., 99 &c.; and our note on Phil. i. 13.

all, or many, of the saints named in a passage (Rom. xvi.) written only a very few years before. Then came the representatives of the Jewish community (Acts xxviii. 17, 23), but apparently never to return, as such, after the long day of discussion to which they were first invited. Then from time to time would come Christian brethren, envoys from distant Churches, or personal friends; Epaphroditus from Philippi, Aristarchus from Thessalonica, Tychicus from Ephesus, Epaphras from Colossæ, John Mark, Demas, Jesus Justus. Luke, the beloved physician, was present perhaps always, and Timotheus, the Apostle's spiritual son, very frequently. One other memorable name occurs, Onesimus, the fugitive Colossian slave, whose story, indicated in the Epistle to Philemon, is at once a striking evidence of the perfect liberty of access to the prisoner granted to anyone and everyone, and a beautiful illustration both of the character of St Paul and the transfiguring power and righteous principles of the Gospel.

"No doubt the visitors to this obscure but holy lodging were far more miscellaneous than even this list suggests. Through the successive Prætorian sentinels some knowledge of the character and message of the prisoner would be always passing out. The right interpretation of Phil. i. 13[1] is, beyond reasonable doubt, that the true account of Paul's imprisonment came to be 'known in the Prætorian regiments, and generally among people around'; and Phil. iv. 22 indicates that a body of earnest and affectionate converts had arisen among the population of slaves and freedmen attached to the Palace of Nero. And the wording of that passage suggests that such Christians found a welcome meeting place in the rooms of the Apostle; doubtless for frequent worship, doubtless also for direct instruction, and for the blessed enjoyments of the family affection of the Gospel. Meanwhile (Phil. i. 15, 16) there was a section of the Roman Christian community, probably the disciples infected with the prejudices of the Pharisaic party (see Acts xv., &c.), who, with very few exceptions (see Col. iv. 11 and notes), took sooner or later a position of trying antagonism to St Paul; a trial over which he triumphed in the deep peace of Christ.

"It is an interesting possibility, not to say probability, that from time to time the lodging was visited by inquirers of intellectual fame or distinguished rank. Ancient Christian tradition[2] actually makes the renowned Stoic writer, L. Annæus Seneca, tutor and counsellor of Nero, a convert of St Paul's; and one phase of the legend was the fabrication, within the first four centuries, of a correspondence between the two. It is quite certain that Seneca was never a Christian, though his language is full of startling superficial parallels to that of the N.T., and most full in his latest writings. But it is at least very likely that he heard, through his many channels of information, of St Paul's existence and presence, and that he was intellectually interested in his teaching; and it is quite possible that he cared to visit him. It

---

[1] See Bp Lightfoot, *Philippians*, pp. 99 &c., and our notes on Phil. i. 13.
[2] The first hint appears in Tertullian, cent. ii—iii.

is not improbable, surely, that Seneca's brother Gallio (Acts xviii. 12) may have described St Paul, however passingly, in a letter; for Gallio's religious indifference may quite well have consisted with a strong personal impression made on him by St Paul's bearing. Festus himself was little interested in the Gospel, or at least took care to seem so, and yet was deeply impressed by the *personnel* of the Apostle. And, again, the Prefect of the Imperial Guard, A.D. 61, was Afranius Burrus, Seneca's intimate colleague as counsellor to Nero, and it is at least possible that he had received from Festus a more than commonplace description of the prisoner consigned to him[1].

"Bp Lightfoot, in his Essay, 'St Paul and Seneca' (*Philippians,* pp. 270, &c.), thinks it possible to trace in some of the Epistles of the Captivity a Christian adaptation of Stoic ideas. The Stoic, for example, made much of the individual's *membership* in the great Body of the Universe, and *citizenship* in its great City. The connexion suggested is interesting, and it falls quite within the methods of Divine inspiration that materials of Scripture imagery should be collected from a secular region. But the language of St Paul about the Mystical Body, in the Ephesian Epistle particularly, reads far more like a direct revelation than like an adaptation; and it evidently deals with a truth which is already, in its substance, perfectly familiar to the readers[2].

"Other conspicuous personages of Roman society at the time have been reckoned by tradition among the chamber-converts of St Paul, among them the poet Lucan and the Stoic philosopher Epictetus[3]. But there is absolutely no evidence for these assertions. It is interesting and suggestive, on the other hand, to recall one almost certain case of conversion about this time within the highest Roman aristocracy. Pomponia Græcina, wife of Plautius the conqueror of Britain, was accused (A.D. 57, probably), of 'foreign superstition,' and tried by her husband as domestic judge. He acquitted her. But the deep and solemn seclusion of her life (a seclusion begun A.D. 44, when her friend the princess Julia was put to death, and continued unbroken till her own death, about A.D. 84), taken in connexion with the charge, as in all likelihood it was, of Christianity, 'suggests that, shunning society, she sought consolation in the duties and hopes of the Gospel[4],' leaving for ever the splendour and temptations of the world of Rome. She was not a convert, obviously, of St Paul's; but her case suggests the possibility of other similar cases."

Commentary on the Epistle to the Ephesians (in *Cambridge Bible for Schools*), Introduction, pp. 16—19.

---

[1] We cannot but think that Bp Lightfoot (*Philippians,* p. 301) somewhat underrates the probability that Gallio and Burrus should have given Seneca an interest in St Paul.

[2] It appears in the First Ep. to the Corinthians, written a few years before the Ep. to the Ephesians. See 1 Cor. xii.

[3] For the curiously Christian tone of Epictetus' writings here and there, see Bp Lightfoot, *Philippians,* pp. 313 &c. The *Manual* of Epictetus is a book of gold in its own way, but still that way is not Christian.

[4] Bp Lightfoot, *Philippians,* p. 21.

B. "SAINTS AND FAITHFUL BRETHREN." (Ch. I. 1.)

"It is universally admitted...that Scripture makes use of presumptive or hypothetical language....It is generally allowed that when all Christians are addressed in the New Testament as 'saints,' 'dead to sin,' 'alive unto God,' 'risen with Christ,' 'having their conversation in heaven,' and in other like modes, they are addressed so hypothetically, and not to express the literal fact that all the individuals so addressed were of this character; which would not have been true.... Some divines have indeed preferred as a theological arrangement a secondary sense of [such terms] to the hypothetical application of it in its true sense. But what is this secondary sense when we examine it? It is *itself* no more than the true sense hypothetically applied.... Divines have...maintained a Scriptural secondary sense of the term '*saint*,' as 'saint by outward vocation and charitable presumption' (Pearson *on the Creed*, Art. ix.); but this is in very terms only the real sense of the term applied hypothetically."

J. B. Mozley: *Review of Baptismal Controversy*, p. 74 (ed. 1862).

C. BISHOPS AND DEACONS. (Ch. I. 1.)

These words have suggested to Bp Lightfoot an Essay on the rise, development and character of the Christian Ministry, appended to his Commentary on the Epistle (pp. 189—269), and now included also in his *Biblical Essays*. The Essay is in fact a treatise, of the greatest value, calling for the careful and repeated study of every reader to whom it is accessible. Along with it may be usefully studied a paper on the Christian Ministry in *The Expositor* for July, 1887, by the Rev. G. Salmon, D.D., now Provost of Trinity College, Dublin.

All we do here is to discuss briefly the two official titles of the Philippian ministry, and to add a few words on the Christian Ministry in general.

Bishops, ἐπίσκοποι, i.e. *Overseers*. The word occurs here, and Acts xx. 28; 1 Tim. iii. 2; Tit. i. 7; besides 1 Pet. ii. 25, where it is used of our Lord. The cognate noun, ἐπισκοπή, occurs Acts i. 20 (in a quotation from the O.T.); 1 Tim. iii. 1; and in three other places not in point. The cognate verb, ἐπισκοπεῖν, occurs Heb. xii. 15 (in a connexion not in point); 1 Pet. v. 2.

On examination of these passages it appears that within the lifetime of SS. Peter and Paul there existed, at least very widely, a normal order of Church-officers called *Episcopi*, Superintendents. They were charged no doubt with many varied duties, some probably semi-secular. But above all they had spiritual oversight of the flock. They were appointed not by mere popular vote, certainly not by self-designation, but in some special sense " by the Holy Ghost" (Acts xx. 28). This phrase may perhaps be illustrated by the mode of appointment of the "Seven" (Acts vi. 3), who were presented by the Church to the Apostles, for confirmatory ordination, as men already (among other marks of fitness) "full of the Holy Ghost."

The ἐπίσκοπος was evidently not an official comparatively rare; there were more ἐπίσκοποι than one in the not very large community of Philippi.

Meanwhile we find another designation of Church-officers who are evidently in the same way shepherds and leaders of the flock; πρεσβύτεροι, *Elders.* They are mentioned first, without comment, at the time of the martyrdom of James the Great. See Acts xi. 30, xiv. 23, xv. 2, 4, 6, 22, 23, xvi. 4, xx. 17, xxi. 18; 1 Tim. v. 1, 17, 19; Tit. i. 5; Jas v. 14; 1 Pet. v. 1 (and perhaps 5). See also 2 John 1; 3 John 1. These elders appear Acts xiv. 23; Tit. i. 5; as "constituted" in local congregations by an Apostle, or by his immediate delegate.

It would appear that the N.T. ἐπίσκοπος and πρεσβύτερος are in fact the same official under differing designations; ἐπίσκοπος, a term borrowed mainly from the Gentiles, with whom it signified a superintending commissioner; πρεσβύτερος, from the "Eldership" of the Jews. This appears from Acts xx. 17, 28, where St Paul, addressing the Ephesian "elders," says that they have been appointed "bishops" of the flock. In the Pastoral Epistles it is similarly plain that the titles coincide. See also 1 Pet. v. 1, 2, in the Greek.

Whether both titles were from the first in use everywhere we cannot be sure. But it is not improbable. In the very earliest post-apostolic writings we find "presbyters" at Corinth (Clem. Rom. to the Corinthians, i. cc. 42, 44, but also references to ἐπίσκοποι, ἐπισκοπή), and "bishops" (*with* "*deacons,*" as in Phil. i. 1) in the further East (*Teaching of the Twelve Apostles,* c. 15).

We trace the same spiritual officials under more general designations, 1 Thess. v. 12, 13; Heb. xiii. 17; and perhaps 1 Cor. xii. 28 (κυβερνήσεις), and Eph. iv. 11 (ποιμένες καὶ διδάσκαλοι).

Deacons, διάκονοι, i.e. *Workers.* The title does not occur in the Acts, nor anywhere earlier than this Epistle, except Rom. xvi. 1, where *Phœbe* is called a διάκονος of the church at Cenchreæ[1]. Here only and in 1 Tim. iii. 8, 12, is the word plainly used of a whole ministerial order. But in Acts vi. we find described the institution of an office which in all likelihood was the diaconate. The functions of the Seven are just those which have been ever since in history, even till now, assigned to deacons. And tradition, from cent. ii. onwards, is quite unanimous in calling the Seven by that title.

Deacons are very possibly indicated by the word ἀντιλήψεις in 1 Cor. xii. 28.

The deacon thus appears to have been primarily the officer ordained to deal with the temporal needs of the congregation. But he was

---

[1] There is evidence of the existence in apostolic times of an organized class of female helpers in sacred work (see 1 Tim. v. 3—16). A little later the famous letter of Pliny to Trajan shews that such helpers (*ministræ*) were known in the Churches of Asia Minor. The order of "deaconesses" was abolished before cent. xii.

assumed to be a "spiritual man," and he was capable of direct commissioned spiritual work.

It thus appears then that during the lifetime of SS. Peter and Paul the word ἐπίσκοπος did not yet designate a minister presiding over and ruling other ministers; a "bishop" in the later and present sense. The ἐπίσκοπος was an "overseer" of not the shepherds but simply the flock, and might be (as at Philippi) one of several such in the same place.

This fact, however, leaves quite open the question whether such a presiding ministry, however designated at first, did exist in apostolic times and under apostolic sanction. That it did so may be inferred from the following evidence, very briefly stated.

It is certain that by the close of cent. ii. a definite presidential "episcopacy" (to which the word ἐπίσκοπος was then already appropriated, seemingly without the knowledge that it had once been otherwise) appears everywhere in the Church. As early probably as A.D. 110 we find it, in the Epistles of St Ignatius, a prominent and important fact of Church life, at least in the large circle of Churches with which Ignatius corresponded[1]. Later Church history presents us with the same constitution, though occasionally details of system vary[2], and the conceptions of function and power were highly developed, not always legitimately. Now between Ignatius and St John, and even St Paul, the interval is not great; 30 or 50 years at the most. It seems, to say the least, unlikely that so large a Church institution, *over whose rise we have no clear trace of controversy or opposition,* should have arisen quite out of connexion with apostolic precedent. Such precedent we find in the N.T., (*a*) in the presidency of Apostles during their lifetime, though strictly speaking their unique office had no "successors"; (*b*) in the presidency of their immediate delegates or commissioners (perhaps appointed only *pro tempore*), as Timothy and Titus; (*c*) in the presidency of St James the Lord's Brother in the mother-church of Christendom; a presidency more akin to later episcopacy than anything else in the N.T.

We find further that all early history points to Asia Minor as the scene of the fullest development of primitive episcopacy, and it consistently indicates St John, at Ephesus, as in a sense its fountainhead. It is at least possible that St John, when he finally took up his abode in Asia, originated or developed there the *régime* he had known so well at Jerusalem.

Meanwhile there is reason to think that the episcopate, in this latter sense, rather grew out of the presbyterate than otherwise. The primeval bishop was *primus inter pares.* He was not so much one of another order as the first of his order, for special purposes of

---

[1] He does not mention the bishop in writing to the *Roman* Church. But there is other good evidence for the then presence of a bishop at Rome.

[2] At Alexandria, till at least A.D. 260, the bishop appears to have been chosen and ordained by the presbyters. In the Church of Patrick (cent. v.) in Ireland and Columba (cent. vi.) in Scotland, the bishop was an ordainer, but not a diocesan ruler. See Boultbee, *Hist. of the Church of England,* p. 25.

government and ministration. Such, even cent. v., is St Jerome's statement of the theory. And St Jerome regards the bishop as being what he is not by direct Divine institution, but by custom of the Church.

Not till late cent. ii. do we find the sacerdotal[1] idea familiarly attached to the Christian ministry, and not till cent. iii. the age of Cyprian, do we find the formidable theory developed that the bishop is the channel of grace to the lower clergy and to the people.

On the whole, the indications of the N. T. and of the next earliest records confirm the statement of the Preface to the English Ordinal that "from the Apostles' time there have been these orders of ministers in Christ's Church, Bishops, Priests, and Deacons." On the other hand, having regard to the essentially and sublimely spiritual character of the Church in its true idea, and to the revealed immediate union of each member with the Head, by faith, we are not authorized to regard even apostolic organization as a matter of the first order in such a sense as that we should look on a duly ordained ministry as the indispensable channel of grace, or should venture to unchurch Christian communities, holding the apostolic faith concerning God in Christ, but differently organized from what we believe to be on the whole the apostolic model[2]. On the other hand, no thoughtful Christian will wish to forget the sacred obligations and benefits of external harmony and unity of organization, things meant to yield only to the yet greater claims of the highest spiritual truth.

D. EBIONITE CHRISTOLOGY. (Ch. I. 15.)

THE allusion in our note to "lowered and distorted views" of the Person of our Lord on the part of later Judaizers more or less Christian, has regard mainly to *Ebionism*, a heresy first named by Irenæus (cent. ii.) but which seems to have been the direct descendant of the school which specially opposed St Paul. It lingered on till cent. v.

It appears to have had two phases; the Pharisaic and the Essene. As regards the doctrine of Christ's Person, the Pharisaic Ebionites held that Jesus was born in the ordinary course of nature, but that at His Baptism He was "anointed by election, and became Christ" (Justin Martyr, *Dial.*, c. xlix.); receiving power to fulfil His mission as Messiah, but still remaining man. He had neither pre-existence nor Divinity. The Essene Ebionites, who were in fact Gnostics, held (at least in many instances) that Christ was a super-angelic created Spirit, incarnate at many successive periods in various men (for instance, in Adam), and finally in Jesus. At what point in the existence of Jesus the Christ entered into union with Him was not defined.

See Smith's *Dict. of Christian Biography, &c.*, art. *Ebionism.*

---

[1] It will be remembered that the word ἱερεύς, *sacerdos*, is never in N.T. a designation of the Christian minister as such.

[2] This was fully owned by the great Anglican writers of cent. xvii See Bp Andrewes writing to Du Moulin; Bp Cosin to Basire; and Bp Hall's *Peace Maker*, § 6. Cp. Bp J. J. S. Perowne, *Church, Ministry, and Sacraments*, pp. 6, 7, and the Editor's *Outlines of Doctrine*, ch. x.

E. CHRISTOLOGY AND CHRISTIANITY. (Ch. II. 5.)

"A CHRISTIANITY without Christ is no Christianity; and a Christ not Divine is one other than the Christ on whom the souls of Christians have habitually fed. What virtue, what piety, have existed outside of Christianity, is a question totally distinct. But to hold that, since the great controversy of the early time was wound up at Chalcedon, the question of our Lord's Divinity has generated all the storms of the Christian atmosphere, would be simply an historical untruth.

"Christianity...produced a type of character wholly new to the Roman world, and it fundamentally altered the laws and institutions, the tone, temper and tradition of that world. For example, it changed profoundly the relation of the poor to the rich...It abolished slavery, and a multitude of other horrors. It restored the position of woman in society. It made peace, instead of war, the normal and presumed relation between human societies. It exhibited life as a discipline... in all its parts, and changed essentially the place and function of suffering in human experience...All this has been done not by eclectic and arbitrary fancies, but by the creed of the Homoousion, in which the philosophy of modern times sometimes appears to find a favourite theme of ridicule. The whole fabric, social as well as personal, rests on the new type of character which the Gospel brought into life and action."

W. E. GLADSTONE (*'Nineteenth Century,'*
May 1888; pp. 780—784).

F. ROBERT HALL ON PHIL. II. 5—8.
BAUR'S THEORY. (Ch. II. 6.)

THE Rev. Robert Hall (1764—1831), one of the greatest of Christian preachers, was in early life much influenced by the Socinian theology. His later testimony to a true Christology is the more remarkable. The following extract is from a sermon "preached at the (Baptist) Chapel in Dean Street, Southwark, June 27, 1813" (*Works*, ed. 1833; vol. vi., p. 112):

"He was *found* in fashion as a man: it was a wonderful discovery, an astonishing spectacle in the view of angels, that He who was in the form of God, and adored from eternity, should be made in fashion as a man. But why is it not said that He WAS *a man?* For the same reason that the Apostle wishes to dwell upon the *appearance* of our Saviour, not as excluding the reality, but as exemplifying His condescension. His being in the form of God did not prove that He was not God, but rather that He was God, and entitled to supreme honour. So, His assuming the form of a servant and being in the likeness of man, does not prove that He was not man, but, on the contrary, includes it; at the same time including a manifestation of Himself, agreeably to His design of purchasing the salvation of His people, and dying for the sins of the world, by sacrificing Himself upon the Cross."

BAUR (*Paulus*, pp. 458—464) goes at length into the Christological passage of our Epistle, and actually contends for the view that it is written by one who had before him the developed Gnosticism of cent. ii., and was not uninfluenced by it. In the words of ver. 6, he finds a consciousness of the Gnostic teaching about the Æon *Sophia*, striving for an absolute union with the absolute being of the Unknowable Supreme; and again about the Æons in general, striving similarly to "grasp" the πλήρωμα of Absolute Being and discovering only the more deeply in their effort this κένωμα of their own relativity and dependence.

The best refutation of such expositions is the repeated perusal of the Epistle itself, with its noon-day practicality of precept and purity of affections, and not least its high language (ch. iii.) about the sanctity of the body—an idea wholly foreign to the Gnostic sphere of thought. As regards this last point, it is true that Schrader, a critic earlier than Baur (see Alford, *N.T.* iii. p. 27), supposed the passage iii. 1—iv. 9 to be an interpolation. But, not to speak of the total absence of any historical or documentary support for such a theory, the careful reader will find in that section just those minute touches of harmony with the rest of the Epistle, e.g. in the indicated need of internal union at Philippi, which are the surest signs of homogeneity.

G. THE 'KENOSIS' OF THE SON OF GOD. (Ch. II. 7.)

"If we seek the true import of the word *Kenosis,* as applied to our Incarnate Lord, the Philippian passage (ii. 7), its original source for us, must be consulted. And it seems to guide us in a line exactly opposite to that which would make fallibility an element in our Lord's Humiliation. Ἐκένωσεν ἑαυτὸν μορφὴν δούλου λαβών. If we interpret the Greek by well recognised facts of idiom, we should take the aorist verb, ἐκένωσεν, and the aorist participle, λαβών, as conspiring to give us, from two sides, one idea. 'He made Himself void,' not anyhow, but thus—'taking Bondservant's form.' The 'making void' was in fact just this—the 'taking.' It was—the assumption of the creaturely Nature, the becoming, in Augustine's words (*ad Dardanum*), 'Creature, as Man' (*quoad hominem, creatura*); and the assumption of it in just *this* respect, that in it, and by the fact of it, He became δοῦλος, Bond-servant. Now what is the implication of that unique, that absolute, unreserved, unhindered Bondservice of the Incarnate Son? What does it say to us about His capacity to do the Father's work, and convey His mind and message? The absolute subjection of the

Perfect Bondservant gives us an absolute warrant—not of the precariousness but of the perfection of His deliverance of His commission from His Father and Master. '*He whom God hath sent speaketh the words of God.*'

"His own servant Paul was one day to claim complete *authority* as messenger because of the absoluteness of his *slavery* to the Lord. 'Let no man trouble me, for I bear in my body the στίγματα, the brands, of the Master, Jesus.' The supreme Bondservant, the Bearer of the Stigmata of the Cross, has He not as such the right to claim our unreserved, our worshipping silence, when He speaks? He, in perfect relation to His Sender, perfectly conveys His Sender's mind. He says *nothing* otherwise than as His Sender bids Him say it. '*He whom God hath sent*, speaketh the words *of God.*'"

From a University Sermon by the Editor.

H. THE WORSHIP PAID TO JESUS CHRIST. (Ch. II. 9.)

"Upon this worship of Jesus Christ as we meet it in the apostolical age, [let us observe, that] it cannot be accounted for, and so set aside, as being part of an indiscriminating cultus of heavenly or supernatural beings in general. Such a cultus finds no place in the New Testament, except when it, or something very much resembling it, is expressly discountenanced. By the mouth of our Lord Jesus Christ the New Testament reaffirms the Sinaitic law which restricts worship to the Lord God Himself. St Peter will not sanction the self-prostrations of the grateful Cornelius lest Cornelius should think of him as more than human....When St John fell at the feet of the angel in the Apocalypse...he was peremptorily checked on the ground that the angel too was only his fellow-slave, and that God was the one true Object of worship....Certainly the New Testament does teach that we Christians have close communion with the blessed angels and with the sainted dead....But the worship claimed for, and accepted by, and paid to, Jesus, stands out in the New Testament in the sharpest relief...not softened or shaded off by any instances of an inferior homage paid, whether legitimately or not, to created beings. We do not meet with any clear distinction between a primary and secondary worship, by which the force of the argument might have been more or less seriously weakened."

Liddon, *Bampton Lectures*, Lect. VII.

I. "HOLDING FORTH THE WORD OF LIFE." (Ch. II. 16.)

The late Dr F. Field (*Otium Norvicense, pars tertia*, p. 118) has an interesting note on λόγον ζωῆς ἐπέχοντες. He points out that ἐπέχειν where we might expect προσέχειν is a usage unexampled, or at best supported by remote examples. And he adduces from later Greek authors examples (collected by Wetstein) of the phrase λόγον ἐπέχειν τινός in the sense of "correspond to," "play the part of." E.g. Diogenes Laertius, VII. 155, about a theory of the universe: μέση ἡ γῆ, κέντρου λόγον ἐπέχουσα, "*doing duty as a centre*"; St Basil, *Hexaëmeron* IX. (tom. i. p. 83 E), κακὸν δὲ πᾶν ἀρρωστία ψυχῆς, ἡ δὲ ἀρετὴ λόγον ὑγιείας ἐπέχει, "all evil is a sickness of the soul; *virtue is as it were its health.*" He compares the better-known phrases, τάξιν or τόπον ἐπέχειν τινός : e.g. Theodoret (tom. III. p. 489), ἡ εὐαγγελικὴ πολιτεία σώματος ἐπέχει τάξιν, ὁ δὲ νόμος σκιᾶς. And he quotes the Syriac Peshitto of this passage of Philippians, which is, "*to whom ye are in place of life.*" His own rendering of the passage would be, "In the midst of a crooked and perverse generation, among whom ye shine as lights in the world, *being (to it) in the stead of life.*" "To the last clause a marginal note might be added : 'Gr., *holding the analogy of life.*'"

The suggestion is important, and from a source which must always command attention. Yet the quotation from Homer, in the notes on ch. ii. 16, still seems on review pertinent, and need not be called "remote," coming from the great Poem. With some hesitation we recommend adherence to the more ordinary rendering.

K. "THE RIGHTEOUSNESS WHICH IS OF GOD BY FAITH." (Ch. III. 9.)

THE following extract from the Editor's running Commentary on Romans (*Expositor's Bible*), p. 32 (on Rom. i. 17), may be appended to the remarks in the notes above:

"This message of power unfolds first, at its foundation, in its front, '*the Righteousness of God,*' not first His Love, but 'His Righteousness.' Seven times elsewhere in the (Roman) Epistle comes this phrase (iii. 5, 21, 22, 23, 26 ; x. 3 twice); rich materials for ascertaining its meaning in the spiritual dialect of St Paul. Out of these passages, iii. 26 gives us the key. There 'the righteousness of God,' seen as it were in action, ascertained by its effects, is that which secures '*that He shall be just, and the Justifier of the man who belongs to faith in Jesus.*' It is that which makes possible the mighty paradox that the Holy One, eternally truthful, eternally rightful, infinitely 'law-abiding' in His jealousy for that Law which is in fact His Nature expressing itself in precept, nevertheless can and does say to man, in his guilt and forfeit, 'I, thy Judge, lawfully acquit thee, lawfully accept thee, lawfully embrace thee.'...Thus it stands practically equivalent to God's way of justifying the ungodly, His method for liberating His love while He magnifies His law. In effect, not as a translation but as an explanation, God's Righteousness is God's Justification.

"Then again we note the emphasis and the repetition here of the thought of *faith.*...Here, if anywhere, we shall find ample commentary in the (Roman) Epistle. Only let us remember from the first that... we shall see "faith" used in its natural and human sense ; we shall find that it means personal reliance....It is in this sense that our Lord Jesus Christ, in the Gospels, invariably uses the word. For this is its human sense, its sense in the street and the market; and the Lord, the Man of men, uses the dialect of His race. Faith, infinitely wonderful...from some points of view, is the simplest thing in the world from others. That sinners...should be brought so to see their Judge's heart as to take His word of peace to mean what it says, is miracle. But that they should trust His word, having seen His heart, is nature—illuminated and led by grace, but nature still....(Faith) is not a faculty for mystical intuitions. It is our taking the Trustworthy at His word....Hence the overwhelming prominence of faith in the Gospel. It is the correlative of the overwhelming...prominence of Jesus Christ. Christ is all. Faith is man's acceptance of Him as such. 'Justification by Faith' is not acceptance because faith is...a merit...a virtue. It is acceptance because of Jesus Christ, whom man, dropping all other hopes, receives."

See this last point admirably explained by Hooker, *A Disc. of Justification*, § 31. And see Julius Hare, *The Victory of Faith* (1847), p. 21:

"It was with the fullest right that Luther and Melanchthon, when the true idea of Faith and of its power was reasserted at the Reformation, were anxious to urge again and again that *faith is trust*, that *faith signifies trust: fides est fiducia ; fides significat fiduciam*. This was only to assert that the faith required in the New Testament is a feeling of the same kind with the trust enjoined in the Old Testament; as is proved—to take a single instance—by the passage in the Gospels, where the disciples are frightened by the tempest, while their Master is asleep..., and where...He rebukes them for their want of faith (Matth. viii. 26), that is...for their want of confidence in Him."

The Editor ventures to refer to his Tract, *Justifying Righteousness* (Seeley, 1885), for a discussion in some detail, with quotations.

L.   ST PAUL'S USE OF ATHLETIC METAPHORS[1].

(Ch. II. 16, III. 14.)

In his constant illustration of the Christian life by the requirements and rewards of the Greek athletic contests, St Paul at once displays his own Hellenic sympathies and appeals to the noblest enthusiasm of the national life of his Greek converts. The Olympian games were closely connected with all that was most precious in the contribution made by Greece to the providential education of the world. Once in every four years the perpetually quarrelling states of the Panhellenic union proclaimed a solemn armistice for a single summer month, and met on the sacred plain of Olympia in a brotherly contest, city against

---

[1] Contributed almost entirely by the kindness of Dr J. Armitage Robinson.

city as well as man against man, for the highest glory that life could offer. Nothing might take precedence of this supreme festival. Even the sending of forces to support the heroes of Thermopylæ[1] must wait till the sacred month was over. Round this centre of Greek life religion, literature and art ranged themselves spontaneously in their most splendid forms. Historians read their histories to the assembled multitudes; poets proclaimed the glories of the successful champions, and sculptors perpetuated their noble forms. Time for the next four years was marked by the name of the victor in the foot-race, who though he carried off but a crown of wild olive returned to his city to receive substantial honours for the remainder of his days.

Something may be usefully noted here as to the training, the testing of candidates, and the actual contest. The training extended over ten months. A strict diet was enforced (ἀναγκοφαγία). The length and severity of this preparatory discipline led to a professionalism which is sharply criticized by several Greek writers. Athletes as such became marked off from ordinary competitors. Euripides[2] denounces the uselessness of the mere athlete's life, and Galen[3] (cent. ii.) its brutalizing tendency. Extreme exertion, even flagellations, inordinate overfeeding, and as a consequence excessive sleep—these were the exaggerations which accompanied the athletics of a baser period. Yet a certain moral witness was given by the necessity of abstinence from unchaste lusts: and the discipline and self-control demanded by these labours were in striking contrast with the lightness and carelessness which characterized so much of the Greek citizen's life.

A month before the contest all the candidates were tested by the Hellanodicæ. Every competitor must be able to shew that he was a pure Greek, and that he had undergone the regular training. He must further declare his determination to abide by the customary rules, and take a solemn oath to this effect.

Of the contest itself two forms only need be noticed here. The Foot-race, in the Stadium, was the central event of the Festival; the Olympiad was marked by the name of the winner. The Herald proclaimed:

> "Foot by foot
> To the foot-line put."

The starting-rope (ὕσπληξ), the race, the goal, the revel, the hymn— all these are familiar from the splendid verse of Pindar. And it is to this race that St Paul most frequently refers. But the severer contest of the Boxing-match, sometimes even fatal in its issue, also finds a place in his vocabulary of illustration. The Boxer's hands and arms were furnished with the dangerous cestus of twisted leather loaded

---

[1] Herod. VII. 206. The advance force under Leonidas was to be supported πανδημεί by the Spartans after the Carneia, the Spartan festival which coincided with the Olympia; and the other States were purposing the like action: but ἦν κατὰ τὠυτὸ Ὀλυμπιὰς τούτοισι τοῖσι πρήγμασι συμπεσοῦσα.
[2] In a long fragment of his tragedy of Autolycus (in Athenæus x. p. 413: Dindorf, Poetæ Scenici, Fragmenta).
[3] In his περὶ Ἰατρικῆς κτλ., c. xlvi. (Galeni opp., v. 894, ed. Kühn), and often.

with metal[1]. In training the competitors would practise even upon "dummies," or upon nothing, "striking the air": but their crushed ears attested more serious and painful preparations[2].

The following passages in St Paul present more or less distinctly athletic metaphors. The passing character of the allusion in some cases serves to shew how familiar, and how instinctive, was the illustration.—The words printed in thicker type recall, often with unmistakable intention, sometimes perhaps half unconsciously, the phraseology of the games.

1 Thess. ii. 1—4. αὐτοὶ γὰρ οἴδατε, ἀδελφοί, τὴν **εἴσοδον** ἡμῶν τὴν πρὸς ὑμᾶς ὅτι οὐ **κενὴ** γέγονεν· ἀλλὰ **προπαθόντες** καὶ ὑβρισθέντες...ἐν Φιλίπποις ἐπαρρησιασάμεθα...λαλῆσαι πρὸς ὑμᾶς...**ἐν πολλῷ ἀγῶνι**...καθὼς **δεδοκιμάσμεθα** ὑπὸ τοῦ θεοῦ...οὕτω λαλοῦμεν...ὡς...ἀρέσκοντες...τῷ θεῷ τῷ **δοκιμάζοντι** τὰς καρδίας ἡμῶν.

1 Thess. ii. 18, 19. ἠθελήσαμεν ἐλθεῖν...ἀλλὰ **ἐνέκοψεν** ἡμᾶς ὁ Σατανᾶς. τίς γὰρ ἡμῶν...**στέφανος** καυχήσεως; ἢ οὐχὶ καὶ ὑμεῖς κτλ.;

2 Thess. iii. 1. ἵνα ὁ λόγος τοῦ Κυρίου **τρέχῃ** καὶ δοξάζηται.

Gal. ii. 2. μή πως **εἰς κενὸν τρέχω** ἢ **ἔδραμον**;

,, v. 7. **ἐτρέχετε** καλῶς· τίς ὑμᾶς **ἐνέκοψεν**;

Phil. i. 27, 30. **συναθλοῦντες**...τὸν αὐτὸν **ἀγῶνα** ἔχοντες.

,, ii. 16. οὐκ **εἰς κενὸν ἔδραμον** οὐδὲ **εἰς κενὸν ἐκοπίασα**.

,, iii. 12, 14. οὐχ ὅτι ἤδη **ἔλαβον**...**διώκω** δέ, εἰ καὶ **καταλάβω**...τὰ μὲν ὀπίσω ἐπιλανθανόμενος τοῖς δὲ ἔμπροσθεν ἐπεκτεινόμενος κατὰ **σκοπὸν διώκω εἰς τὸ βραβεῖον** κτλ.

Col. i. 29, ii. 1. **εἰς ὃ καὶ κοπιῶ ἀγωνιζόμενος**...θέλω γὰρ ὑμᾶς εἰδέναι ἡλίκον **ἀγῶνα** ἔχω κτλ.

Col. ii. 18. μηδεὶς ὑμᾶς **καταβραβευέτω**.

,, iii. 15. ἡ εἰρήνη τοῦ Χριστοῦ **βραβευέτω** κτλ.

1 Tim. iv. 7—10. **γύμναζε** σεαυτὸν πρὸς εὐσέβειαν· ἡ γὰρ **σωματικὴ γυμνασία** πρὸς ὀλίγον ἐστὶν ὠφέλιμος...εἰς τοῦτο γὰρ καὶ **κοπιῶμεν** καὶ **ἀγωνιζόμεθα** (ita leg.) κτλ.

1 Tim. vi. 11, 12. **δίωκε** δικαιοσύνην...**ἀγωνίζου τὸν καλὸν ἀγῶνα**... **ἐπιλαβοῦ** τῆς αἰωνίου ζωῆς...ἐνώπιον πολλῶν μαρτύρων.

Cp. Heb. xii. 1. ἔχοντες περικείμενον ἡμῖν **νέφος** μαρτύρων, ὄγκον ἀποθέμενοι πάντα...δι' ὑπομονῆς **τρέχωμεν** τὸν προκείμενον ἡμῖν **ἀγῶνα**.

2 Tim. ii. 5. ἐὰν δὲ καὶ **ἀθλῇ** τις, οὐ **στεφανοῦται** ἐὰν μὴ νομίμως **ἀθλήσῃ**.

2 Tim. iv. 7, 8. **τὸν καλὸν ἀγῶνα ἠγώνισμαι, τὸν δρόμον τετέλεκα** ...λοιπὸν ἀπόκειταί μοι ὁ τῆς δικαιοσύνης **στέφανος**.

Cp. Acts xiii. 25. ὡς ἐπλήρου ὁ Ἰωάνης **τὸν δρόμον**. xx. 24. **τελειῶσαι τὸν δρόμον** μου.

---

[1] See e.g. Theocritus, *Idyll.* XXII. 80, and cp. Virg. *Æn.* v. 400.
[2] Theocr. XXII. 45, δεινὸς ἰδεῖν, σκληραῖσι τεθλασμένος οὔατα πυγμαῖς.

By far the most elaborate illustration is found in 1 Cor. ix. 24—27, where almost every word receives its signification from the Greek games.

Οὐκ οἴδατε ὅτι οἱ ἐν σταδίῳ τρέχοντες πάντες μὲν τρέχουσιν, εἷς δὲ λαμβάνει τὸ βραβεῖον; οὕτω τρέχετε ἵνα καταλάβητε. πᾶς δὲ ὁ ἀγωνιζόμενος πάντα ἐγκρατεύεται· ἐκεῖνοι μὲν οὖν ἵνα φθαρτὸν στέφανον λάβωσιν, ἡμεῖς δὲ ἄφθαρτον. ἐγὼ τοίνυν οὕτω τρέχω, ὡς οὐκ ἀδήλως· οὕτω πυκτεύω, ὡς οὐκ ἀέρα δέρων· ἀλλ' ὑπωπιάζω μου τὸ σῶμα καὶ δουλαγωγῶ, μήπως ἄλλοις κηρύξας αὐτὸς ἀδόκιμος γένωμαι.

It is interesting to set beside this the splendid appeal on behalf of purity in Plato, *Laws*, Bk viii. p. 840. After recording instances of famous athletes and their temperance in the period of training, the Athenian stranger says :

"And yet, Cleinias, they were far worse educated in their minds than your and my fellow-citizens, and in their bodies far more lusty.

"*Cleinias.* No doubt this fact has been often affirmed positively by the ancients of these athletes.

"*Ath.* And shall they be willing to abstain from what is ordinarily deemed a pleasure for the sake of a victory in wrestling, running, and the like; and our young men be incapable of a similar endurance for the sake of a much nobler victory, which is the noblest of all, as from their youth upwards we will tell them ? " (Jowett's *Plato*, Vol. v., p. 409.)

M. AD. MONOD ON ST PAUL'S TEARS. (Ch. III. 18.)

"What is the Gospel of St Paul ? Is it but a refined deism, announcing as its whole doctrine the existence of God and the immortality of the soul, as its whole revelation the fatherhood of God and the brotherhood of man, as its only mediator Jesus Christ living as prophet and dying as martyr ? Or is this Gospel a religion unlike all others (*une religion tout à part*)...proclaiming a God unknown, promising an indescribable deliverance, demanding a radical change, compassionate and terrible at once,...high as heaven, deep as hell ? You need not, for your answer, consult the writings of the Apostle; you have but to see him weeping at your feet."

Saint Paul, Cinq Discours (ed. 1859), p. 62.

N. FAMILY AFFECTION OF CHRISTIANITY. (Ch. IV. 1.)

"While the great motives of the Gospel reduce the multiplicity and confusion of the passions by their commanding force, they do, by the very same energy, expand all sensibilities; or, if we might so speak, send the pulse of life with vigour through the finer vessels of the moral system : there is far less apathy, and a far more equable consciousness in the mind, after it has admitted Christianity, than before; and, by necessary consequence, there is more individuality, because more life. Christians, therefore, while they understand each other better than other men do, possess a greater stock of sentiment to make the subject of converse, than others. The comparison of heart to heart knits heart to heart, and communicates to friendship very much that is sweet and intense....

"So far as Christians truly exhibit the characteristics of their Lord, in spirit and conduct, a vivid emotion is enkindled in other Christian bosoms, as if the bright Original of all perfection stood dimly revealed....The conclusion comes upon the mind...that this family resemblance...springs from a common centre, and that there exists, as its archetype, an invisible Personage, of whose glory all are, in a measure, partaking."

Isaac Taylor, of Ongar; *Saturday Evening*, ch. xix.

O. **PHILIPPI AND THE EPISTLE.** (Ch. IV. 18.) From an essay by Prof. J. Agar Beet, in *The Expositor* (January, 1889), I extract the closing sentences:—

"With this reply [the Epistle], a gift infinitely more precious than that he brought from Philippi, Epaphroditus starts on his homeward journey. The joy caused by his return, and the effect of this wonderful letter when first read in the Church at Philippi, are hidden from us. And we may almost say that with this letter the Church itself passes from our view. To-day, in silent meadows quiet cattle browse among the ruins which mark the site of what was once the flourishing Roman colony of Philippi, the home of the most attractive Church of the apostolic age. But the name and fame and spiritual influence of that Church will never pass. To myriads of men and women in every age and nation, the letter written in a dungeon at Rome and carried along the Egnatian Way by an obscure Christian messenger, has been a light Divine, and a cheerful guide along the most rugged paths in life. As I watch, and myself rejoice in, the brightness of that far-shining light, and glance at those silent ruins, I see fulfilled an ancient prophecy : *The grass withereth, the flower fadeth : but the word of our God shall stand for ever.*"

INDICES.

I. GENERAL.

II. GREEK.

CAMBRIDGE: PRINTED BY JOHN CLAY, M.A. AT THE UNIVERSITY PRESS.

The Cambridge University Press

THE CAMBRIDGE BIBLE FOR SCHOOLS AND COLLEGES

GENERAL EDITORS:

A. F. KIRKPATRICK, D.D., Dean of Ely

R. ST JOHN PARRY, D.D., Fellow of Trinity College

With Introductions, Notes and Maps. Cloth. Extra fcap. 8vo.

An Introduction to the Pentateuch. By the Rev. A. T. CHAPMAN, M.A. 4*s. net.*

The Book of Genesis. In the Revised Version. Edited by HERBERT E. RYLE, D.D. With 2 Maps and 5 Plates. 5*s. net.*

The Book of Exodus. In the Revised Version. Edited by the Rev. S. R. DRIVER, D.D. With 11 Illustrations and 4 Maps. 4*s. net.*

The Book of Leviticus. In the Revised Version. Edited by A. T. CHAPMAN, M.A., and A. W. STREANE, D.D. 3*s. net.*

The Book of Numbers. In the Revised Version. Edited by the Rev. A. H. McNEILE, D.D. With 2 Maps. 2*s. 6d. net.*

The Book of Joshua. Edited by the Rev. G. F. MACLEAR, D.D. With 2 Maps. 2*s. 3d. net.*

The Book of Judges. Edited by the Rev. J. J. LIAS, M.A. With Map. 2*s. 3d. net.*

The Book of Judges. In the Revised Version. Edited by the Rev. G. A. COOKE, D.D. With Map. 2*s. 3d. net.*

The Book of Ruth. In the Revised Version. Edited by the Rev. G. A. COOKE, D.D. 1*s. 3d. net.*

The Books of Judges and Ruth. In the Revised Version. As above, in one volume. 3*s. net.*

The First Book of Samuel. Edited by the Very Rev. A. F. KIRKPATRICK, D.D. With Map. 2*s. net.*

The Second Book of Samuel. Edited by the Very Rev. A. F. KIRKPATRICK, D.D. With 2 Maps. 2*s. net.*

The First Book of the Kings. In the Authorised Version. Edited by the Rev. J. R. LUMBY, D.D. With 3 Maps. 2*s. net.*

The Second Book of the Kings. In the Authorised Version. Edited by the Rev. J. R. LUMBY, D.D. With 3 Maps. 2*s. net.*

The First and Second Books of the Kings. In the Authorised Version. Edited by the Rev. J. R. LUMBY, D.D. In one vol. With 5 Maps. 3s. 6d. net.

The First Book of the Kings. In the Revised Version. Edited by the Rev. W. E. BARNES, D.D. With Map. 2s. net.

The Second Book of the Kings. In the Revised Version. Edited by the Rev. W. E. BARNES, D.D. With 2 Maps. 2s. net.

The First and Second Books of the Kings. In the Revised Version. Edited by the Rev. W. E. BARNES, D.D. In one vol. With 2 Maps. 3s. 6d. net.

The First and Second Books of Chronicles. Edited by the Rev. W. E. BARNES, D.D. With 2 Maps. 3s. 6d. net.

The Books of Chronicles. In the Revised Version. Edited by W. A. L. ELMSLIE, M.A. With 4 maps. 4s. 6d. net.

The Books of Ezra and Nehemiah. Edited by the Right Rev. H. E. RYLE, D.D. With 3 Maps. 3s. net.

The Book of Esther. In the Revised Version. Edited by the Rev. A. W. STREANE, D.D. 1s. 6d. net.

The Book of Job. Edited by the Rev. A. B. DAVIDSON, LL.D., D.D. 3s. 6d. net.

The Psalms. Edited by the Very Rev. A. F. KIRKPATRICK, D.D.

    Book I. 1—41. 2s. net.

    Books II. and III. 42—89. 2s. net.

    Books IV. and V. 90—150. 2s. net.

The Book of Proverbs. Edited by the Ven. T. T. PEROWNE, B.D. 2s. net.

Ecclesiastes; or, the Preacher. Edited by the Very Rev. E. H. PLUMPTRE, D.D. 3s. net.

The Song of Solomon. Edited by the Rev. ANDREW HARPER, D.D., Edin. 1s. 6d. net.

Isaiah. Vol. I. Chapters i—xxxix. In the Revised Version. Edited by the Rev. J. SKINNER, D.D. With Map. 3s. 6d. net.

Isaiah. Vol. II. Chapters xl—lxvi. Edited by the Rev. J. SKINNER, D.D. 3s. net.

The Book of Jeremiah together with the Lamentations. In the Revised Version. Edited by the Rev. A. W. STREANE, D.D. With Map. 3s. 6d. net.

The Book of Ezekiel. In the Revised Version.
Edited by the Rev. A. B. DAVIDSON, D.D., revised by the
Rev. A. W. STREANE, D.D. 3s. 6d. *net.*

The Book of Daniel. Edited by the Rev. S. R.
DRIVER, D.D. With Illustrations. 3s. *net.*

Hosea. Edited by the Rev. T. K. CHEYNE, M.A.,
D.D. 1s. 6d. *net.*

The Books of Joel and Amos. By the Rev. S. R.
DRIVER, D.D. Adapted to the text of the Revised Version,
with a few supplementary notes, by the Rev. H. C. O.
LANCHESTER, M.A. With Illustrations. 2s. 6d. *net.*

Obadiah and Jonah. Edited by the Ven. T. T.
PEROWNE, B.D. 1s. 6d. *net.*

Micah. Edited by the Rev. T. K. CHEYNE, M.A.,
D.D. 1s. *net.*

Nahum, Habakkuk and Zephaniah. Edited by
the Rev. A. B. DAVIDSON, LL.D., D.D. 1s. 6d. *net.*

Haggai, Zechariah and Malachi. Edited by the
Rev. W. E. BARNES, D.D. 2s. 6d. *net.*

The New Testament complete

The Gospel according to St Matthew. Edited
by the Rev. A. CARR, M.A. With 2 Maps. 2s. 3d. *net.*

The Gospel according to St Mark. Edited by
the Rev. A. PLUMMER, D.D. With 4 Maps. 2s. 3d. *net.*

The Gospel according to St Luke. Edited by
the Very Rev. F. W. FARRAR, D.D. With 4 Maps.
3s. 6d. *net.*

The Gospel according to St John. Edited by
the Rev. A. PLUMMER, D.D. With 4 Maps. 3s. 6d. *net*

The Acts of the Apostles. Edited by the Rev. J.
RAWSON LUMBY, D.D. With 4 Maps. 3s. 6d. *net.*

The Epistle to the Romans. Edited by the Right
Rev. H. C. G. MOULE, D.D. With Map. 3s. *net.*

The First Epistle to the Corinthians. In the
Revised Version. Edited by the Rev. R. St JOHN
PARRY, D.D. 2s. 6d. *net.*

The Second Epistle to the Corinthians. Edited
by the Rev. A. PLUMMER, D.D. 1s. 9d. *net.*

The Epistle to the Galatians. Edited by the Rev.
A. LUKYN WILLIAMS, B.D. 1s. 9d. *net.*

The Epistle to the Ephesians. Edited by the
Right Rev. H. C. G. MOULE, D.D. 1s. 6d. *net.*

The Epistle to the Philippians. Edited by the
Right Rev. H. C. G. MOULE, D.D. 1s. 6d. *net.*

The Epistles to the Colossians and Philemon.
Edited by the Right Rev. H. C. G. MOULE, D.D. 1s. 6d. net.

The Epistles to the Thessalonians. Edited by
the Rev. G. G. FINDLAY, D.D. With Map. 1s. 9d. net.

The Epistles to Timothy and Titus. Edited by
the Rev. A. E. HUMPHREYS, M.A. With Map. 2s. 3d. net.

The Epistle to the Hebrews. Edited by the Very
Rev. F. W. FARRAR, D.D. 3s. net.

The Epistle of St James. Edited by the Very
Rev. E. H. PLUMPTRE, D.D. 1s. net.

The Epistles of St Peter and St Jude. Edited
by the Very Rev. E. H. PLUMPTRE, D.D. 2s. net.

The Epistles of St John. Edited by the Rev. A.
PLUMMER, D.D. 2s. net.

The Revelation of St John the Divine. Edited
by the Rev. WILLIAM HENRY SIMCOX, M.A. 2s. 3d. net.

The Book of Psalms. With Introduction and Notes
by the Very Rev. A. F. KIRKPATRICK, D.D. Crown 8vo,
cloth, gilt top. 7s. net.

The edition of the Psalms prepared by Dr Kirkpatrick for
the "Cambridge Bible for Schools" having been completed and
published in three volumes, the whole work is now also published
in a single volume. The page is larger than in the separate
volumes, and, a thinner paper being used, this edition will be
found convenient in size, and it is thought that many readers
will prefer it to the separate volumes.

The Wisdom of Solomon. In the Revised Version.
Edited by the Rev. J. A. F. GREGG, M.A. 3s. net.

The Wisdom of Jesus the Son of Sirach, or
Ecclesiasticus. In the Revised Version. Edited by the
Rev. W. O. E. OESTERLEY, D.D. 7s. net.

The First Book of Maccabees. In the Revised
Version. By the Rev. W. FAIRWEATHER, M.A., and J.
SUTHERLAND BLACK, LL.D. With Map and Illustrations.
3s. net.

In preparation (completing the series of the books
of the Old and New Testaments)

Deuteronomy. Edited by the Rev. G. ADAM SMITH,
D.D., Professor of Old Testament Language, Literature and
Theology, United Free Church College, Glasgow.

THE REVISED VERSION FOR SCHOOLS

Edited with Introductions, Notes and Maps.
Fcap. 8vo. 2s. net each

THE SMALLER CAMBRIDGE BIBLE FOR SCHOOLS

Revised and enlarged edition

With Introductions, Notes and Maps.   1s. 6d. net each

The Book of Joshua.   Edited by J. SUTHERLAND BLACK, LL.D.

The Book of Judges.   Edited by J. SUTHERLAND BLACK, LL.D.   And **The Book of Ruth.**   Edited by the Rev. A. W. STREANE, D.D.   In one volume.

The First Book of Samuel.   Edited by the Very Rev. A. F. KIRKPATRICK, D.D.

The Second Book of Samuel.   Edited by the Very Rev. A. F. KIRKPATRICK, D.D.

The First Book of the Kings.   Edited by the Rev. T. H. HENNESSY, M.A

The Second Book of the Kings.   Edited by the Rev. T. H. HENNESSY, M.A.

The Books of Ezra and Nehemiah.   Edited by the Right Rev. HERBERT EDWARD RYLE, D.D.

The Book of Proverbs.   Edited by the Rev. J. R. COATES, B.A.

The Books of Joel and Amos.   Edited by the Rev. J. C. H. HOW, M.A.

The Gospel according to St Matthew.   Edited by the Rev. A. CARR, M.A.

The Gospel according to St Mark.   Edited by the Rev. G. F. MACLEAR, D.D.

The Gospel according to St Luke.   Edited by the Very Rev. F. W. FARRAR, D.D.

The Gospel according to St John.   Edited by the Rev. A. PLUMMER, D.D.

The Acts of the Apostles.   Edited by the Rev. H. C. O. LANCHESTER, M.A.

The Gospel according to St Mark.   The Greek Text.   Edited with Introduction and Notes for Beginners by Sir A. F. HORT, Bart., M.A.   With 2 Maps.   3s. net.

The Gospel according to St Luke.   The Greek Text.   Edited with Introduction and Notes for Beginners by the Rev. W. F. BURNSIDE, M.A.   With 2 Maps. 3s. 6d. net.

The Acts of the Apostles.   The Greek Text. Edited with Introduction and Notes for Beginners by the Rev. W. F. BURNSIDE, M.A.   With 8 Illustrations and Maps.   4s. net.

THE CAMBRIDGE GREEK TESTAMENT FOR SCHOOLS AND COLLEGES

General Editor: R. St John Parry, D.D.

With Introductions, Notes and Maps. Extra fcap. 8vo, cloth

The Gospel according to St Matthew. Edited by the Rev. ARTHUR CARR, M.A. 4s. net.

The Gospel according to St Mark. Edited by the Rev. A. PLUMMER, D.D. 4s. 6d. net.

The Gospel according to St Luke. Edited by the Very Rev. F. W. FARRAR, D.D. 5s. net.

The Gospel according to St John. Edited by the Rev. A. PLUMMER, D.D. 5s. net.

The Acts of the Apostles. Edited by the Rev. J. R. LUMBY, D.D. 5s. net.

The Epistle to the Romans. Edited by R. St J. PARRY, D.D. 4s. net.

The First Epistle to the Corinthians. Edited by the Rev. R. St JOHN PARRY, D.D. 4s. 6d. net.

The Second Epistle to the Corinthians. Edited by the Rev. A. PLUMMER, D.D. 3s. net.

The Epistle to the Galatians. Edited by the Rev. A. LUKYN WILLIAMS, B.D. 3s. net.

The Epistle to the Ephesians. Edited by the Rev. J. O. F. MURRAY, D.D. 3s. 6d. net.

The Epistle to the Philippians. Edited by the Right Rev. H. C. G. MOULE, D.D. 3s. net.

The Epistles to the Colossians and Philemon. Edited by the Rev. A. LUKYN WILLIAMS, B.D. 3s. net.

The Epistles to the Thessalonians. Edited by the Rev. GEORGE G. FINDLAY, D.D. 3s. net.

The Pastoral Epistles. Edited by the Very Rev. J. H. BERNARD, D.D. 3s. 6d. net.

The Epistle to the Hebrews. Edited by the Very Rev. F. W. FARRAR, D.D. 3s. 6d. net.

The General Epistle of St James. Edited by the Rev. ARTHUR CARR, M.A. 3s. net.

The First Epistle General of St Peter. Edited by the Very Rev. G. W. BLENKIN, M.A. 3s 6d. net.

The Second Epistle General of St Peter and the General Epistle of St Jude. Edited by M. R. JAMES, Litt.D. 3s. net.

The Epistles of St John. Edited by the Rev. A. PLUMMER, D.D. 4s. net.

The Revelation of St John the Divine. Edited by the late Rev. WILLIAM HENRY SIMCOX, M.A. Revised by G. A. SIMCOX, M.A. 5s. net.

The Cambridge Companion to the Bible.
Containing the Structure, Growth, and Preservation of the Bible, Introductions to the several Books, with Summaries of Contents, History and Chronology, Antiquities, Natural History, Glossary of Bible Words, Index of Proper Names, Index of Subjects, Concordance, Maps, and Index of Places.

Pearl Type, 16mo. from 1s. 3d. *net*; Ruby Type, 8vo. from 3s. *net*; Nonpareil Type, 8vo. from 4s. *net*.

A Companion to Biblical Studies. Being a revised and re-written edition of *The Cambridge Companion to the Bible*. Edited by W. EMERY BARNES, D.D. With 8 illustrations and 10 maps. Royal 8vo. 15s. *net*.

A Concise Bible Dictionary, based on the Cambridge Companion to the Bible, and containing a Bible Atlas consisting of 8 maps, and a complete Index. Crown 8vo. 1s. 3d. *net*.

The History of the English Bible. By JOHN BROWN, D.D. Royal 16mo. With 10 plates. 1s. 6d. *net* in cloth, 3s. *net* in lambskin.

The Bible of To-Day. By the Rev. ALBAN BLAKISTON, M.A. Demy 8vo. 3s. 6d. *net*.

A Short History of the Hebrews to the Roman Period. By R. L. OTTLEY, D.D. Crown 8vo. With seven maps. 6s. *net*.

The Religion of Israel. A Historical Sketch. By R. L. OTTLEY, D.D. Second edition. Crown 8vo. 4s. 6d. *net*.

A Short Syntax of New Testament Greek. By the Rev. H. P. V. NUNN, M.A. Second edition. Crown 8vo. 3s. *net*.

The Elements of New Testament Greek. By the same author. 3s. 6d. *net*. **Key.** 2s. 3d. *net*.

Scripture Teaching in Secondary Schools. Papers read at a Conference held in Cambridge 10—13 April, 1912. First Year. Edited by N. P. WOOD, M.A., B.D. With a Preface by F. C. BURKITT, M.A., F.B.A. Crown 8vo. 1s. 6d. *net*.

Scripture Teaching in Secondary Schools. A Report of a Conference held at Oxford 22—23 April, 1913. Second Year. Edited by H. CRADOCK-WATSON, M.A. Crown 8vo. 1s. 6d. *net*.

CAMBRIDGE UNIVERSITY PRESS
C. F. CLAY, MANAGER
LONDON : FETTER LANE, E.C. 4
EDINBURGH : 100, PRINCES STREET